Praise for Lee Gutkind

"Gutkind is the Godfather Behind Creative Nonfiction." —*Vanity Fair*

"The Leading Figure in the field." —*Harper's*

"An electrifying anthology that covers the creative nonfiction universe from the personal essay to nature writing, literary journalism, and science writing." —*Booklist*, Starred Review, on *In Fact*

Praise for *Almost Human*:

"A crazy suspense story about these kids at Ca[...] their leader making robots . . . fascinating stuf[...]

"A fascinating look inside a place where sci-f[...] made real. . . . High tech at its most exh[...]

"A compelling account that reveals h[...] come, but how far they have yet to trave[...] human sensibilities and gumption." —[...]

Praise for *Forever Fat*:

"This collection of beautifully crafted personal essays . . . demonstrates the author's mastery over his chosen genre. Always engrossing, the pieces convey emotional pain leavened with humor and are written with piercing honesty." —*Publishers Weekly*

"Gutkind strides openly into any subject. His essays combine humor, pathos, confession, insight. They attract for their openness and style. . . . Entertaining reading, any one of the essays could also serve as a model for exemplary nonfiction, lending the volume to use as a text for classes or individual study in contemporary writing." —*University Press Book Reviews*

"Gutkind's writing is deceptively simple. It's a clean, sleek style, with sentences as black-and-white as the cover photo. But they pack a wallop." —*Naples (FL) Daily News*

"Lee Gutkind writes, 'Trusting other people is the easy part.' But the truth is, whether he's writing of Plantar's warts, coffee in a Pittsburgh diner, or even divorce and fatherhood, Lee Gutkind is the one it's easy to trust. He takes care with the word in all its glory."
—Bret Lott, author of *Jewel* and *Fathers, Sons, and Brothers*

"*Forever Fat* is a deeply moving account of one man's physical and spiritual transformation, where the words, "Never, never, never give in' have particular resonance for anyone who has tried to piece together the truth of one's life on the page, against the doubting voices that surround us."
—Terry Tempest Williams, author of *Leap* and *Refuge: An Unnatural History of Family and Place*

"A book about identity, the cruel threats one's family can make to one's sense of self, and the courage and clarity of vision it takes to transcend the injury. The essays are brimming with dramatic intensity, astute observation, wit, and narrative skill."
—Lee Martin, author of *From Our House*

Praise for *Almost Human*:

"*Almost Human* is an eloquent meditation on the fragile and increasingly friable line between flesh and metal, dendrites and wires. This book tells the tale of mad scientists and the strangely sane machines they create; in doing so, it illuminates the rarified world of computer science while simultaneously transcending it, or widening it, by bringing to light the essential questions robots raise for us–questions of autonomy, of cognition, of ambition and the toll it takes."
—Lauren Slater, author of *Welcome to My Country, Prozac Diary*, and *Opening Skinner's Box*

YOU CAN'T MAKE THIS STUFF UP

ALSO BY LEE GUTKIND

Almost Human: Making Robots Think

Anatomy of Baseball

The Art of Creative Nonfiction

At The End of Life: True Stories About How We Die

*Becoming a Doctor: From Student to Specialist,
Doctor-Writers Share Their Experiences*

The Best Creative Nonfiction, Volumes 1, 2, and 3

The Best Seat in Baseball, But You Have to Stand

Bike Fever

Creative Nonfiction: How to Live It and Write It

The Essayist at Work

Forever Fat: Essays by the Godfather

God's Helicopter

Healing

*An Immense New Power to Heal:
The Promise of Personalized Medicine*

*Keep It Real: Everything You Need to Know About
Researching and Writing Creative Nonfiction*

Many Sleepless Nights

One Children's Place

On Nature: Great Writers on the Great Outdoors

Our Roots are Deep with Passion

The People of Penn's Woods West

Silence Kills

Stuck in Time: The Tragedy of Childhood Mental Illness

Surviving Crisis

Truckin' with Sam

The Veterinarian's Touch

A View from the Divide

You Can't Make This Stuff Up

The Complete Guide to
Writing Creative Nonfiction—
from Memoir to Literary Journalism
and Everything in Between

LEE GUTKIND

DA CAPO PRESS/LIFELONG BOOKS
A Member of the Perseus Books Group

This book is dedicated to Gay Talese in appreciation of his talent, his integrity, his unwavering dedication to his work, and most of all his friendship. Gay Talese is an inspiration to writers of all genres, everywhere.

Designed by Timm Bryson
Set in 11 point Arno Pro by the Perseus Books Group

Cataloging-in-Publication data for this book is available from the Library of Congress.
   Gutkind, Lee.
   You can't make this stuff up : the complete guide to writing creative nonfiction, from memoir to literary journalism and everything in between / Lee Gutkind.—
1st Da Capo press ed.
      p. cm.
   Includes bibliographical references and index.
   ISBN 978-0-7382-1554-9 (hardcover : alk. paper)—ISBN 978-0-7382-1586-0
(e-book) 1. Reportage literature—Technique. 2. Creative nonfiction—
Authorship. 3. Exposition (Rhetoric) 4. Creative writing. 5. Authorship. I. Title.
   PN3377.5.R45G89 2012
   808'.02—dc23

                                                                    2012018586

First Da Capo Press edition 2012
Published by Da Capo Press
A Member of the Perseus Books Group
www.dacapopress.com

Da Capo Press books are available at special discounts for bulk purchases in the U.S. by corporations, institutions, and other organizations. For more information, please contact the Special Markets Department at the Perseus Books Group, 2300 Chestnut Street, Suite 200, Philadelphia, PA 19103, or call (800) 810–4145, ext. 5000, or e-mail special.markets@perseusbooks.com.
10 9 8 7 6 5 4 3 2 1

CONTENTS

ACKNOWLEDGMENTS

Thanks so much to Gay Talese, Rebecca Skloot, Eve Joseph, Lauren Slater, Meera Lee Sethi, and Adam Briggle, whose work we will be studying in depth in this book. Thanks to the staff of *Creative Nonfiction* for joining me as the collective voice of the genre: Stephen Knezovich, Patricia Park, Jenelle Pifer, Ginny Levy, and especially Hattie Fletcher, who single-handedly put together "Then and Now: Great (and Not So Great) Moments in Creative Nonfiction," the appendix at the back of this book. Thanks to my "onward and upward" agent, Andrew Blauner, and my "onward" editor, Renee Sedliar. Thanks to Anjali Sachdeva, also of *Creative Nonfiction,* for reading and commenting on the initial draft of this book. Thanks to the Consortium for Science Policy & Outcomes and the Hugh Downs School of Human Communication at Arizona State University for supporting me and believing in my work. Thanks to my assistant at ASU, Michael Zirulnik, for fact checking the manuscript, proofreading, and putting together the bibliography. Thanks to Michele Pasula for inspiration. Thanks to Kathryn Lang for reading the book multiple times, for making many helpful suggestions, and for nitpicking me to death. And thanks to my readers, who are helping me put my son through college, grad school—and beyond.

INTRODUCTION: HOW TO READ THIS BOOK

This book is divided into two parts. Part I defines creative nonfiction, tells you how and when creative nonfiction evolved, who the prime movers are, what the primary challenges are, and why creative nonfiction has become so popular and important in the literary, scholarly, journalistic, and publishing worlds.

I've titled Part I "What Is Creative Nonfiction?" If there were a subtitle, it would read: "Everything You Ever Wanted to Know, Everything That Is Important to Know, and Everything I Can Think of Related to Creative Nonfiction to Tell You, Except—How to Write It."

Writing is an integral aspect of every page in Part I, which provides the parameters that will guide you as you conceive of your creative nonfiction writing product, whether it be essay, article, memoir, or book. Part I will help you as you choose a subject to write about, decide how and why you will or will not be a character in it, how you will research it, flesh it out for the first time on paper or computer display, fact-check it, edit it, polish it, pray for it—and continuously revise it.

All the rules of the game are here for you to contemplate so that you are well aware of the legal, ethical, and moral lines between factual creativity and over-the-line fabrication. All of this, including the writing process itself, will be discussed in detail, along with the passion, the spirituality, the painful frustrations, and the irreplaceable rewards of the creative nonfiction way of writing and living.

Which brings us to Part II. It guides and encourages you as you put pen to paper, fingers to keyboard and experience the magic moment of creation.

Composers are informed and motivated by music, artists by the work of the masters, Da Vinci, Van Gogh, Picasso. They may have been painting or composing before actually becoming grounded in their artistry, but they did not do their best work, were not recognized, and did not achieve greatness or professional credibility until they were thoroughly steeped in the background of their profession. So too with the art of creative nonfiction as delineated in Part I, which prepares you for Part II.

In Part II, you'll incorporate the insight and knowledge you gained in Part I, and as the classic Nike advertising campaign challenged consumers: Just Do It!

"Doing it" means "writing—rewriting—revising" and then, when you're finished—doing it again: turning your life or the lives of the people about whom you are writing into hard-hitting, compelling, informative, truthful, and accurate drama with vivid scenes, electrifying characters, and unforgettable messages.

On the last page of this book (but before the appendix), you can read my final message to you, specifying how you will achieve such a standard of excellence: write, revise, and rewrite until you are certain that you can't go any farther, that you have achieved your best work. And then writing, revising, and rewriting again. Start something new but hold on to what you have just written for a while longer so that you can revisit each draft with perspective.

My goal in Part II is to teach you, inspire you, give you the confidence to write with courage and conviction and to nurture your work until it can stand as a testament to your persistence, your talent, and the inherent power of your story.

Because both parts of this book are essential, it hardly matters which you read first. Read spontaneously where the muse strikes your fancy—from beginning to end, from back to front—or start with some of the readings scattered throughout the text. After all, this is the way we write. We move in and out of the stories we tell, capturing the reader with the power of our words and the intensity and scope of our vision.

And speaking of reading, there are lots of great essays and excerpts in this book by new and established writers. Some of the work is mine, but mostly it's from other writers like Gay Talese, Rebecca Skloot, Lauren Slater. I will ask you to read this work (and learn to read all creative writing) with a "double eye"—learn to read from the point of view of the reader, your reader. It's a kind of golden rule: writing for others in a way you might want others to write for you. That's one eye. The other eye is teaching yourself to read like a writer, to understand the approach, the craft, the tricks of the trade of the writer you are reading. I will deconstruct some of the

EXERCISE 1

No matter how old you are—eighteen or eighty—there have been significant moments in your life that represent something you have learned. It could be the scene at the dinner table when your parents announced to the family that they were divorcing—or the day you turned forty and felt old, or the moment you crossed the finish line of the Marine Corps Marathon, when you were fifty, and felt young.

In Part II, I devote a lot of time and attention to the elements and techniques that the writer needs to use when writing scenes. But for now, let me say that scene writing is true storytelling. A scene is an incident, an experience, a happening that the writer captures as cinematically as possible.

The experience—or the scene you are recreating—could actually come from someone you are writing about. A story you heard or an incident you observed. If you're writing memoir, the event probably happened to you. And this is what we will focus on for now—you!

Begin to jot down experiences that you vividly remember. Sketch them out, reconstruct them in your own mind, and write them. What do they mean to you—or what might they mean to your readers? How might descriptions of those experiences help others? Go to work on that assignment, for you will revisit and expand it throughout the book.

Meanwhile, in Part I (page 3), I will recreate for you something that happened to me—the day, the moment, I became the Godfather. Life changed for me in the blink of an eye and provided me with an opportunity to spread the word about nonfiction storytelling, the literature of reality, and in the process, help readers and writers discover and develop a new avenue of expression.

readings in this book, and then I will ask you to deconstruct some of the other readings on your own—with my help, of course.

So jump into this book wherever you choose. Learn what you need to know about creative nonfiction in any order—and begin to fulfill your mission as a writer, to tell your story, share your knowledge and wisdom, make an impact, and influence opinions and change lives.

By the way, in addition to readings, there will be periodic question and answer boxes. I do this once in a while because I am trying to relate to my readers and to anticipate your thoughts and questions while you are reading. It is also always good for a writer to change the pace of the book once in a while; it helps both the reader and the writer to focus and refocus, to think and review. This is part and parcel of what we want to do as creative nonfiction writers—to make our readers think more deeply about the stories we are telling and to make ourselves delve more deeply into the inherent meaning and clarity of our message. Capturing a story and connecting the story with our readers is what we are trying to do.

And please take note of the repetition of the word "story" and the idea of storytelling. As you will discover, many parts of this book are written in the creative nonfiction style, which is anchored in story, to demonstrate the genre it portrays. This is what creative nonfiction is all about—the basic, anchoring elements, whether it is personal essay, intense immersion, lyric essay, memoir, whatever subcategory you may want to label it. In the end, creative nonfiction means true stories, well told. That is what I intend to do—and exactly what I intend to help motivate you to do.

I work hard to help you along. There are two basic approaches to creative nonfiction—memoir/personal essay and immersion nonfiction. I have designed a series of exercises that will help you write one example of each kind of creative nonfiction.

By the time you finish this book, especially if you read it more than once, you will have written an immersion and a memoir. I am not saying it will be ready to send to an editor or agent, but you will have a solid draft to begin to shape and polish—and revise and revise.

So much for this introduction. Now let's begin to read, think, and write.

Part I

WHAT IS CREATIVE NONFICTION?

The Birth of the Godfather

I'm in the elevator in the University of Pittsburgh's Cathedral of Learning, the tallest classroom building in the world. I'm heading for the English Department on the fifth floor where I'm teaching. But I'm uncomfortable and ill at ease because of what's recently happened.

Then the elevator doors glide open and there standing before me is my colleague Bruce Dobler, a short, broad-shouldered fellow with a toothy smile. When he notices me, he raises his eyebrows and then drops to his knees, grabs my hand, and says, with breathless reverence, "I kiss your hand, Godfather."

And then as I watch, confused and astounded . . . he does just that—with a loud, wet *smmmack!*

In the moment I had no idea why he was acting so crazily—but then it hit me. Bruce must have read James Wolcott's *Vanity Fair* article making me look like a snake oil salesman and (maybe worse) a "navel gazer." I was embarrassed to be presented to the world in that context—in *Vanity Fair*, with its more than a million readers (1,157,653 in 1997), to the chic literati, the movers and shakers, so to speak. That's why I'd been so out of sorts that day.

The article was an ambush; neither Wolcott nor *Vanity Fair* had interviewed or contacted me. A former student had discovered it the night before my elevator encounter with Dobler while she was browsing through the new magazines at a supermarket checkout counter. She'd telephoned me with the news that morning. I'd considered hiding out and not leaving my house for a while, but I soon realized how silly that was. And then at the Cathedral of Learning elevator, Bruce Dobler showed me how I would need to adjust to and appreciate my fifteen minutes of fame and celebrity.

Wolcott had also ridiculed others in his diatribe against the genre I'd been writing, editing, and championing for years—creative nonfiction—but he'd singled me out as the worst of a bad bunch. Wolcott had said it in big bold letters, and it was an unforgettable label to be stuck with. Not only was I a "navel gazer," I was something worse. He'd dubbed me the "godfather behind creative nonfiction."

When I first read the article I was mortified. It wasn't good to be roasted in such a prestigious national magazine, not good for my image as an English professor and my rapport with my conservative academic colleagues—or so I thought. But Dobler got the picture and made me remember what Oscar Wilde had said about criticism: "The only thing worse than being talked about—is not being talked about."

On the upside, being lambasted in *Vanity Fair* attracted attention to the genre. Over the next few years, many people began to read and experiment with creative nonfiction. As a result it enjoyed unprecedented growth and was transformed into an expanding literary movement with an unbridled momentum—it became the fastest-growing genre in the literary and publishing worlds.

In 1997, when Wolcott disparaged me as the godfather, many people were writing and reading creative nonfiction, which, of course, is why it was a topic to target. But Wolcott didn't realize that few people knew what to call the form, how to write it, or where to try to publish their work. With Wolcott's article and *Vanity Fair's* million-plus readers, people began to understand that what they were reading and writing had a name—a label—as well as a rationale and a burgeoning audience. From that time on, creative nonfiction became the genre to contend with in the literary world—the literature of reality.

The Definition Debate

James Wolcott was not the only one ridiculing creative nonfiction, although the reasons for the ridicule varied. Mostly, at least at the outset, the problem was the word "creative." On the one hand, it was thought to be pretentious. Academics especially found this to be troubling. Their mantra was that you don't *tell* people that you're being creative—they're supposed to recognize it and tell you.

Journalists also opposed the term "creative," although for different reasons. Creativity, they insisted, meant making things up—fabricating facts—something journalists are never supposed to do. (Just ask William Randolph Hearst or Jason Blair!) To avoid the word "creative," some academics and reporters began calling the genre "literary nonfiction" or "literary journalism." Neither label caught on.

"Literary" sounds as pretentious as "creative." And although most creative nonfiction contains a journalistic element (depending, of course, on how you define journalism), the assumption that all creative nonfiction was also journalism was inaccurate.

Prior to the use of the term "creative nonfiction," this kind of writing had gained popularity as the "new journalism," due in large part to Tom Wolfe, who published a book by that title in 1973. But that term led to debate about the use of the word "new." A.J. Liebling, George Orwell, James Baldwin, and Lillian Ross, to name only a few masters of the literature of reality, were publishing their work a half century before Tom Wolfe—so what was new about the "new journalism"?

Recently the word "narrative"—as in "narrative journalism" and "narrative nonfiction"—has gained popularity. Everyone has personal stories or narratives: politicians, movie stars, businessmen and women. Yet creative nonfiction does not strictly adhere to one narrative form; there's the lyric essay, the segmented essay, and the prose poem, all of which can be nonfiction.

But in the end, the name game is a waste of time and energy. It doesn't matter what you call it; much more important is how you define it—and how you make it work.

WHAT IS IT—OR ISN'T IT?

The banner of the magazine I'm proud to have founded and I continue to edit, *Creative Nonfiction,* defines the genre simply, succinctly, and accurately as "true stories well told." And that, in essence, is what creative nonfiction is all about.

In some ways, creative nonfiction is like jazz—it's a rich mix of flavors, ideas, and techniques, some of which are newly invented and others as old as writing itself. Creative nonfiction can be an essay, a journal article, a research paper, a memoir, or a poem; it can be personal or not, or it can be all of these.

The words "creative" and "nonfiction" describe the form. The word "creative" refers to the use of literary craft, the techniques fiction writers, playwrights, and poets employ to present nonfiction—factually accurate prose about real people and events—in a compelling, vivid, dramatic manner. The goal is to make nonfiction stories read like fiction so that your readers are as enthralled by fact as they are by fantasy. But the stories are true.

The word "creative" has been criticized in this context because some people have maintained that being creative means that you pretend or exaggerate or make up facts and embellish details. This is completely incorrect.

It is possible to be honest and straightforward and brilliant and creative at the same time. Albert Einstein, Jacques Cousteau, Stephen Hawking, and Abraham Lincoln are just a few of the brilliant leaders and thinkers who wrote truthful, accurate, and factual material—and were among the most imaginative and creative writers of their time and ours.

The word "creative" in creative nonfiction has to do with how the writer conceives ideas, summarizes situations, defines personalities, describes places—and shapes and presents information. "Creative" doesn't mean inventing what didn't happen, reporting and describing what wasn't there. It doesn't mean that the writer has a license to lie. The word "nonfiction" means the material is true.

The cardinal rule is clear—and cannot be violated. This is the pledge the writer makes to the reader—the maxim we live by, the anchor of creative nonfiction: "You can't make this stuff up!"

WHO COINED THE TERM "CREATIVE NONFICTION"?

Nobody knows, exactly. I've been using it since the early 1970s, although if I were to pinpoint a time when the term became "official," it would be in 1983, at a meeting convened by the National Endowment for the Arts to deal with the question of what to call the genre as a category for the NEA's creative writing fellowships. Initially, the fellowships bestowed grant money ($7,500 at the time; today, $20,000) to poets and fiction writers only, although the NEA had long recognized the "art" of nonfiction and was trying to find a way to describe the category so writers would understand what kind of work to submit for consideration.

"Essay" was the term used to describe this "artful" nonfiction, but that didn't quite capture the essence of the genre. Technically, scholars of all sorts were writing "essays," but these were usually academic critiques—not accessible in style or content to the general public, even the most informed. Newspaper columnists were writing "essays" in a way, but these were mostly short opinion pieces, lacking the narrative and the depth of research artful essays demanded.

The word "journalism" didn't fit the category either, although the best creative nonfiction does require a significant aspect of reportage. For a while the NEA used the term "belles-lettres," a kind of writing that favors style over substance. If nothing else, the pomposity of the term was off-putting. None of these labels captured the essence of the compelling, character-driven, story-oriented literature they were seeking. Eventually one of the NEA members in the meeting that day pointed out that a rebel in his English Department was campaigning for the term "creative nonfiction." That rebel was me. From that time on, the commonly accepted name for the kind of writing we're examining in this book was "creative nonfiction."

The Fastest-Growing Genre

Despite the controversy over its name—or perhaps because of it—creative nonfiction has become the most popular genre in the literary and publishing communities.

These days the biggest publishers—HarperCollins, Random House, Norton, and others—are seeking creative nonfiction titles more vigorously than literary fiction and poetry. (I'm distinguishing here between "literary" and "popular" fiction; the latter includes work by master storytellers like John Grisham and James Patterson.) Recent creative nonfiction titles from major publishers on the best-seller lists include Laura Hillenbrand's *Unbroken*, Dave Eggers's *Zeitoun*, Rebecca Skloot's *The Immortal Life of Henrietta Lacks*, and Jeannette Walls's *The Glass Castle*. Even small and academic (university) presses that previously would have published only books of regional interest, along with criticism and poetry, are actively seeking creative nonfiction titles these days. The University of Nebraska Press, Other Press, McSweeney's, Feminist Press, Graywolf Press, and many more have won major publishing awards, such as the National Book Award or the National Book Critics Circle Awards, and attracted new literary audiences for their creative nonfiction titles.

In the academic community generally, creative nonfiction has become the popular way to write. Through creative writing programs mostly within English departments at small colleges and large universities, from Princeton to Iowa to Columbia, students can earn undergraduate degrees, MFA degrees, and PhDs in creative nonfiction—not only in the United States but in Australia, New Zealand, and throughout the world. Creative nonfiction is the dominant form in publications like the *New Yorker, Esquire,* and *Vanity Fair.* You will even find creative nonfiction stories featured on the front page of the *New York Times* and the *Wall Street Journal.* We will look at some examples of that later in this book.

If you leaf through magazines published in the 1960s and 1970s (you may have to use microfiche), you'll see that creative nonfiction was dominant then as well. Gay Talese, Truman Capote, Lillian Ross, and Norman Mailer regularly contributed what we now call creative nonfiction to the magazines noted above as well as to magazines that no longer exist, like *Collier's* and the *Saturday Review.*

The big difference between then and now is that this artful nonfiction is rapidly growing, while readership and sales of literary and popular (paperback) fiction have remained stagnant or decreased—and that the genre now has a name most everyone accepts.

SUBGENRES

Just like poetry and fiction, creative nonfiction includes subgenres. In poetry, subgenres have to do with form, while in fiction subject matter and voice often signify divisions. "Chick lit" is mainly written by women for women, addressing women's issues often in a lighthearted manner, such as *The Devil Wears Prada* by Lauren Weisberger. Detective, spy, and mystery novels, like John Grisham's *The Firm* or Tom Clancy's *The Hunt for Red October,* invariably appear on fiction best-seller lists.

Like these titles, most fiction published today is "popular." These books appeal to a broad audience and focus more on plot than characterization and style, which are more "literary." Jonathan Franzen's *The Corrections* and *Freedom* are examples of literary fiction that has managed to attract a popular audience, perhaps because Franzen is able to probe and criticize, in an amusing way, the American middle class.

Many categories in nonfiction storytelling—creative nonfiction—relate to specific subjects, such as baseball, business, science, and law. If your work belongs to a particular subject matter, you have a built-in audience that can be pinpointed and categorized. The bookstore buyer or manager will know exactly where to place your book. The downside to categorization is that your book can be isolated from the general browser/reader who is not interested in, say, psychology or golf. However, bookstore categorization may not matter as much in this age of online browsing and electronic book buying. The challenge is to target your niche audience by concentrating on subject while, at the same time, enticing the general reader by making the subject seem secondary and the characters and the narrative primary and irresistibly compelling. This dual appeal to a dual audience can be very effective—and profitable.

CROSSING GENRES

Some people refer to creative nonfiction as the fourth genre—behind drama, poetry, and fiction. But creative nonfiction is also a second genre for some prestigious writers. Ernest Hemingway, the Nobel laureate best known for fiction, wrote stirring creative nonfiction like *Death in the Afternoon*, his paean to bullfighting. George Orwell, James Baldwin, John Updike, Phillip Roth, Truman Capote, and David Mamet have distinguished themselves equally in fiction or drama, and in creative nonfiction. Mary Karr, Diane Ackerman, and Terry Tempest Williams were poets first before discovering the potential of creative nonfiction, which has brought them fame and fortune.

Creative nonfiction is not only the second genre for some authors but it's also the second profession for many distinguished men and women. Scientists like Oliver Sacks, historians like Edmund Morris, movie stars like Rob Lowe, comedians like Tina Fey, journalists like Bob Woodward, and baseball players like Jim Bouton are all writing or have written successful and compelling works of creative nonfiction.

POETRY IS (OFTEN) CREATIVE NONFICTION

Poetry can be closer to nonfiction than you might imagine. Many poets contend that their poems are, in essence, nonfiction—spiritual and literal truth—presented in free form or verse. What some people refer to as the "lyric" essay can be poetry. In composing the lyric essay, writers emphasize artfulness over information. Meditation takes precedence over narrative, logic, and persuasion. Poets Claudia Rankine (*Don't Let Me Be Lonely*), Lia Purpura (*On Looking*), and anthologist/writer John D'Agata (*The Next American Essay*) have been championing the lyric essay most recently. The skills and objectives of the best poets are the skills and objectives most vital for those who write factual pieces.

One of the most formidable challenges of the nonfiction writer is to learn to develop a targeted focus. We devote weeks, months, and sometimes years to the study and observation of different subcultures, places, and ideas. For any given piece, journalists and essayists can tell many stories, go off on dozens of tangents, while gradually coming to focus on the meaning of their research, ideas, and interviews.

The best poets consistently control not only the structure of their poems but also the scope and range of vision. They are able to translate and communicate complicated ideas with compact specificity, even as they are being informative and dramatic, which is what good creative nonfiction is all about. Some poets are oriented toward the subtle (and sometimes not so subtle) propagation of a social cause; this is also in the deepest and noblest of journalistic traditions. Poetry and journalism can pursue the same ends and are not as far apart as you might think. Poets and journalists are often in sync, seeking "larger truths."

FLEXIBILITY, FREEDOM, AND THE LARGER TRUTH

Gay Talese, in the introduction to *Fame and Obscurity* (1970), his landmark collection of profiles of public figures including Frank Sinatra, Joe DiMaggio, and Peter O'Toole, described his work specifically and the new journalism generally, in this way: "Though often reading like fiction, it is not fiction. It is, or should be, as reliable as the most reliable reportage, although it seeks a *larger truth* [my italics] than is possible through the mere compilation of verifiable facts, the use of direct quotations, and adherence to the rigid organizational style of the older form."

This may be creative nonfiction's greatest asset: it offers flexibility and freedom while adhering to the basic tenets of reportage. In creative nonfiction, writers can be poetic and journalistic simultaneously. Creative non-fiction writers are encouraged to use literary and cinematic techniques, from scene to dialogue to description to point of view, to write about themselves and others, capturing real people and real life in ways that can and have changed the world.

What is most important and enjoyable about creative nonfiction is that it not only allows but also encourages writers to become a part of the story or essay they are writing. This personal involvement creates a special magic that can help alleviate the anxiety of the writing experience; it provides satisfaction and self-discovery, flexibility, and freedom.

Truth Or . . .

James Frey was an alcoholic, a drug addict, and a criminal. He went to prison for three months where he endured torturous experiences, including a series of root canals—without painkillers—but he survived and in the end courageously rehabilitated himself. He then wrote a raw confessional book so moving and life changing that Oprah Winfrey was seduced by its power and drama. Oprah featured him on her show as "the man who kept Oprah up all night." The book, *A Million Little Pieces* (2003), became a national best-seller. It made millions of dollars and catapulted the writer from invisibility to fame and fortune.

The Smoking Gun, a website that specializes in investigative reportage, later published an in-depth exposé of the book. Based on a six-week investigation, it outed Frey as a liar and phony—the biggest literary fake since the early 1970s when Clifford Irving pretended to have written a biography of the reclusive billionaire Howard Hughes. Among the many exaggerations and fabrications, Frey had not gone to jail for more than half a day, the root canals without pain medication never happened, and his description of a friend's suicide was untrue. The moral of the Frey tale is that if you make stuff up, you very likely will get caught and there will be consequences. Frey has blamed his addiction for his miscues.

Since being outed, James Frey has published other books, fiction and nonfiction, which have sold fairly well. But his credibility remains seriously damaged. Oprah lambasted him on her show and he was criticized on a TV special devoted to the controversy on CNN's *Larry King Live.*

James Frey was not alone in deceiving readers. Stephen Glass, fresh out of the University of Pennsylvania, became a sought-after young reporter in the nation's capital, producing breathtaking pieces for the *New Republic*, *Rolling Stone*, and the *New York Times*. But his most significant talent was his ability to fabricate stories and then cover up his lies. By creating fictitious websites and sketching out invisible and nonexistent sources, along with phony URLs and telephone numbers, Glass maintained his charade. According to H. G. (Buzz) Bissinger, author of *Friday Night Lights*, who profiled Glass for *Vanity Fair*, it was "the most sustained fraud in modern journalism."

Glass disappeared for five years, attending law school, and emerged in 2009 to promote a novel based on his life, *The Fabulist*. CBS's *60 Minutes* also profiled Glass in 2009 as he promoted his book. Glass was hoping to pass the New York state bar at that time. He had passed the written exam, but "there are questions about his character and his fitness to pass the bar," according to *60 Minutes*. Glass will probably not easily—and perhaps never—return to the journalism field. Leon Wieseltier, literary editor of the *New Republic*, told *60 Minutes*: "He's a worm. I have no place in my heart for him any longer."

Glass was contrite in his *60 Minutes* interview. But in response to interviewer Steve Croft's question, Is the person being interviewed "really Stephen Glass or just another character that he has invented?" former *New Republic* executive editor Charles Lane, who eventually helped expose Glass, replied: "If it was sunny outside and Steve and I were both standing outside in the sun and Steve came to me and said, 'It's a sunny day,' I would immediately go check with two other people to make sure it was a sunny day."

HALL OF FAME OF FAKERS

Frey and Glass were rank amateurs compared to Clifford Irving, whom *Time* magazine named "The 1972 Con Man of the Year," after being caught trying to fool the world with his fake biography of Howard Hughes. Irving went to prison for seventeen months.

Not long after the Irving/Hughes scandal, Lillian Hellman, the respected playwright, published her memoir *Pentimento* (1973) that, among other things, detailed how she smuggled money to her childhood friend Julia, who was resisting the Nazis in Vienna. The book was made into a movie in 1977 (*Julia*) starring Jane Fonda and Vanessa Redgrave. But ten years later, Yale University Press published Muriel Gardiner's memoir, *Code Name "Mary,"* which was so close to *Julia*'s story that most critics believe Hellman lifted the story from Gardiner.

Other popular stories scrutinized for truth and accuracy include *Midnight in the Garden of Good and Evil,* John Berendt's best-seller about a murder in Savannah. Berendt has admitted to making up dialogue and rearranging the story chronology. Oprah was fooled a second time by Herman Rosenblat. His manuscript "Angel at the Fence," under contract but not yet published, dramatized a Holocaust love story, depicting Rosenblat's first encounter with Roma, the woman who was to become his wife. He was in a concentration camp and she, disguised as a Christian farm girl, tossed apples over the camp's fence to him.

Rosenblat wrote that he never forgot this wonderful woman—and when they met on a blind date a decade after the war, he embraced and married her. Oprah was so moved that she hosted the Rosenblats twice, calling their romance "the single greatest love story" ever written. When it was discovered that the story was fiction, Berkeley Books canceled publication in 2008.

> **Question:** But why didn't the editor—or the publisher—make certain Frey and Rosenblat were telling the truth?
> **Answer:** Publishers usually shift responsibility to the author. Publishers contend that they cannot afford to take the time or spend the money to do the necessary fact checking. They require the writer to sign a contract attesting to the manuscript's veracity.
> **Question:** So they're off the hook?

Answer: They hope they're off the hook—but they can be sued as easily as can the writer.

Question: But this doesn't make sense. The publisher has so much more to lose than the lowly writer.

Answer: Publishers also have more attorneys to protect them.

Question: Well, isn't it the case that a disclaimer protects everybody— writer and publisher? Just print it in the front or the back of the book that the story is true to the best of your ability. Like the old TV show *Dragnet:* "The names have been changed to protect the innocent."

Answer: It might help, but it is no guarantee you are protected.

Question: And I can also get the people I am writing about to sign a permission disclaimer form which pretty much grants me freedom to use their names and stories and to write about them in ways I feel are most effective. That's the other thing I can do to protect myself, right?

Answer: Let's say it is not totally wrong. Disclaimers and permissions may help your case if you are sued, but there's really no guarantee that the terms you define will be recognized and enforced in a legal dispute. And asking people you are writing about to sign a permission/disclaimer form might make them think a second time about cooperating with you. It will put them on edge.

Question: So what's a writer to do?

Answer: Read the upcoming fact-checking section (as well as the sections on slander and libel and truth telling) and protect yourself in every way possible. Don't rely on your editor or publisher to come to your defense—especially when you are under attack by the media, an attorney, or a person about whom you have written. You're on your own. And in some ways, this is best, for you are the master of your own destiny. It is up to you to safeguard the covenant between you and your reader by being responsible for your own credibility.

Truth and Fact

Say you're sitting in a local Starbucks with my most recent ex-wife and she's telling you all of the reasons she decided to divorce me. She names my flaws one by one. By the end of the conversation, you understand how difficult it was to live with me, a workaholic, always traveling, constantly complaining, and never wanting to settle down. And even when I'm home, I insist on waking up at 4:30 AM seven days a week. I was too difficult to be married to, so it's understandable that she had to divorce me.

Now that you know her side of the story, you say good-bye to my ex-wife and walk down the street to another coffee shop for your meeting with me. This place is called The Coffee Tree Roasters. The front window can be lifted automatically, kind of like a garage door. It's sunny and warm today so we sit and talk by the open window, enjoying the comfort of the sun, refreshed from time to time by a cool breeze.

Meanwhile, I sip my fifth cup of coffee so far today—it's only 11:00 AM—while I tell you, detail by detail, reason after reason, why my latest marriage collapsed. She knew I was a writer, and she knew what kind of life I led before we were married; after all, we'd lived together for five years before we made it official. But she was always complaining, wanting me to change—and her mother hated me and made our lives miserable. Yes, it was her decision to get divorced, but the marriage was her problem, not mine.

Less than an hour later, you're out the door, waving good-bye to me through the window. You think as you walk down the street and get into your car, after listening to both of those stories, it almost seems like two different marriages, so opposite were the perceptions of the former spouses. For a moment, you wonder which of us to believe. Who's telling the truth? And then you realize: possibly we both are.

Truth is personal—it is what we see, assume, and believe, filtered through our own lens and orientation. Although it may revolve around the same subject or issue, the truth as one person perceives it may not be the same truth another person sees. I didn't make anything up about my ex-wife. I told you honestly how I saw the dissolution of our marriage. And my ex-wife was equally honest with you about me; she gave you her perspective on why our marriage failed.

There are many truths to a story and many versions of the same story. Here in the United States, juries often hear eyewitnesses testifying under oath about the same murder or robbery scene or incident; these witnesses often give many conflicting details. Jurors may be left with an impression of two or three different men or women committing the same crime.

Let's contrast truth with willful fabrication. James Frey lied. His six hours in jail may have *seemed* like three months—but they weren't and he knew the facts. Stephen Glass lied and went through elaborate machinations to mislead his editors and his readers. He simply made stuff up. These authors weren't writing creative nonfiction. They weren't even writing fiction. They were dishonest, violating the trust between writers, editors, publishers, and readers. Glass and Frey knew the truth and altered it for their own benefit.

My ex-wife and I—and most creative nonfiction writers—tell stories as we remember them, even though aspects of our stories may conflict. Our perceptions are different, as was yours when you heard both of our stories. Your perception of our marriage will probably fall somewhere between the two versions you heard. And your recollections of your encounters with us on that particular morning, and the stories we told, may be as flawed and conflicting as ours were about one another.

FACT CHECKING

This does not mean that you as a creative nonfiction writer have a clear field to write anything you remember—or anything others remember, if you're telling someone else's story. There are facts in all stories that cannot be blurred or changed by perception. Description and detail—like how many floors are in the Cathedral of Learning at the University of Pittsburgh—can be confirmed. The date of the *Vanity Fair* article, the words I attribute to both Wolcott and Wilde—all of that can be confirmed and much more, usually with research.

Is that really the Coffee Tree around the corner from Starbucks in my neighborhood? Does it have a front window that can be raised like a garage door? It's the responsibility of the creative nonfiction writer to confirm every fact that can be confirmed. Is the English Department at the University of Pittsburgh on the fifth floor? And was it located there at the time this incident occurred? If not, and a reader is aware of this inaccuracy, then how can the reader be sure of my credibility?

Then there's truth that can only be confirmed by memory and perception. Did Bruce Dobler drop to his knees or just bend down? Did he kiss my hand or just feign kissing it and make a smacking sound with his lips? Was he having fun with me or making fun of me? Was this an act of respect and appreciation—or derision? We could ask Bruce, of course, and he'd give you his interpretation, which may well differ from mine. However he responds, we'd both be telling the truth from our perspective. (Bruce Dobler died in 2010, so for purposes of verification, the only remaining eyewitness to this event, as far as I know, is me.)

Because a blurry line exists between fact and truth, readers will usually make a judgment about the veracity of the stories being told and ideas presented based on their faith in the narrator. The higher the credibility of the storyteller, the more accepting readers will be. Making stuff up, no matter how minor or unimportant, or not being diligent in certifying the accuracy of the available information, endangers the bond between writer and reader. You don't have to be objective or balanced in presenting your narrative, but you must be trustworthy and your facts must be right if you're going to be a credible writer of creative nonfiction.

Fact Checking Sedaris

Readers love David Sedaris. He's clever, funny, and self-effacing. His books have sold more than 7 million copies, and when Sedaris performs in person, he knocks the audience dead.

But Alex Heard, a veteran magazine editor who once worked with Sedaris, thought that some of Sedaris's stories seemed far-fetched, that his characters were conveniently eccentric—perfect to write about—and that the dialogue was sometimes too precious and perfect to believe. So Heard fact-checked many classic moments in Sedaris's books and wrote a three-part article about what he found out, which was published in 2007 in the *New Republic*. Heard retraced Sedaris's childhood, from which much of Sedaris's classic work emerged, and he interviewed his relatives and friends, including Sedaris himself. Heard discovered that Sedaris radically embellishes many of the situations he describes and often fabricates dialogue, a fact that Sedaris, when confronted, admits: "I exaggerate wildly, for the sake of the story. Mostly in dialogue," he once told the New Orleans *Times-Picayune*.

Three examples follow, first from *Naked*. Heard visited Empire Haven, a woodsy retreat in the Finger Lakes region of New York, the nudist colony Sedaris profiled. He interviewed Empire Haven's co-owner, Marleen Robinson, who was able to identify Dusty, a *Naked* character whose comic function in the story is to ridicule Sedaris about his citified ways.

"Oh," Dusty sputters at one point, "you're all just so sophisticated sitting in your little cafés and looking up at the Empire State Building while the rest of us lie around in haystacks smoking our corncob pipes."

In another story, Sedaris writes: "Here's a woman on a bus ride from North Carolina to Oregon, hollering about her baby's shiftless father: 'I said, I got a good mind to call him Cecil Fucking Fuckwad, after his daddy, you ugly fucking fuckwad.'"

And finally in a third piece, here's David's mom, Sharon Sedaris, discussing David's nervous tics with his second grade teacher: "I know exactly what you're talking about. The eyes rolling every which way, it's like talking to a slot machine. Hopefully, one day he'll pay off, but until then, what do you say we have ourselves another glass of wine?"

Are they true? Did these conversations take place and was the dialogue accurate? Sedaris told Heard that the Dusty quote is partly fabricated and the other two are totally made up.

Sedaris fabricated not only conversations but descriptions of places, characters, and entire situations. Not always, Heard points out. For example, Sedaris "really did hitchhike from Ohio to North Carolina with a girl in a wheelchair," described in "The Incomplete Quad." Heard's point was that Sedaris is funny and more or less harmless in most instances, but he is an untrustworthy narrator. Sedaris not only admitted to his *sins* (my italics) but didn't seem to care that he had been outed by Heard. He told a reporter from *Newsday*, "I'm probably lucky the person [Heard] who wrote it is so incompetent."

Heard's investigation triggered a dialogue about the latitude humorists should be allowed. "Exaggeration and embellishment are what allow humor to suggest larger truths," according to the *Raleigh News Observer*, and the *San Francisco Chronicle* said, "A humorist has lots of latitude because funny things don't usually write funny."

But these are shallow and inadequate observations. Real stories, factual stuff, reported accurately and skillfully, can evoke many emotions, from humor to tragedy to fear. It doesn't follow that humorists alone should receive a free pass—and a shortcut to larger truths. There are countless larger truths in politics, war, or science that can be illuminated and made more raw and poignant through fabrication and exaggeration. I have no problem with Sedaris (or James Thurber, for example, or Woody Allen) radically embellishing true stories, but let's call them what they are: fiction. Humor is not subject to another set of rules in nonfiction.

HAVE I TOTALLY D'AGATA-ED THIS?

Am I making a big deal out of truth, accuracy, and fact checking in creative nonfiction? Yes! And for good reason: honesty and credibility are the bone and sinew, the essential irrefutable anchoring elements of nonfiction. Besides, it doesn't make a lot of sense to make stuff up. How can lying to readers do you, the writer—or them—any good?

But this is John D'Agata's premise in the book *The Lifespan of a Fact*. According to D'Agata, changing facts, altering truth is justifiable if you do it in the name of art. This sounds preposterous, but his ideas have attracted some attention—mostly, not surprisingly, animosity.

The book's back story begins in 2003. D'Agata had written an essay on assignment for *Harper's* about a teenager who committed suicide in Las Vegas. The essay was rejected because of factual inaccuracies. This should be the end of the story and the essay. What magazine would want to publish a nonfiction piece rejected because the author was not being truthful? But *The Believer* agreed to publish it.

Jim Fingal, an intern fresh out of college, is assigned to fact-check D'Agata, who rejects the notion that he needs to be fact-checked or for that matter, that he's expected to be truthful. Fingal does his job, calling out D'Agata sentence by sentence, word for word, on what he calls the "factual disputes" (and "factual quibbles" and "factual nudgings"). D'Agata vehemently resists any changes, no matter how blatantly wrong he may be.

For example, when Fingal proves that there are thirty-one strip clubs in Las Vegas and not thirty-four as claimed, D'Agata says: "The rhythm of 'thirty-four' was better in the sentence than the rhythm of 'thirty-one,' so I changed it." And when he swaps the name of a bar from "Boston Saloon" to "Bucket of Blood," it's okay, because "'Bucket of Blood' is more interesting." And when Fingal demonstrates that D'Agata's information about how many heart attacks took place during a certain time period in Las Vegas—there were eight, not four—and asks if the text should be changed, D'Agata replies: "I'd like to leave it as it is."

Fingal is astonished: "But that would be intentionally inaccurate . . . Aren't you worried about your credibility with the reader?"

"I'm not running for public office," D'Agata replies. "I'm trying to write something that's interesting to read."

And so it goes. D'Agata is an associate professor teaching creative nonfiction writing at the University of Iowa, and the author or editor of four books, so he should know better—and I am sure he does. So what is he up to? You could say, as some have, that he is lazy, unwilling to follow through with the heavy and often tedious background work to get it right. You could say he doesn't care about his responsibility as a writer to tell a story and enlighten his readership, or even the people about whom he is writing. You could say—and I would agree—that D'Agata is downright arrogant.

The writer, through history, has always tried to make a difference, to touch readers, to make them aware of what is going on around them. We have learned that information, enhanced by story, can be ammunition: our weapon for change. President Obama made his entire staff read a *New Yorker* essay by Atul Gawande about ways to control the rising costs of health care. Gawande spotlighted the health care system in McAllen, Texas, where patients suffer through twice as many cardiac surgeries as the national average, ambulance spending is four times higher and health care costs during the end of life are eight times higher, and compares health care costs in similar size towns in order to spotlight unnecessary waste and mismanagement. Some of the ideas from Gawande's piece ended up in the Obama health care package, and so the consequences of misreporting— or inaccuracy for any reason—could have been profound.

There are many wonderful books of creative nonfiction that are dramatically, stylistically, rhythmically powerful and factually accurate that have made a difference, some of which are excerpted or discussed here—from Rebecca Skloot's *The Immortal Life of Henrietta Lacks*, most recently, to Susan Sheehan's Pulitzer Prize–winning *Is There No Place on Earth for Me?* We could all make such a list of books and writers whose spellbinding narrative nonfiction has helped influence public opinion while remaining true to fact: Rachel Carson, John Hersey, Ernest Hemingway, Ernie Pyle. They were all reporters.

Not D'Agata, who tells Fingal, "I am not a reporter and I have never claimed to be a reporter." This may be true, on a certain level, but it is nevertheless a ridiculous claim: all nonfiction contains a significant amount of reportage. (For that matter, so does most fiction.) In his essay, D'Agata is—accurately or not—reporting, researching, and interviewing. In creative nonfiction, the reporting may be filtered by a writer's perception and the use of narrative, but that does not mean we are creating characters and situations—nor does it mean that we are willfully altering facts. We are recreating, as vividly as possible, in dramatic form, what we think happened. That said, it's also our responsibility to relate the facts we know—without purposefully altering them.

D'Agata, however, maintains that the information in essays doesn't have to be factually accurate. It may be, in the classic informal essay, that style often takes precedence over substance—but the substance must nevertheless remain reliable and accurate. Fabrication is fiction. Most people recognize that creative nonfiction is a challenge in balancing substance with style—based in the belief that the substance is most important and the style is the vehicle that makes the substance more compelling to a larger readership.

But D'Agata is not really writing for the general public. For what it's worth, he acknowledges this. And this acknowledgment, I believe, answers my earlier question about what he's up to.

As you will see on page 60, D'Agata helped introduce the term "lyric essay" to university creative writing programs. He has vigorously promoted the lyric essay, and the term has captured a bit of cachet. Interestingly, D'Agata's initial definition of the lyric essay conflicts with his current attitude toward fact. The complete definition can be found on page 60, but D'Agata and his mentor Deborah Tall say "the lyric essay has an overt desire to engage with facts, melding its allegiance to the actual with its passion for imaginative form." *Allegiance to the actual*: that, to me, clearly implies a loyalty to truth and accuracy.

Yet he contradicts himself repeatedly, insisting that he has an appreciative audience. As D'Agata tells Fingal during their debate about the importance of four versus eight heart attacks: "The readers who care about the difference between 'four' and 'eight' might stop trusting me. But the readers who care about interesting sentences and the metaphorical effect that the accumulation of those sentences achieve will probably forgive me."

His colleagues will probably forgive him. They may even make jokes (like one of my colleagues, who said that she totally "D'Agata-ed" something she wrote, meaning that she fudged it), and they will speculate about the income D'Agata will make on his book tours and through his interviews.

But can anyone trust him? Frey has salvaged his career to a certain extent and Glass turned his life of lying into a novel. But respect for their character and motives will be illusive, as it will be for D'Agata.

"I guess I'm confused; what exactly are the benefits of using 'four' versus 'eight' in this sentence?" Fingal asks D'Agata at one point. This is a question that D'Agata obviously cannot answer without admitting to the emptiness of his argument. His reply is telling:

"I'm done talking about this."

CREDIBILITY—AND CORRECTNESS

An annoyed reader recently discovered a factual mistake in an essay we published in *Creative Nonfiction*. A description of Lake Tahoe was "absolutely false," he wrote. "Lake Tahoe is NOT 'the largest and deepest body of fresh water in the United States', Lake Superior is the largest, at 31,700 square miles and containing 10% of the fresh water in the world. Crater Lake in southern Oregon . . . is the deepest lake in the United States at 1,932–1,949 feet and over 300 feet deeper than Lake Tahoe. Lake Tahoe is merely the largest ALPINE lake in the United States." It was "a big difference," the disgruntled reader concluded in his email.

Chances are it was not a big difference to most readers, who were probably oblivious to this fact. It didn't seem to make a big difference in the content or impact of the essay, either. So why should we at *Creative Nonfiction* care? What's the big deal?

To this reader, the big deal was that the writer was being lazy. She didn't fact-check herself—an easy task that would have taken her "a couple of clicks with the mouse on the internet." *Creative Nonfiction* was at fault, as well. "Editors and/or fact checkers at your magazine should have caught this blatant mistake. It would have saved the writer from embarrassment in a national literary magazine, since other readers undoubtedly caught it, too, over such an easily recognizable research flub."

Checking for factual accuracy is usually not complicated. You can question or debate "truth"—how I see a certain subject or remember a certain incident may be different from your perception and recollection. But the size or the depth of a lake or the number of floors in a classroom building can and should be researched and confirmed.

Factual accuracy is different from personal truth. A reader who knows that a writer is careful about the facts is often predisposed to accept the writer's version of the truth. If we can't rely on writers to Google the details in their essays, then how can we believe the questionable contentions in their stories, especially in situations where we must take the writer's word? It's a question of credibility.

"I'm not surprised that this writer would make such an error (we all have if we write long enough)," the annoyed reader continued, "nor do I care whether the rest of her writing is marvelous or not . . . but, to be truthful, I didn't finish the piece because if there are obvious errors of fact in the first two pages, you immediately lose me as a reader."

This Lake Tahoe gaffe was a mistake, an oversight, easily correctable, and because it was so easily correctable it shouldn't have been allowed to happen—not by the writer or the editors. The writer lost a reader and the magazine may have lost a subscriber.

WHAT ABOUT THE BOTS?

In 2010, *The King's Speech* starring Colin Firth was the movie to watch— it was the story of King George VI of Britain, his ascension to the throne, and the speech therapist who helped him control his stuttering so that he was able to address the British people with thoughtfulness and power.

Following close behind in attention and vying for Oscar honors was *The Social Network*. This movie begins in the autumn of 2003 when Harvard undergrad and computer programming nerd Mark Zuckerberg, played by Jesse Eisenberg, sits down in his dorm room and creates Facebook, triggering a revolution in communication and a multibillion dollar corporation. In both movies, the viewer learns a great deal about the two protagonists, as well as the cast of characters surrounding them and the temper of the times. Maybe.

Question: Are these movies anchored in fact? Are they true?
Answer: Yes and yes. And no and no. They're a hybrid form of moviemaking called BOTS—based on a true story.

BOTS are a popular and often profitable part of our artistic culture. Directors like Oliver Stone have carved a significant reputation making such films. Stone has produced, so far, a presidential trilogy, beginning most recently with *W* in addition to *JFK* and *Nixon*. There are Academy Award–winning BOTS from past generations, such as *Patton* and *Lawrence of Arabia*, for which George C. Scott and Peter O'Toole, respectively, won best actor Oscars. BOTS contain many factual elements but are mostly fiction.

We're not talking only movies here. Hundreds (and maybe thousands) of novels are based on true stories. Classics like Irving Stone's *The Agony and the Ecstasy*, Leon Uris's *Exodus*, and James Michener's *Hawaii* come immediately to mind. These authors never pretended anything else. They were well aware that "nonfiction" is an absolute. You can't be half dead. And a story described as half true is false—and is therefore categorized as fiction. If your son tells you he took the car, drove to the convenience store, bought a candy bar, and talked to a friend, when in fact he smoked a joint with his friend, despite the fact that everything else in his explanation is accurate, he's in the end not telling the truth and is making stuff up.

This is not to say that the writers and directors and even the actors haven't done their research to capture the period in which the BOT story takes place, through costumes, mood, and spirit. But in all of these stories, as riveting and powerful as they are, the filmmakers turn away from fact

---

EXERCISE 2

You should be reading all the time you are writing. So purchase copies of the magazines you most appreciate, the places where you think you want to see your own work published. We're talking the *New Yorker, Harper's,* and *Creative Nonfiction*, among the best. Begin to study what other writers are doing from a craft point of view and also how they are treating subject matter. And as you go through this book, try to recognize many of the ideas and techniques we are discussing here—from legalities to dialogue to overall structure and connect and relate them to the writing you are doing now. Remember you are teaching yourself to read like a writer, as well as a reader.

---

and construct scenes that never occurred, introduce characters who didn't exist, and often alter the endings to please or shock an audience.

Creative nonfiction cinema—documentary films and docudrama in the theater—is a completely different exploration and experience. The camera is the reporter. The camera's eye reveals the images and ideas, conversations, and confrontations. Who will ever forget the drama, the suspense, the tearful and moving story Morgan Freeman narrated in the 2005 film *The March of the Penguins*? No words, images, or ideas are falsified. Freeman interprets what he or the writers might assume about the penguins' migration or what they say, but he does not fabricate, no matter how tempting.

Yet documentary films don't claim to be objective or balanced. The director chooses what to show a reader and what footage to leave on the cutting room floor. And the narrator or writer interprets for viewers the meaning of the footage they're seeing—at least from his or her point of view. Michael Moore (*Bowling for Columbine, Sicko, Fahrenheit 9/11,* and many more) insists all of his documentaries are fact-checked, which is undoubtedly true. But he selects which ideas, characters, and incidents to present—and which to leave out.

The writer of creative nonfiction can be subjective and establish a personal point of view, as Michael Moore does. But being opinionated can alienate readers. Sometimes, to make a point, a lighter touch can be effective. People who are free to make up their own minds often believe with more fervor and conviction. So remember when you're telling your story, you're not writing an op-ed piece. You may want to influence readers, but you need to do so subtly.

INTERESTING READING

Margaret Robison's memoir *The Long Journey Home* came out in May 2011. Robison is the mother of Augusten Burroughs, the author of his own well-known childhood memoir, *Running with Scissors* (2002). His brother, John Elder Robison, also wrote a memoir about the family and about growing up with Asperger's syndrome, *Look Me in the Eye* (2007). John's book takes place, more or less, during the same time and place as the memoirs of his

---

EXERCISE 3

In Exercise 1, I asked you to recreate a scene or situation from your past that led to something bigger or more significant that you might want to talk about. Something that opened a door to a larger conversation. And I provided you with an example—the day I became a "godfather." This opened the door for me to talk about the genre of creative nonfiction, the definition, the parameters, and even the pitfalls. Now I am about to tell you another story, which will lead to another series of topics that I will discuss in this book. It is a police or mystery story, although not necessarily a crime story, as you will see.

But first, I want you to make your story or stories lead somewhere—shape the narrative so that they segue to a conversation or an examination of issues of substance. Where do the stories take you as a nonfiction writer dispensing information and ideas to a reader? You have your incident or situation. Now make it mean something bigger.

Note: Look carefully at what I have done in the next chapter. I have told a story, and that story leads to the substance of my information and my message.

---

brother and his mother. Each book is very different and each contains differing accounts of key events in the family's life. All three bring their own perspective, style, and talents to their respective memoirs. You might look at these books as a kind Rashomon of memoirs, where the divergent stories offer new insights into one family, while none of them capture the whole truth of the family and none of them are false. The bottom line, as I have said, is that factual accuracy is much easier to achieve than total truthfulness because facts can be nailed down, while truth is elusive and undeniably personal. When writing creative nonfiction, you must attempt to achieve a chain of truths: be true to your story, true to your characters, true to yourself.

WHO WILL TAKE CHARGE?

I began this section by introducing famous fakers and exaggerators of the creative nonfiction/journalism world and the punishments and pitfalls of crossing the line from nonfiction to fiction—taking the leap.

By "leap," I mean taking chances, pushing the boundaries too far, crossing the line, purposely or mistakenly. And I have tried to present ideas and actions to help you safeguard yourself and the people about whom you are writing.

But who or what will be the final arbiter if things go wrong? Where is the Clint Eastwood–like enforcer, the guy who knows the rules and devotes his life to making certain no one breaks them?

You will soon meet the creative nonfiction police officer—sort of!

The Creative Nonfiction Police

I've just completed a reading at St. Edward's University in Austin, Texas. It's a Thursday evening after a day of classes and now I'm answering questions about essay writing. Writing nonfiction so that it reads like fiction, I tell the audience, is challenging. Some critics say it is virtually impossible, unless the author takes liberties in style and content that may corrupt the nonfiction, making it untrue or partially true. A comment from John Berendt, author of *Midnight in the Garden of Good and Evil*, is indicative of the danger inherent in the form. Berendt says he made up transitions in order to move from scene to scene in his book to make the experience more enjoyable for his readers, a process he called "rounding the corners."

This is the subject we're discussing in the auditorium after my reading—what writers can or can't do in walking the blurred line between fiction and nonfiction. The questions pile up as the audience becomes engaged. "How can you be certain the dialogue you're recreating from an incident that occurred months ago is accurate?" asks one audience member. Another demands, "How can you look through the eyes of your characters if you aren't inside their heads?"

I try to explain that such questions have a lot to do with the believability of your narrative and a writer's ethical and moral boundaries. After a while, I throw up my hands in exasperation and say, "Listen! I'm not the creative nonfiction police."

There's a woman in the audience, someone I'd noticed earlier during my reading. She's in the front row—hard to miss—older than most of the undergraduates, blonde, attractive, in her late thirties maybe. She has the alert yet composed look of a nurse, a person only semirelaxed, always ready to act or react. She's taken her shoes off and propped her feet on the stage; I remember how her toes wiggled as she laughed at the essay I'd been reading.

Many people chuckle when I say, "I'm not the creative nonfiction police." But this woman suddenly jumps to her feet, whips out a badge, and points in my direction. "Well, I am," she announces. "And you're under arrest."

Then she scoops up her shoes and storms barefooted from the room. The Q and A ends and I rush into the hallway, but she's gone. My host says the woman is a stranger. No one knows her. She's a mystery to everyone, especially me.

This incident occurred about a decade ago—and I have returned to read and teach in Austin twice since then. And each time I keep expecting the woman with the badge to reappear—and arrest me. Wherever I go, she's on my mind, lurking in the shadows of my consciousness and making me aware that in some ways I am being watched, forced always to consider the ethical and moral boundaries inherent in creative nonfiction.

How do we distinguish between right or wrong, exaggeration and fabrication, true and untrue, honest and dishonest—decisions so challenging to writers of creative nonfiction? Fact checking is a vital beginning, along with doing what's right—following the old-fashioned golden rule by treating your characters and their stories with as much respect as you would want them to treat you and the important people in your life. But there's more to it than that. The mystery woman—call her *conscience*—is a reminder and an invisible arbiter over us all.

THE OBJECTIVITY DEBATE

The hard facts of the Watergate scandal were reported in an explosive series of articles in the *Washington Post* by Bob Woodward and Carl Bernstein.

But anyone who reads their 1974 book *All the President's Men* will be presented with a complete and well-rounded story. They describe their characters with three-dimensional perspective, and they analyze and debate intricacies and conflicts inherent in the story from the characters' points of view.

Much of this is missing in their *Post* accounts, as are the adventures and challenges of the reporters themselves as they reconstruct the Watergate break-in, fight to discover the reason it happened, and try to identify the perpetrators of the crime as well as the people who masterminded the failed caper. That personal dimension is part of the story the *Post* missed— which is the privilege and leeway of creative nonfiction.

Journalists are often most critical of creative nonfiction because of this truth-fact separation. And certainly there's a measure of doubt, when credibility is at issue. But there's also a dark side to journalism. The reporter's mission is to report the news with objectivity and balance, not take sides or give one aspect of a story more attention than the other. We all know by reading the *New York Times* or watching Fox News that objectivity in journalism doesn't exist—it's merely empty rhetoric. Objectivity is impossible unless, perhaps, you're a robot. Even then, the software that helps robots think is written by men and women who have ideas and opinions of their own.

The creative nonfiction writer need not worry about being balanced and objective. The creative nonfiction writer is encouraged to take a side, to have a point of view, to demonstrate that he or she can think, evaluate, summarize, and persuade—within the boundaries of truth, accuracy, and good taste. This subjective orientation is one of many ways to distinguish between the traditional nonfiction writer and the creative nonfiction writer. While it is best for the creative nonfiction writer to seem fair, fairness, like objectivity, is nearly impossible to achieve. How a creative nonfiction writer tells a story, even when using the same facts as a traditional journalist, can influence a reader in many different ways.

COMPOSITES

We all know the story. Robinson Crusoe, the protagonist of Daniel Defoe's 1719 book, is marooned for twenty-eight years on a desert island, completely isolated from civilization and sporadically threatened by cannibals, pirates, and mutineers.

Many readers once thought *Robinson Crusoe* was a true story—some still do—and the author probably based part of his novel on at least two different real-life castaway characters. The book was a composite of their adventures, heavily embellished by Defoe's imagination. Despite the authentic connection, Defoe was writing fiction and didn't try to fool people into thinking otherwise.

More than 250 years later, however, Janet Cooke, a reporter for the *Washington Post*, was awarded the 1981 Pulitzer Prize for her depiction of an eight-year-old boy dealing drugs on the streets of the nation's capital. But curious reporters searching for the subject of the story eventually forced Cooke to admit he didn't exist. He was a composite of a number of kids she had met. Cooke lost her job—her reputation was ruined. Unfortunately, some have not learned from her mistakes.

In February 2002, the *New York Times Magazine* revealed that a boy profiled in its pages, an Ivory Coast laborer who cut weeds on a cocoa plantation for slave wages, was a composite. The author, Michael Finkel, a contributing writer for the magazine, was fired. At first Finkel was defiant and dramatic. "I hope readers know that this was an attempt to reach higher—to make something beautiful, frankly," he told *New York* magazine. A half dozen years later he admitted in his 2006 book, *True Story: Murder, Mayhem, Mea Culpa*: "I thought I'd get away with it. I was writing about impoverished, illiterate teenagers in the jungles of West Africa. Who would be able to determine that my main character didn't exist?"

Sometimes it is the editor, sometimes a critic, but usually it is the reader who ferrets out a phony. Which is why you can't make stuff up. You are violating the overarching mission of creative nonfiction—to tell true stories and to provide your audience with unforgettable and impactful factual insight and information. It is unethical, immoral, and downright unnecessary to make stuff up, since truth is usually more evocative and certainly more convincing than fantasy.

COMPRESSION

Henry David Thoreau lived for two years on Walden Pond, but he conflated those two into one in his book *Walden*, published in 1854. Which part of the two years did he choose? How often, in his painstaking process of revision, did he combine two or three days—or even four weeks—into one?

Thoreau employed "compression," combining multiple incidents or situations in order to flesh out the narrative. This technique allows a writer to build a compelling, three-dimensional story with more ease and fluidity.

In her book *In the Freud Archives* (1984) Janet Malcolm combined a series of conversations with Jeffrey Moussaieff Masson, former projects director of the Sigmund Freud Archives, into one long conversation. Masson subsequently sued Malcolm and the *New Yorker* magazine, which published an excerpt from the book, contending that Malcolm manufactured quotes in this conversation. He wasn't aware of her use of compression until he saw their conversation in print much later. Malcolm didn't admit to altering facts in their conversations—only when and how the conversations occurred.

The case took nearly ten years to play out, ending up in the U.S. Supreme Court. Masson lost his suit, although Malcolm was criticized for her sloppy reporting. Some of the quotes attributed to Masson were in fact wrong, but use of the technique of compression, although debated vigorously by opposing counsels, was deemed legal. So does compression violate an ethical or moral bond with the reader or the subject? Probably not, as long as the information isn't manufactured—which is another subject entirely. But it is always a good idea to tell your reader if you've compressed the events in your work. You can do this easily in an author's note at the beginning or end of the book or you can insert the information into the text. But you don't want readers to think, in the end, that they have been misled.

MANUFACTURING DIALOGUE

There is a question that always comes up when creative nonfiction is discussed: "How do you know, if you weren't there, that such a conversation went on and what the participants said?" Or, "How can you remember, word for word, even if you were there, what everyone said?" Or finally, "Don't the quotation marks mean that the dialogue is accurate word for word?"

The use of quotation marks traditionally signifies authenticity. Some writers, like Sebastian Junger in the 1997 best-seller *The Perfect Storm*, write dialogue without using quotation marks. And Frank McCourt, in his blockbuster 1996 memoir *Angela's Ashes,* chose to italicize dialogue. Many writers see nothing wrong with using quotation marks in recreated scenes, contending that readers know the writer didn't (as with McCourt during the Great Depression) carry around a tape recorder or video camera to record every memorable conversation in his life.

I like using quotation marks in recreated dialogue. Since my readers know it is recreated, it's clear I am not trying to bamboozle them—and I think quotes make text read more smoothly. Readers have been programmed to hear the words in their mind when they see the "quotes" and I want to establish and maintain such authenticity.

But I can appreciate the use of italics or some other signal that the quotes are recalled or recreated speech, if the writer feels it's important to send such a message ("this is not totally reliable, not word for word") to the reader. Which is the better way is kind of a coin toss. The idea is to replicate the conversation vividly and to mirror memory and speculation with trust and good judgment.

NAME CHANGING

Question: You can probably say anything you want about a person in a book or an essay if you change that person's name. Then you're protected from lawsuits, right?

Answer: Many people think that—but it isn't true. You aren't protected from their temper; they can still hit you over the head with a frying pan. And you aren't necessarily protected legally, either.

Question: I can just say I am writing fiction, right?

Answer: If a person is identifiable, if you've left a birthmark on his right cheek or a tattoo on his forearm, or he has a recognizable accent, you could be in big trouble. Just because you contend that you are writing fiction, even if your contention is legitimate, you are not shielded from litigation.

In 1993 David Leavitt wrote *While England Sleeps,* the story of a relationship between two homosexual men right before World War II. The book triggered controversy because of its graphic gay sexual encounters. This was 1993, after all. The book's notoriety led to the discovery that it was a thinly veiled life of the respected British poet Stephen Spender. Leavitt eventually admitted that the book was based on Spender's 1951 autobiography, *World Within World.* In Leavitt's version, the protagonist— Spender—was presented in a way that could well have harmed the poet's illustrious reputation. Spender filed a lawsuit that ordered Leavitt's book off the shelves in England—and forced Leavitt to do a significant rewrite for a second edition published in the United States.

Spender is more or less famous, so it didn't take much work to identify him as the model for Leavitt's character, but what about people who are not famous? If a person is recognizable to friends, families, colleagues, and business associates, and is portrayed in a way that would damage his reputation and therefore his livelihood, then the writer can also be liable in the same was as Leavitt was. Truth, of course, is the best defense, although not as good as demise.

LIBEL, DEFAMATION—AND WRITING ABOUT THE DEAD

Let's get back to one of my ex-wives. No matter what I say about her—no matter how scurrilous my remarks may be—if what I say is true, it's not libel. And even if what I say is false, if I utter these falsehoods only to her or write them to her in a letter or an email, it's still not libel. On the other hand, if I write something scurrilous and untrue about my ex-wife and share my views with others in an article or blog or letter, then I could be in trouble, guilty of libel . . . maybe.

Maybe? Well, technically speaking, libel is a false and defamatory statement in writing about a third party. If what I've said embarrasses or annoys my ex-wife, she may not forgive me, but she won't win a lawsuit against me. But if my remarks are untrue and hurt her reputation in a way that she'll be harmed personally or professionally, then that would be defamatory and it would be time for me to call my attorney to defend myself, or cut a deal.

So lesson 1 is to be honest, accurate, and ever so careful. And lesson 2 is to understand the caveats and exceptions inherent in the law. In certain situations, there's a difference between stating an opinion and stating a fact, for example.

A fact can be verified, but if my ex-wife says something about me that can't be verified, then it's probably an opinion. *Hustler* magazine once maintained that evangelist Jerry Falwell had sex with his mother. Falwell sued and the case was eventually dismissed, the court ruling that the statement was too outlandish (it was parody) to be true. Falwell's mother was unable to deny the accusation, since she was dead.

The libel bar is much higher for public figures—movie stars, politicians, sports figures—than for the average person. This is why so many people could accuse Barack Obama of not being a U.S. citizen and get away with it (an ongoing accusation prior to his election in 2008, continuing even into 2012), even if it hurt his reputation and caused him to lose his next election. On the other hand, since I'm not a public figure, if my ex-wife stated that I wasn't a U.S. citizen and my reputation was harmed by her assertion—readers spurned my books, for example—then I might be serving her papers.

Is anyone immune from defamation and libel? No one who's alive, that's for certain. But writing about dead people is generally a good safety zone. In most states, you can't libel a dead person no matter how hard you try. There are, however, a few exceptions. Under certain circumstances, in a few states, like Rhode Island, California, or Texas, false or defamatory statements about a dead person can lead to litigation. In all circumstances, when lawyers are involved, it is best to be super careful and check out the state statutes to cover your bases.

INTERESTING BUT NOT SO AMUSING FUDGING

In 1999 there was a national debate over the legitimacy of the work of Pulitzer Prize–winning biographer Edmund Morris. While working on the authorized biography of Ronald Reagan, he wrote himself into the book as a fictional character to flesh out Reagan's hidden and puzzling personality.

To be fair, Morris wasn't misleading his readers; he made clear that he was fictionalizing himself in the text of *Dutch*. This decision, however—to fictionalize an important aspect of an authorized biography—created an uproar that was covered in the *New York Times*, on *60 Minutes*, and elsewhere. Over the years, historians have come to accept the scholarship of *Dutch*, but Morris's leap of style—from nonfiction to fiction—remains controversial and in some viewpoints unacceptable in academia. However, Morris wasn't writing for his colleagues. *Dutch* was serious but targeted to a general audience.

Share Your Work with Your Subjects

One way to protect the characters in your book, article, or essay, as well as to allow them to defend themselves—is to share what you've written about them before publication. Few writers go to this trouble, but sharing your narrative with the people about whom you're writing doesn't mean you have to change what you say about them; it only means that you're being particularly responsible to your characters and their stories.

I understand why you might not want to share your narrative with your subject; it could be dangerous. It could ruin your friendship, your marriage, or your future, or it could ignite resistance and lead to litigation even before your book or essay is published. But by the same token so could publication of your book or article, if the information is incorrect—with serious damage. This is the kind of responsible action you might appreciate if the situation were reversed.

I have on occasion (not always) shared parts of my books prior to publication with people I've written about—with positive results—by reading excerpts to them. This is a good practice to consider. Characters appreciate hearing and considering what I have written, and have corrected mistakes. But more importantly, when I come face-to-face with a character, I'm able to communicate on a more intimate level. When I show or reveal to my subjects what I think and feel—when they hear what I've written about them—some of them get angry, which is also interesting to observe and write about. But most of the time they're gratified to be brought into the process before the work is published.

Notice that I have read excerpts to my characters so that they may "hear" what I have written about them. This is because I don't surrender hard copy. I make it a point *not* to allow my subjects to share what I've written about them with others. Attorneys, spouses, friends, even neighbors, then become part of the dialogue. You lose control. So instead of asking them to read and review, I read what I've written to my subjects and tape-record their remarks. They hear what I've written—and we can go off on valuable tangents at the same time—but they can't nitpick my work at their leisure.

COVERING YOURSELF

Lauren Slater, whose work you'll read later in this book, often protects herself this way. At one point in her controversial 2004 book, *Opening Skinner's Box*, Slater writes that the distinguished Harvard University psychologist Jerome Kagan, to illustrate a point he was making about free will, suddenly jumped up and ducked under his desk. After the book was published, Kagan was annoyed, perhaps embarrassed by his actions, and told a writer from *The Guardian* the event didn't happen. He said that ducking under his desk *could* happen, if he chose to do so. Some weeks later, a reporter from the *New York Times* confronted Slater with Kagan's denial—and she handed him a transcript from an email exchange she'd had with Kagan. Slater had sent Kagan a prepublication fact-checking list in which she'd written "in demonstrating to me that people do, indeed, have free will, you jumped under your desk," to which Kagan had responded: "I was trying to demonstrate that when humans have a choice of actions, they can select an act that has never been rewarded in the past." Slater had thought ahead, suspecting that such a prestigious academic might not like to look foolish, even if it was his own doing—or in this case, his undoing.

FINAL THOUGHTS ABOUT ETHICAL, LEGAL, AND MORAL BOUNDARIES

There are no rules, laws, specific prescriptions—that's the first thing to remember—and there's no one person who can be considered the creative nonfiction police or the final arbiter, not even the godfather. The gospel according to Lee Gutkind or anyone else doesn't and shouldn't exist. It's more a question of doing the right thing, being fair, following the golden rule. Treating others with courtesy and respect and using common sense.

Rounding corners or compressing characters or incidents isn't absolutely wrong, but if you do experiment with these techniques, make certain you have a justifiable reason. Making literary decisions based on good narrative principles is often legitimate—you are, after all, a writer. And you and your work can benefit when you take chances and break rules. But be careful and give your actions significant thought. No harm in trying and experimenting, but consider the consequences to you and the people about whom you are writing before you click "send."

More than in any other literary genre, the creative nonfiction writer must rely on his or her own conscience and sensitivity to others and display a higher morality and a healthy respect for fairness and justice. We may harbor resentments, hatreds, and prejudices; but being writers doesn't give us a special dispensation to behave in a way unbecoming to ourselves and hurtful to others. This sounds simple—yet it's so difficult. Write both for art's sake and for humanity's sake. In other words, we police ourselves. As writers we intend to make a difference, to alter people's lives for the greater good. To say something that matters—this is why we write, to have an impact on society, to put a personal stamp on history. Art and literature are the legacies we leave to succeeding generations. We'll be forgotten, but our books and essays, our stories and poems can survive us, whether on the shelves of libraries or in the ether of the Internet age.

Wherever you draw the line between fiction and nonfiction, you need to remember the basic rules of good citizenship: don't create incidents and characters who never existed; don't write to do harm to innocent victims. Don't forget your own story, but while considering your struggle and your achievements, think about how your story will affect your reader. Beyond the creation of a seamless, engaging narrative, you're trying to touch and affect someone else's life—which is the goal creative nonfiction writers share with novelists, storytellers, and poets. We all want to connect with other human beings in such a way that they'll remember us and perhaps share our legacy with others.

Someday I hope to connect face-to-face with the woman in the Austin audience at St. Edward's, the one with the police badge and the bare feet. I've never forgotten her. She has, in some strange way, become an accoutrement to my conscience, standing over me as I write, forcing me to ask the questions about my work that I'm recommending to you now. I'm hoping you too will feel her shadow over your shoulder each time you sit down, approach your keyboard or notebook, and begin to write.

Schedules

I have asked you to write and have provided some exercises to help you get started. I am well aware of challenges that you may be facing. Writing is difficult, time-consuming, sometimes painful or tedious, and almost always frustrating. And certainly not as profitable as you'd like. So how do you keep writing on a regular basis so that you produce the work you intend to—and make the impact your work deserves? As I have already pointed out, there is no enforcer character to help you tow the line. But you can motivate and energize and excite yourself by being your own police person. Listen to Annie Dillard.

In her book *The Writing Life* (1989) Dillard writes about schedules—hers and others': "A schedule defends from chaos and whim. It is a net for catching days. It is a scaffolding on which a worker can stand and labor with both hands at sections of time."

She describes the routines of many writers, including poet Wallace Stevens who regularly got up at 6:00 AM, read for two hours, and then walked three miles to his office at the Hartford Insurance Company where he dictated poems to his secretary before selling the policies that generated his income.

Jack London wrote twenty hours a day; he set his alarm to wake him after four hours of sleep. "Often he slept through the alarm," says Dillard, "so . . . he rigged it to drop a weight on his head." Dillard confesses that she doesn't believe this story, though she jokes that "a novel like *The Sea*

Wolf is strong evidence some sort of weight fell on his head with some frequency."

On Cape Cod, Dillard, who won the 1975 Pulitzer Prize in nonfiction for her book *Pilgrim at Tinker Creek*, worked in a prefabricated tool shed, eight by ten feet, crammed with her computer, printer, copier, air conditioner/heater, and coffeemaker. When she became too interested in the world outside her shed she cut out squares of paper and pasted them over each pane of glass in the windows. Then, so as not to feel so boxed in, she painted birds, trees, and wildflowers on the paper.

You do what you can, whatever works for you, to keep writing on a regular basis. You need to create a writing schedule and keep it sacrosanct. If becoming a writer means enough to you as a person, then, as I have said, you will police yourself. But more importantly, writing should become a voluntary part of your life—not a forced internment. Many writers complain about the agony of the writing experience, but the mere thought of giving it up, even for a week, would be anathema.

Slave to Routine

John McPhee, who has written more than thirty books and traveled around the world, is mostly a person of regimentation and routine. He has an office on the Princeton University campus where he writes and, when he's not on the road, arrives there every morning at about 8:00 AM. With rare exceptions, he'll stay there throughout the day—writing or thinking about writing.

He admits that sometimes during those long solitary days waiting for the words to come he'll fall asleep, but he knows by the end of the day he's expected—he expects himself—to produce one to two thousand words to add to his growing manuscript. He'll walk home with the new pages tucked into his tote bag, have a martini, and perhaps read some of what he's written to his wife, his most trusted critic, for comment or criticism.

We can't all be fortunate enough to have offices on college campuses or the time to write most of the day, but McPhee's routine demonstrates what writers must do to progress and produce. Writing for a living is not like staying up all night to write a paper for a college professor. Writing is a process that requires slow and steady building and shaping.

A regular schedule is essential. I've never known a writer who's published regularly who doesn't write regularly—and have some sort of idiosyncratic routine, with or without martinis. Hemingway preferred wine and whiskey to martinis, but he always bragged that he was up in the morning pounding away at his typewriter no matter how late he was out "living the writer's life" the night before.

I don't expect most of my readers to be full-time writers, although I'm hoping to help you get there one day. If you have some flexibility, it's best to choose a time and place that's comfortable and quiet and allows you to experience as much clarity as possible. For me, it's the predawn hours, but for others it may be midnight—or later. When I suffered from insomnia, I'd walk by my neighbor's house and see his third floor attic light on at 3:00 AM, his prime time for clarity. He was an academic and a single dad, but also a writer—and after he said good night to his children, he began his most serious work.

The need for a regular schedule isn't limited to writers. One early spring morning many years ago, when I got up and out of bed and dressed, with my first steaming mug of coffee in hand, I heard the sweet music of a woodwind wafting through the silence. It was beautiful and entrancing as I went to my keyboard and started my work. I listened to the music as I wrote. Far from disturbing me, it enhanced my experience that day. But in the back of my mind I wondered where it was coming from and why I was hearing it that day. Finally I put the puzzle together. My new neighbor Tom, who'd moved into the little carriage house behind my house, was principal flutist of the renowned Pittsburgh Symphony.

Later Tom and I discussed the similarities of our work. "But don't you rehearse every afternoon at Heinz Hall or wherever you are performing?" I asked him.

"Yes," Tom replied. "But you have to practice regularly—not just to get better, but to maintain your high standards."

His statement helped me understand that every draft I wrote was practice for the next draft I wrote. My final manuscript was like Tom's performances—some magnificent and others only marginal. Practice may never make perfect, but it certainly makes you better.

Michael Jordan, one of the world's greatest living athletes, once explained his philosophy and outlook on life: "I have missed more than 9,000 shots in my career. I have lost almost 300 games. On 26 occasions I have been trusted to take the game winning shot and I missed. I have failed over and over again in my life . . . that is how I have succeeded."

Writers and athletes are similar in this way. It doesn't matter how much raw talent we have if we don't exercise our muscles and our brains in a sustained and uninterrupted effort to hone our skills. Michael Jordan and Tiger Woods were not born superstars. They worked and practiced with sustained and concentrated dedication in order to achieve greatness. This intense commitment to dedication and practice begins with passion.

PASSION AND PRACTICE

Most every writer has a special way of preparing to get to work and keep working, and a goal for a satisfying stopping point for the day. Some writers, like McPhee, need to fight their way through the piece from beginning to end, producing a rough draft before going back to the manuscript to add shape and clarity. But William Styron once told me his goal was to write a page a day, and to write it again and again on that day, until it was the best page he thought he could write—and then he wouldn't return to it again. Because he had a bad back, Hemingway wrote standing up, as did Thomas Wolfe. Since Wolfe was a giant of a man at 6 feet 7, he often wrote on top of his icebox, which was higher than any table he could find.

Wolfe wrote with brute passion, for days at a time, sometimes flinging the pages of his manuscript onto the floor of his kitchen apartment in New York's West Village, forgetting to number them. It's said that his editor, the famous Maxwell Perkins, was often seen rooting around Wolfe's apartment, looking for the lost flying pages and trying to figure out where in Wolfe's deep and intense narratives they belonged. When he could write no more, Wolfe roared into the streets of the city, living life with the same passion and abandon that animated his writing.

There was a time when I experienced similar explosions of exhilaration and exhaustion as Thomas Wolfe's paper slinging. After writing through a day or night, I'd leap onto my motorcycle and thunder into the country, feeling the cold night air blowing in my face—as I contemplated the dark anonymity of the highway. Hours later, sipping coffee in a truck stop or diner, I sketched with words the tired faces and recorded the conversations of my fellow travelers. These were wonderful, formative experiences for me, although frenetic and wild, especially when I soared through those dark country roads on two wheels.

Passion is what's required of a creative nonfiction writer—passion for people, passion for the written word, passion for knowledge, passion for spontaneity of experience, passion to understand how things work. As Joan Didion said in a *New York Times Magazine* article titled "Why I Write" (1976), "I write to find out what I am thinking, what I am looking at, what I see, and what it means."

I know it is easy to provide examples of famous writers (and athletes), but what about people laboring alone and in the dark, who have yet to achieve success? They may be reluctant to tell people they are writers, lest someone ask what they have published and whether they have appeared on the bestseller list. This is a difficult barrier to cross—to have faith and confidence in yourself, knowing in your heart that someday you will prove your worth and that your practice and passion will lead to satisfaction and success. This is the challenge almost all writers confront: their own unique "rope test."

THE ROPE TEST

I'd assumed, as did most of my friends and family, that when I enlisted in the U.S. Coast Guard I'd have an easy time of it, physically. After all, Guardsmen were the shallow water sailors. Little did I know that because we were operating on the coast (protecting our shores from enemy aggression), we were always running like hell on land instead of powering through the waves in a boat like true seamen.

A signal on the bell tower—three staccato chimes—triggered a favorite drill in basic training. When we heard these chimes, we recruits were obliged to grab our rifles and bayonets, dash to meet an invading enemy, and do combat in the water. Traditional Coast Guard boot camp when I was a grunt in the 1960s was twelve weeks, versus the Army's nine-week stint. This was because people who came into the Guard were usually in suboptimal physical condition and because we had more instructional classes, such as semaphore and maritime law.

After twelve weeks of basic, I was the only member of my company who didn't graduate and join a unit. I'd lost some eighty pounds at this point—I'd entered weighing 220 pounds—and was now as fit as I'd ever been. Needless to say, the food was not as appealing as my mother's cooking.

But no matter how hard or how often I tried, I couldn't pass the rope test. We were supposed to climb a fifty-foot rope, with knots spaced evenly for handholds; we had to get to the top and then control our descent. There are other ways of boarding an invading ship, but when a rope is the only answer, a Coast Guardsman must be prepared.

After boot camp graduation ceremonies (from which I was barred), I said good-bye to my fellow recruits, now assigned to units across the country and abroad. I would be anchored to the boot camp base until I could pass the rope test. "We'll keep you in this compound," Chief Petty Officer O'Reilly assured me, "for however long it takes."

During the day I worked with a maintenance crew—men who were in the brig for minor offenses—inside a large abandoned furnace, chiseling away at the burned-on soot and debris without seeing natural light between breakfast and lunch and lunch and supper. At that time, masks were unheard of. I breathed in the coal dust all morning and coughed it out at night. Working so long and hard while breathing that sooty material, by day's end I lacked the energy and will to climb the rope or even work out with free weights to strengthen my upper body. I began to think I'd serve my entire hitch as a "boot." The rope test seemed beyond me.

In the recreation hall one Saturday afternoon, I wandered aimlessly toward a door in the back of the room behind the pool hall and saw a plaque that read "Library." I entered a new world.

The books I found in the library were the same stuff I'd been reading at home: Hemingway's *Nick Adams Stories*; Frank Slaughter's novels about physicians in every conceivable milieu; Arthur Miller's *Death of a Salesman* (I identified with Biff, not an admirable character, but what a stupendous nickname); Herman Wouk's *Marjorie Morningstar*; *The Diary of Anne Frank*; Mark Twain's *Huckleberry Finn*.

This library allowed me some privacy, a place to sit in a soft chair and think, with no one talking or telling me what to do or forcing me to salute. Books were stories, and the stories I read took me to another dimension of time and place where people, some of whom I could identify with, were confronting problems similar to those plaguing me.

My involvement in the stories of other people's lives, real or make-believe, helped me assess and eventually reshape my own priorities. Here was Philip Roth's protagonist in *Goodbye, Columbus* (1959), frustrated by his inability to be accepted in a world that, ironically, he knew in his heart he did not want to be a part of, as I had wanted to be accepted in my school and neighborhood.

Ernest Hemingway's 1925 story "Big Two Hearted River" (published in his first story collection, *In Our Time*) captured and reinforced my search for solitude, which Hemingway experienced on the Upper Peninsula in Michigan. Within weeks, I could feel myself changing. Reading the stories of others gave me the self-confidence I needed to become stronger and more independent—and I was physically shrinking. The uniforms I'd been issued hung from my body like curtains.

I never made a conscious decision to try to lose weight; it just started happening. I started to get up early in the morning and do hundreds of extra push-ups and sit-ups before reveille. At lunch, instead of eating or smoking, I'd take long walks around the compound, reading as I walked. Or I went into the men's room and practiced pull-ups on the toilet stall walls. I stayed behind closed doors because the guys with whom I shared furnace-cleaning duty were in detention, not because they were too fat or couldn't pass the rope test. They wouldn't have taken kindly to my public display of extra physical training. Their attitude was that we had enough PT in our regular routine. In the evening I was back in my private library sanctuary, reading and working out.

After following my secret regimen for six weeks, I surprised my superiors and myself by showing up at the gym one evening and literally bounding up the rope from floor to ceiling, almost effortlessly. I touched the top with one sure hand and then skittered down again without using my feet.

When I got to the bottom the first time, I showboated by going up again—and back. It was a triumphant moment, not just because I succeeded but because I pulled it off with ease.

Suddenly the possibilities and potential of my life became evident. Passing the rope test more than satisfied Chief O'Reilly. I could now go on to other postings and other challenges—like writing creative nonfiction.

FALL DOWN NINE TIMES—GET UP TEN

The rope test had been a life test for me. I'd never forget—I'd never permit myself to forget—that there were few limitations to my potential, as long as I had a goal in mind and I persisted. I could and would climb the rope, any rope, anywhere, no matter how long it took, how much effort it required.

Along the way, I adopted two slogans that became guiding principles for me. The first comes from an organ transplant surgeon I met while I was doing research for one of my books, *Many Sleepless Nights* (1988). He was talking with a patient who was waiting for an organ transplant—and slowly dying. He paraphrased Winston Churchill's appeal to the British people in 1941 in the darkest days of the German blitzkrieg, telling his patient, "Never give in, never give up. Never. Never. Never. Ever."

Later I looked up Churchill's exact words: "Never give in, never give in. Never. Never. Never. Never. In nothing great or small, large or petty, never give in, except to convictions of honor and good sense."

I remember that the patient somehow responded; he managed to live a few more days until a heart became available. I lost touch with this man after his surgery, and I don't know if he lived or for how long, but the message his heart surgeon told him remained imprinted on my mind. I'll never give in and I'll never forget how much I might achieve in my life if I keep trying. Not trying means capitulation.

The second slogan comes from another sick person, an old friend who had battled depression throughout his life and slit his wrists on his wedding day. His new wife discovered him bleeding nearly to death in the bathroom. Paramedics saved his life.

A few weeks later, when I visited him at home, I asked him why he was able to look so cheerful and how he was managing to project a positive image after what he'd been through. He chanted for me the little song he'd heard in the suicide unit—the ward where every patient was under twenty-four hour observation—in the psychiatric facility where he'd recuperated.

While he was lying in bed in the dark, the door to his room wide open so nurses could maintain constant surveillance, he could hear a man singing to himself. This man, he found out later, had lost his wife and child in an auto accident some years ago. He'd been driving. Since then he'd suffered severe and paralyzing fits of depression. He'd frequently tried to hurt himself, but, according to the nurses, he always seemed to rally and recover and try to get on with his life. He was strong enough to leave the hospital—frequently—but not strong enough to manage his depression at home for a sustained period of time. His song was simple and relentless, my friend said, and eerie to hear again and again, but the message, so clear and simple, struck home with him: "Fall down nine times . . . get up ten."

This is the lesson every writer must learn—each piece of creative writing is a separate challenge. Writing a book is like having a baby and raising it to adolescence. A long-form essay, say 5,000 words, is comparable to a surgical procedure. Okay, perhaps I'm exaggerating. But the writer is the mother or the father of the book. It's your creation, even if you're writing nonfiction. You'll describe and shape the lives of your characters, plan for their future, and suffer when they take you off course—which they will.

Question: What about preparing an outline before starting to write?

Answer: Even if you begin writing with an outline of your essay or book, from Roman numeral I to X or XX, you don't really know where the numerals will take you. And I hope that your outline is just a guide and not a straitjacket. You're a writer, and writers, especially those using the artful form of creative nonfiction, are often guided by instinct, as are most creative people in the world. So go with your instinct, especially when writing a first draft, and worry later about fine-tuning the details.

John McPhee often begins the writing process, whether he's working on a book or essay, a long or short form, with the end. McPhee says he likes

---

EXERCISE 4

My experience with the rope test and the meaningful and memorable lessons I took from it prompted my writing students to refer to my approach to scheduling as "the boot camp way of writing." This is because I preached the mantra of the regular schedule in all my classes—and my regular routine mirrored the schedule the military had indoctrinated in me during my Coast Guard days. For years, since adopting the writing life, my reveille has come at 4:30 or 5:00 AM. I had many jobs when I was a beginning writer—truck driving, shoe selling, advertising copywriting, and finally teaching, but by getting up in the early morning I was able to attend to my "real" work—my creative writing—when I was the freshest and most clear-minded before I went about the practical responsibilities of my day.

Some of you are already writing on a regular schedule; for those who are not, now is the time to devise one. Think about your life and decide when you are most clear-headed, where you can find a space undisturbed, and what part of your life (early morning, late night, lunch hour with your colleagues) you are most willing to sacrifice. Try all of the combinations until one works best.

---

to write his last sentence or paragraph right at the beginning so that, from the start of the first draft of his essay or book, he knows where he's supposed to end up. This doesn't mean he can predict his conclusion and foresee his final scene at the beginning. But wherever the story takes him, he knows the general direction he will travel. The ending may change by the time he gets there—but he needs to have a road map of sorts in order to get started. Beginning at the ending is his method.

I work differently. I begin my story at the point I feel most excited and involved. I have an idea in the beginning of what I want to say, but I try to let my words and ideas guide me as they burst out onto the page. In the end, there are probably as many writing routines as there are serious writers. The important thing to remember is that the only way you are going to write successfully is to keep on writing until you get it right.

A FINAL WORD ABOUT SCHEDULES

"When I am working on a book or story I write every morning as soon after first light as possible. There is no one to disturb you, and it is cool or cold and you come to your work and warm as you write. You write until you come to a place when you still have your juice and know what will happen next, and you stop and try to live through until the next day when you hit it again.

"When you stop you are as empty, and at the same time never empty, but filled as when you have made love to someone you love. Nothing can hurt you, nothing can happen, nothing means anything until the next day when you do it again. It is the wait until the next day that is so hard to get through" (Ernest Hemingway).

The Creative Nonfiction Pendulum:
From Personal to Public

One simple way to approach creative nonfiction is by gauging the relationship of the writer to the subject.

Imagine a pendulum swinging expansively from left to right.

The pendulum swings between what can be called "public" or "issue-oriented" or "big idea" creative nonfiction at one extreme, and on the other "personal" or "private" creative nonfiction. The pendulum can swing radically from one side to the other, strictly personal or strictly public. Or it can swing moderately, merging the public and the private into a rich and compelling prose mixture. When that happens, the jazz of creative nonfiction can become a literary symphony.

THE PERSONAL: THE KISS THAT CAUSED THE CRAZE

The girl is very pretty—blonde, pale, lithe, shy, and sensitive. She's twenty when it begins, and she knows from the start what she's doing is wrong, very wrong. But she's obsessed, can't seem to stop herself.

She meets him in train stations and airports, art museums and national monuments, and they often rendezvous in the dark confines of her apartment. The trysts go on sporadically for two agonizing years, until finally one day she summons up the courage and resolve to end it.

He takes it badly—he doesn't want to stop seeing her. But in his heart he knows that sooner or later it would come to a bad end, for nothing good can ever come from having an affair with your daughter. Especially when you have another family—a wife and three children hundreds of miles away who have no idea where you go when you disappear and who you are meeting.

Especially when you are a Presbyterian minister and have a congregation of souls to watch over.

Twenty years later, the girl goes public. When Kathryn Harrison's memoir, *The Kiss*, was published in 1997, it was a literary sensation because it was so intimate and revealing. And now she was a married woman and the mother of two young children.

Considering what we see every day on reality TV nowadays or read in the tabloids, Kathryn Harrison's revelations don't seem that shocking to us. But in 1997, the critics went crazy. Jonathan Yardley of the *Washington Post* was so obsessed he reviewed *The Kiss* three times and could hardly find enough invective for his attack. *The Kiss*, according to Yardley, was "shameful, slimy, repellent, meretricious, cynical and revolting."

Mary Eberstadt theorized in England's *Weekly Standard* that Harrison concocted the story because her novels (she'd published three novels prior to the publication of *The Kiss*) weren't selling well. James Wolcott (the guy who named me the godfather), writing in the *New Republic* and wearing his psychotherapist's hat, accused Harrison of "inviting humiliation upon her own children . . . as misery was invited on her."

This is the danger of writing so personally and revealing such intimacies. People will not take you seriously, will contend that you are just trying to attract attention to yourself, or that you are lonely and wallowing in self-pity. But Harrison's book changed the lives of generations of women who had spent a lifetime hiding similar secrets from friends and families, suffering in silence. It is a prime example of the very personal and powerful side of the creative nonfiction pendulum. *The Kiss* was an instant bestseller—and it remains in print today. But, as Harrison discovered, such honesty bred contempt in response to this work but not to the other fine books of fiction and nonfiction she has published since *The Kiss*.

THE MEMOIR CRAZE

James Wolcott was incensed by what he called navel gazing. "Creative nonfiction," Wolcott said in *Vanity Fair*, was "civic journalism for the soul—a sickly transfusion whereby the weakling sensitive voice of fiction is inserted into the beery carcass of nonfiction." What he meant was that in creative nonfiction, writers talk too much about themselves, look inside instead of outside—are self-indulgent, whiny, boring people with their own neuroses. In a recent article in *Creative Nonfiction*, Robin Hemley, who writes both fiction and creative nonfiction, makes the point that poets (and fiction writers) are constantly engaging in excess introspection and that the interiority of their ruminations makes their work powerful and provides connectivity to the ordinary reader. It's a good thing. So why aren't creative nonfiction writers permitted the same interiority?

It's true that "public" nonfiction writers like Michael Pollan (*The Omnivore's Dilemma* 2006; *The Botany of Desire* 2001) or Dexter Filkins (*The Forever War* 2008) write books that take on big issues like war and politics, food and football. The big issue books will entertain, surprise, and inform you—but they won't move you in the way a short story or a poem or a memoir may. That's why memoirs can be so effective. Memoirs reveal the intimacies of ordinary lives—ideas and information that some may criticize as less important than nuclear peril or other major issues. But many writers are convinced small personal issues are just as important as major themes and ideas.

"Back when I was in graduate school in the late 1980s," writes Hemley, "my friends and I used to classify writers into two types: windows and mirrors. The fiction writers were the windows, writers who looked out on the wide world, and wrote about what they saw. The mirrors were the poets, writers of reflection and meditation. . . . We even named our softball teams accordingly, the Windows vs. the Mirrors."

But what team included the poor nonfiction writers, the memoirists in particular?

"They could play on neither team," says Hemley, "because memoirists as we know them today didn't exist." That was then and this is now. Times have changed.

The Kiss didn't change the literary landscape by itself, of course. It was published around the same time a half dozen other intimate memoirs were published. Together they triggered what the publishing industry and the book critics referred to with surprise and derision as the "memoir craze."

Angela's Ashes (1996) by Frank McCourt and *This Boy's Life* (1989) by Tobias Wolff were both made into major motion pictures; the British actress Emily Watson starred as McCourt's mother, Angela, and the Academy Award winner Robert De Niro played Wolff's stepfather, Dwight Hansen. *The Liars Club* (1995) by Mary Karr, another of these best-selling tell-all memoirs, rode the new interest in the genre.

Memoirs are not new to the literary world. Henry David Thoreau's *Walden* is a classic of the form as is Isak Dinesen's *Out of Africa*, first published in this country in 1938. *The Kiss*, however, pushed into new territory, with the subject of incest scandalizing both critics and ordinary readers. Even in 1997, book-reviewing venues were drying up, and any controversy that might help sell a few more magazines or newspapers was a boon at the time. Yardley and Wolcott predicted the demise of the memoir as a form, but it remains a significant presence on the literary landscape.

Today the memoir craze continues in full force. Celebrities, politicians, athletes—victims and heroes alike—are making their private lives public. And readers can't get enough of these books. The literature of reality, with all of the pain and the secrets that authors confess, is helping to connect the nation and the world in a meaningful and intimate way.

BETWEEN MEMOIR AND AUTOBIOGRAPHY

"Am I writing memoir or autobiography?" I'm often asked.

"Are you writing about your entire life, more or less, from the beginning up to the present day?" I inquire. If the answer is yes, then it's probably an autobiography.

A memoir, in contrast, is autobiographical but focuses on one aspect or one period or one incident in your life. Let's say your marriage is falling apart. Week after week, you and your partner can feel your relationship disintegrating. You fight and then you make up, which works for a while, but the damage is done. The arguing and the name-calling overwhelm the pleasure of making up and coming back together. That significant aspect of your life, the break-up or the threatened break-up of your marriage, may be the window on your life that your memoir will open to your reader.

We won't learn about your great job in the banking industry or your frustrations as a golfer or your problems with acne as an adolescent—unless they relate in some way to the crumbling state of your marriage. If you think of a writer as a camera, a memoirist documents a close-up through the zoom lens, revealing the most intimate and personal details, while the autobiographer shoots a whole landscape with a panoramic lens.

Reading *The Kiss,* we learn very little about Kathryn Harrison except for her two-year affair with her father. The recent best-seller *Eat Pray Love* focuses mostly on Elizabeth Gilbert's odyssey to find herself after a messy divorce. Where she grew up and went to school, what career she had before writing her book are mostly omitted. The only other information Gilbert provides relates to the trauma and challenges of her romantic life.

In Lauren Slater's essay "Three Spheres," included in this book, the reader peers through a window into Slater's life for a few days. But those days are excruciatingly vivid. The power of the memoir is in its concentration, the narrowness of its scope, and the intensity and clarity of its revelations.

Another frequent question I'm asked is this: "What's the difference between a memoir and the personal essay?"

The term "memoir" usually refers to a book. A shorter piece, standing alone, is usually referred to as a personal essay. "Three Spheres," for example, is one of seven essays in Slater's first memoir, *Welcome to My World* (1995). She's written several others: *Prozac Diary* (1999), *Lying: A Metaphorical Memoir* (2000), and *Love Works Like This: Moving from One Kind of Life to Another* (2002).

DON'T GET TANGLED IN TERMINOLOGY

Academics often refer to the formal and informal essay. What are they? In the introduction to his anthology *The Art of the Personal Essay* (1994), Phillip Lopate quotes C. Hugh Holman and William Harmon's *A Handbook to Literature* in order to define and distinguish between formal (or impersonal) and informal essays. Holman and Harmon characterize the informal essay as containing "very personal elements, including self-revelation, individual tastes and experiences, humor . . . freshness of form, freedom from stiffness and affectation . . . incomplete treatment of topic." I think the informal essay, the personal essay, and the memoir are very close in content and can be referred to indiscriminately. They fit comfortably under the creative nonfiction umbrella.

In the formal essay "literary effect is secondary to serious purpose." Formal essays are less personal—or personal in a different way—and are on the other side, the "public" or "big idea" side of the creative nonfiction pendulum. They too fall under the creative nonfiction umbrella: true stories well told.

"Lyric essay" is a term that confounds many people, perhaps because "lyric," a poetic term, and "essay," a more fact-oriented term, don't seem to fit together. But they can fit and often do, as John D'Agata demonstrates in his 2002 anthology, *The Next American Essay*. D'Agata brings together work from such creative nonfiction masters as John McPhee, Susan Sontag, Joan Didion, and Annie Dillard to demonstrate the scope of the lyrical form of creative nonfiction, blending biography, poetry, philosophy, and memoir.

As I have mentioned on page 25, D'Agata, along with his mentor, poet Deborah Tall, helped introduce the lyric essay in a literary journal, the *Seneca Review* (a publication of Hobart and William Smith colleges), which Tall edited from 1982 until her death in 2006. Since then, D'Agata has promoted the idea and it's caught on, primarily in creative writing classrooms. How to define or describe the lyric essay—and distinguish it from poetry? Tall and D'Agata did so with clarity in the *Seneca Review* in 1997. "The lyric essay partakes of the poem in its density and shapeliness, its distillation of ideas and musicality of language. It partakes of the essay in its weight, in its overt desire to engage with facts, melding its allegiance to the actual with its passion for imaginative form."

Eve Joseph's essay "Yellow Taxi," reprinted in this book (page 169), is an example of a personal essay with strong lyric elements.

The Public or "Big Idea"

One distinction between the personal and the public—or the opposite sides of the pendulum—is that the memoir is *your* particular story, nobody else's. It's personal. You own it. In contrast, the public side of creative nonfiction is mostly somebody else's story; anybody, potentially, owns it, anybody who wants to go to the time and trouble to write about it. Or, conversely, it could be your story in that you have a theory or an idea or a larger point to make about the world. A bigger and more universal idea.

Every week, the *New Yorker* publishes "fact pieces": creative nonfiction about virtually any subject—from bullfighting to death and dying to transcontinental trucking to poverty in India or game hunting in Africa. There are no limits to the subject matter—except any that the writer and the subject may establish or discover. So it may be your story, but it isn't personal—it's a story almost anyone could research and write.

I've included examples of the public kind of creative nonfiction in this book, including my essay "Difficult Decisions," published in the literary review *Prairie Schooner* in 1996, and "Fixing Nemo" by Rebecca Skloot, published in 2004 by the *New York Times*. The first is about a day in the life of Wendy Freeman, a large animal veterinarian. The second documents surgery on a goldfish. Although it took a considerable amount of work on my part to gain access to the vet and on Skloot's to interview the fish surgeon, almost any writer could have made the contacts, invested the time and energy, and written these pieces. So each is a public story with an idea behind it.

Because they're so personal, memoirs have a limited audience, while the public kind of creative nonfiction—when authors write about something other than themselves—has a larger audience. These essays are more sought after by editors and agents.

Each issue of the *New Yorker* includes two and sometimes as many as four or five "fact pieces"—public creative nonfiction essays—and usually only one or possibly two shorter "personal history" pieces, which is another way of saying "memoir." The *New Yorker* is a popular, trendsetting magazine, so the frequency of public versus personal essays in its pages is important. *Harper's*, *Esquire*, and other magazines have a similar mix.

THE UNIVERSAL CHORD: WHEN PERSONAL AND PUBLIC COME TOGETHER

The driving force behind creative nonfiction has everything to do with attracting and keeping the reader interested. On the public or big issue side of the pendulum, the subject matter must capture a reader's attention. Baseball fans love biographies of players such as Mickey Mantle, Joe DiMaggio, and Ty Cobb. Men read and are often obsessed with military history—World War II, especially. These books stay in print and are referred to in the publishing world as backlist books, meaning they're perennial sellers; there's no need to promote these titles. The subjects sell themselves, not a lot of copies, perhaps, but enough to keep making a profit.

The memoir, on the opposite side of the pendulum, has its own draw—an unusual and compelling personal story—and will also show up in the backlist catalog. *The Kiss*, *The Liars Club*, and others like them will be available for a long time because of their unique stories, their intimate revelations, and of course the fine writing. Both sides of the pendulum can be successful.

The ideal creative nonfiction piece is one where the pendulum stops somewhere around the middle—a public subject with an intimate and personal spin. Writers who can choose a public subject and give it a personal treatment are establishing a "universal chord": reaching out and embracing a large umbrella of readership. People from Iowa to Israel and from New York to Indonesia are equally intrigued by such a book. That's the writer's mission: to establish and stretch his potential reading audience.

"Difficult Decisions" and "Fixing Nemo" are public issue/idea pieces. Many writers can profile veterinarians, whether they specialize in goats or goldfish. At its bare bones, even Lauren Slater's "Three Spheres" is a public topic. The essay illustrates how therapists and therapy teams deal with patients and admit them to the proper therapeutic facility. It's also about how borderline personality patients act, and how professionals and treatment teams deal with borderline patients.

"Three Spheres" demonstrates the way writers can modify their distance from the subject and merge dual voices. Slater is not only the therapist and the writer, but she's also been a patient. She is "inside" and "outside" simultaneously.

Another way of achieving this inside and outside middle ground—public and personal—is demonstrated in Susan Sheehan's Pulitzer Prize–winning

---

EXERCISE 5

For the first few exercises, I asked you to choose a personal experience and dramatize it—and then connect the story to something of substance you can talk about and create a dialogue or amplify. Perhaps you have already begun an essay that represents a big idea—a public issue—and the piece you are writing contains that elusive and essential universal chord. If not, then it's time to think more seriously about the direction of your essay and how you can make it more relevant to a larger audience from a substance point of view.

Or better yet—and this is what I prefer—start a second essay—a big idea piece of writing—about something that is very important to you. What turns you on—or off? Politics, food, French wine, sustainability, or big time college sports? What do you want to learn more about—or talk about? How would you like to change the world? Make a list and start to learn everything you can about the subject. Research is often the best way to begin.

Is There No Place on Earth for Me? (1982), first excerpted in the *New Yorker*. The narrative revolves around a schizophrenic patient, Sylvia Frumkin, who, like Slater's patient, is being admitted to a psychiatric facility and discussing the treatment options available to her under the New York state system. Sheehan is a reporter who documented the tragic and sometimes ridiculous details of Frumkin's life.

The book opens with a vivid scene as Frumkin is taking a bath. Sheehan tells us she's washing her brown hair with a combination of shampoo and red mouthwash. At some point in her past, Frumkin had dyed her hair red and liked the way she looked, but became impatient with the coloring process. That morning she concluded that the mouthwash would seep into her scalp and make her hair red forever.

Sheehan describes Frumkin's "frolicking" in the bathtub, blowing bubbles and making a soapy mess on the floor, which causes her to slip and fall and get a cut on the back of her head. She wraps a towel around her head and stumbles into her bedroom where, on her dresser, she sees the bottle of expensive perfume a relative had recently given her for her thirtieth birthday. "She poured the contents of the bottle on her cut," Sheehan writes, "partly because she knew that her perfume contained alcohol and that alcohol was an antiseptic and partly because she suddenly thought that she was Jesus Christ and that her cut was the beginning of a crown of thorns. She also thought that she was Mary Magdalene, who had poured ointment on Christ."

Although the stories by Slater and Sheehan differ in content, the disjointed memories and experiences of Slater as a patient and of Frumkin evoke similar feelings of chaotic disturbance. They could be the same person. Or, stretching it a little, Frumkin could have been the person the young Slater would have grown up to be had circumstances been different. This is a testament to Sheehan's research, her ability to connect with her subjects, and her willingness to devote enough time and attention to understand the issues and ideas in a three-dimensional sense. She's building into the book and her story a universal chord, meaning that she's talking about real issues that concern our country generally and the health care system specifically—a big idea—and personalizing it so that readers can understand and relate in a vivid and unforgettable manner.

Widening the Pendulum's Swing

You can maximize your reading audience and strike a universal chord through research. Or to use a word journalists prefer: reporting. Your story might be too local—too much about your hometown or your neighborhood—to connect with folks who live in Nebraska or Oklahoma or an urban subculture like Boston or New York. Or too personal—about close friends and family, people your readers might not identify with.

To broaden substance and enhance readership, some writers reach back and make historical connections. John Edgar Widemann is the author of "Looking at Emmett Till," in *In Fact: The Best of Creative Nonfiction* (2003). The essay is about the Ku Klux Klan's 1965 murder of teenager Emmett Till in tiny Money, Mississippi. Wideman makes it clear this wasn't an isolated incident; it was a blight upon our nation. He provides many other examples of white hate crimes against blacks in the 1960s and into the present day.

"It was hard to bury Emmett Till," he writes, "hard, hard to bury Carole Robinson, Addie Mae Collins, Denise McNair, Cynthia Wesley, the four girls killed by a bomb in a Birmingham, Alabama, church. So hard that an entire nation began to register the convulsions of black mourning." He continued: "Emmett Till's mangled face could belong to anybody's son who transgressed racial laws; anyone's little girl could be crushed in the rubble of a bombed church. . . . Martin Luther King understood the killing of our children was an effort to murder the nation's future."

In her memoir "Yellow Taxi," published in a collected volume I recently edited, *At the End of Life: True Stories About How We Die* (2012), Eve Joseph, a hospice counselor, writes: "When I was twelve, my older brother was killed in a car accident. It was 1965, the year Allen Ginsburg introduced the term *flower power*, and Malcolm X was shot dead inside Harlem's Audubon Ballroom, the year T.S. Elliot died and Bob Dylan's 'Like a Rolling Stone' was on its way to becoming a new anthem" (see the entire essay on page 169).

These historical extensions connect readers with memories of their own experiences in the 1950s and 1960s, or perhaps with their own relationships with minority groups—incidents that may be dangerous or embarrassing. Jews weren't lynched or murdered for being Jews in this country in 1955, but anti-Semitism was still common enough to frighten them; Japanese Americans felt simmering resentment over the discrimination and internment they experienced during World War II. And thus, even though these groups might not have been persecuted in the overt way African Americans were, they can nonetheless empathize with Wideman's words. And few baby boomers do not have poignant and often gloriously nostalgic memories of Ginsberg and Dylan, making Eve Joseph's reminiscent line hit home.

Including history, when appropriate and relevant, is one way to expand your base audience; so too is adding fascinating ancillary information as texture, to make the facts of whatever you're describing more evocative. Later in "Yellow Taxi" Joseph writes: "At birth a newborn baby has approximately three hundred bones while on the average an adult has two hundred six. Our bones fuse as we grow. We are building our scaffolding without even knowing it. The twenty-four long curved bones of our ribcage form a structure that shelters the heart, lungs, liver and spleen. Like exotic birds, we live within the shelter of our bony cages."

She continues to connect her information to her story: "One summer night, a twenty-eight-year-old patient with bone cancer asked to be wheeled outside in her hospital bed to sleep beneath the stars. In the days preceding her death, the bones in her ribcage were so brittle that one or two broke whenever she rolled over. I was horrified to learn that our bones could snap like dry twigs."

If you're writing about geography or travel, information about location can add substance and allow you to connect to more readers. From my book *Truckin' with Sam* (2010), here's an interesting factoid I found on Google: "We follow the interstate past Fargo to Jamestown, North Dakota, then eventually connect to US 52, which takes us to Portal. North Portal, a sister city, is just over the Canadian border in Saskatchewan. Some time later, I googled Portal and learned that the town is known for its international golf course, the only course in the world in two countries, with the first eight holes in Canada and the final hole in both countries. You tee off in Canada and your ball crosses the 49th parallel and, because of the changing time zones, lands in Portal, North Dakota—an hour later."

Even if you're describing something you know a lot about, it's good to bring in other viewpoints—not only to broaden the topic but also to enhance your own credibility, as Eve Joseph does by invoking a preeminent expert:

> In 1969, with her book *On Death and Dying,* Elisabeth Kübler-Ross brought the subject of death out of the privacy of medical schools and delivered it to the streets. She gave the layperson a language and a framework to understand the process of grief. Her five stages of grief provided new ways to think and speak about loss and helped give a sense of movement to the dying process. Her model is largely responsible for the ubiquitous idea of the "good death," the idea that there is a best way to approach the end of life, that we will reach acceptance before our last breath. A central concept of a good death is one that allows a person to die on his or her own terms, relatively pain free, with dignity. As if we have control. I was regularly asked, by family members, to describe the dying process. I would tell them about how people often lapse into a coma in the days preceding death and how breath moves from the deep and regular to the shallow and intermittent. I would explain apnea and how many people hold their breath for long periods of time, up to three minutes sometimes, and how all others in the room also hold their breath until the gasping breath breaks the silence in the room. I would explain

that people rarely die in the space between breaths, that they return to the body as if they have been on a practice run. I would go over the possibility that phlegm would build up, resulting in what is known as a "death rattle," a term that invokes a kind of dread, a term that conjures up scenes like the one Dostoevsky described in *Crime and Punishment*: "She sank more and more into uneasy delirium. At times she shuddered, turned her eyes from side to side, recognized everyone for a minute, but at once sank into delirium again. Her breathing was hoarse and difficult; there was a sort of rattle in her throat." I would talk about how the hands and feet get cold as blood leaves the extremities and pools around the heart and lungs in a last attempt to protect the vital organs and how those hands and feet turn blue shortly before death. And I would talk about how breath leaves the body, how it moves from the chest to the throat to little fish breaths at the end.

Note how Eve Joseph connects her ideas and experiences with Elisabeth Kübler-Ross, thus enhancing her own credibility. This sort of information—quoting from an expert—is what is expected in a public story, but the pieces quoted here are from memoir or personal essay. This is an important point. By adding research/reportage *even to memoir* we are pushing the pendulum closer to the middle in order to reach more readers and make our own personal story more encompassing.

The memoirist doesn't lose story or intimacy by adding research. On the contrary, research information makes the work more three dimensional and powerful. It's also part of the package. Remember, the term "creative nonfiction" includes two words—and writers sometimes become so obsessed with the first that they forget the second. Combining research and story creates connective tissue and forges the universal chord that we are all seeking in order to reach out to the reader on all levels and maximize our audience.

The Creative Nonfiction Way of Life

Once I thought I was going to become a great American novelist. My heroes were Ernest Hemingway, Philip Roth, Joseph Heller, and Norman Mailer, among others, typical and predictable for a Jewish boy growing up in the 1950s and 1960s at a time when, as Tom Wolfe has pointed out, the novel was "king" of American literature.

But the more I read these terrific authors and their books I so admired, the more ignorant I felt—naive about the world. I knew only the people in my neighborhood in Pittsburgh, Pennsylvania, a nice enough place. But Mailer, Heller, and Hemingway had been to war—or I should say *wars*. Hemingway, especially, had been everywhere—to Africa, Spain, Cuba, and Wyoming. He'd hunted big game and knew all about bullfighting; he'd driven an ambulance at the front during World War I. Me? I'd been nowhere and done nothing to speak of, except attend high school somewhat erratically and sell orthopedic shoes in my father's store.

Instead of going to college like most of my peers, I enlisted in the military, where I lived in a few places other than Pittsburgh and met a lot of people who were very different from me. My first week in boot camp I met the first black person I'd ever known who was my age and the first gay person—or at least the first person I knew was gay—who happened also to be Jewish.

And then there was a big guy named Gall, nearly six and a half feet tall, broad shouldered and surly. He was from Florida, somewhere in the middle of the state. We shared a bunk—he was in the upper and I was in the lower berth, and the moment I arrived and dumped my knapsack on the lower mattress, he dropped down as if he were a vulture, waiting for me to roost. He bent toward me, sticking his hawk-like nose in my face, and demanded: "Are you Jewish?"

And I figured, "Oh my God. Just as my father had warned me: wherever you go there'll be anti-Semites waiting to intimidate you and make your life miserable."

I toyed with the idea of denying my Jewish heritage, but I'd already received my dog tags, and my dog tags said I was Jewish. And anyway Gall might have ripped them from my neck to fact-check me, so I said, in as brave a voice as I could muster, bracing myself for whatever onslaught Gall was planning, "Yes. I'm Jewish."

Gall looked at me for a second, then smiled and jumped back onto his upper berth. Then he bent back down again and said in a friendly manner, "Well okay. As long as you aren't Catholic."

This moment was amazing to me. I'd grown up in a neighborhood of Catholic churches. The families on both sides of our house were Catholic. Billy, the older boy in the house next door, taunted me constantly, not just because I was Jewish but because I wasn't Catholic. His mother once told me, quite nicely and with a great deal of sympathetic understanding, "I feel sorry for you because you are a Jew. You'd be so much happier if you were Catholic."

She may have been right about that, at least in Greenfield, which was what the neighborhood was called, but I was happy to be a Jew in boot camp, with Gall as my mate. Gall was a Baptist who also had grown up surrounded by Catholics—and he got his enjoyment in his hometown by beating the hell out of them.

I came to see very quickly during those four months in boot camp that I had a lot to learn, and the more people I met and the more places I visited as I went though the military, the more I came to realize I knew very little about the world and the people in it. By the time I entered college—I was working my way through school doing odd jobs and attending classes at night—I realized I still didn't know enough to write a good novel. I loved reading novels, but I knew I couldn't write the book I wanted to write without knowing a lot more about the world.

A novel isn't just an adventure story—or a character study. A good novel recreates the world or shapes an aspect of the world in a unique and vivid manner. So I kept reading books and making plans to have new experiences, to meet as many people as possible, and learn about life—my life and the lives of others. At that time I didn't understand that what I was doing was preparing myself for a writing career but in a different form than the novel, in a form that didn't yet have a good and accurate name, but is now called creative nonfiction. I began living the creative nonfiction life.

FROM DREAM TO REALITY

Susan Sheehan was able to tell, vividly and intimately, the story of Sylvia Frumkin because she lived in the same facility and often in the same bedroom as Sylvia Frumkin. Sheehan set up a cot by Frumkin's bedside. She was present the morning Frumkin washed her hair with mouthwash and slipped and fell in the bathroom that led to her eventual committal in Creedmore Psychiatric Hospital. Sheehan had immersed herself in Frumkin's life, off and on, for many months, in order to be able to see the world through Frumkin's eyes—or, at the least, to understand Frumkin's world and the people in it.

Using the technique of immersion, writers can tailor a public story (a larger subject) in a way that allows them to own it—to make it their story. A faithful immersion will ultimately yield intimacy, and the deeper writers immerse themselves, the more targeted, all encompassing, and intimate the immersion will become. Immersion takes courage, commitment, and a great deal of time and concentration. Just like memoir, the idea of immersion is not new—writers and storytellers have been immersing themselves in the lives of other people and in foreign situations for millennia. It's only relatively recently that people have been paying attention to the methods writers use to enhance their work and engage their readers.

Thoreau, of course, immersed himself in nature for two years to capture a year in solitude on Walden Pond. George Orwell literally lost himself in the sub-basements and catacombs of Paris in order to experience and portray what poverty was like for the disenfranchised; laboring for slave wages in the kitchens of fine Paris hotels and restaurants. His 1933 book, *Down and Out in Paris and London,* is a classic of immersion. Hemingway immersed himself in the bullfighting culture for *Death in the Afternoo*n, and more recently John McPhee immersed himself in the pine barrens of New Jersey for a book of the same title and in the Florida wetlands for his 1968 book of reportage, *Oranges.* Tom Wolfe wrote *The Right Stuff* (1979) by hanging around the early NASA astronauts, and Susan Orlean's foray into the orchid world yielded her best-selling work of personal journalism, *The Orchid Thief* (1998). Becoming a part of the story, in one way or another, is a crucial aspect of the creative nonfiction way of life.

Single-Subject Books

John McPhee pioneered the idea of single subject immersion—a type of book that's become very popular. In addition to *Oranges,* he's written books about shad (*The Founding Fish,* 2002), canoes (*The Survival of the Bark Canoe,* 1975), and freight transportation (*Uncommon Carriers,* 2006), to name just a few. Other writers have written single subject books destined for the best-seller lists on subjects ranging from caviar to cod, peaches, apples, cheese, chocolate, and salt. Mark Kurlansky's book *Cod* (1997) is subtitled "The Biography of the Fish That Changed the World." In it he discusses how cod fishing helped inspire the early exploration of North America, and thus it's also a history book, filled with anecdotes and interesting, eccentric characters.

Through Immersion, a Writer Can See the Story As It Happens

It begins with living life vigorously and experiencing as much as possible, whether it's in your hometown, your home state, or throughout the world.

My first book, *Bike Fever* (1973), was about the motorcycle subculture. To learn more about the people who rode motorcycles and how they felt about their experiences, I traveled cross-country, off and on, and lived a life on two wheels for nearly three years. I was inspired during that time by Jack Kerouac's 1957 thinly fictionalized autobiographical novel *On the Road*, the 1969 classic road movie, *Easy Rider* with Peter Fonda and Dennis Hopper, and Hunter S. Thompson's 1967 account of the notorious motorcycle gang, *Hell's Angels*. Thompson had hung out with and lived part of the time with the most vicious Hell's Angels gang in California.

At one time in my life, I loved baseball, and so after *Bike Fever*, I sat down and figured out what kind of baseball book I could write so that I could immerse myself in the baseball subculture. I chose the men in blue—umpires.

In many ways, as I got to know them, these guys were like some of the motorcycle folks I'd met—independent, living on the fringes of society. Umpires were ordinary guys, and in many respects they seemed to me to be the heart and soul of the summer game. But because they were also the game's law enforcers they lived on the fringe of baseball culture, just like the motorcyclists. After I got to know them, they became heroes to me. I devoted a year to traveling around the country with a crew of four umps from the National League for *The Best Seat in Baseball, But You Have to Stand* (1975).

So I lived the life of a motorcyclist and a baseball umpire. Next, I wanted isolation, peace and quiet, grass and trees, so I became a mountain man, spending time in the backwoods of Pennsylvania and West Virginia looking at the world through the eyes of people who knew very little about urban life.

Through a forest ranger, I met Mountain Man McCool, who'd faced down bears, grabbed rattlesnakes by the neck, and wore coon-racker (raccoon testicles) necklaces. He was fearless in the woods but had never ventured more than fifty miles away from home. He'd lived all his life in the mountains; he'd never been to a large city and didn't intend to. He was afraid of traffic, black people, and the mere mention of the drug culture. McCool was operating on the fringes of society—a lifestyle or theme that seems to feed each of my books. This one was *The People of Penn's Woods West* (1984), followed by a documentary film, *A Place Just Right*.

These were immersion books with good topics to investigate—the motorcycle subculture, the rural-urban divide, and umpires which, as it turned out, was not only about baseball but a bigger issue, racism in the summer game. All of this fueled my desire to delve into a bigger idea—a major issue that concerned many more people—and learn and write about it. After doing a lot of reading and thinking about what I was reading about, I turned to health care and subsequently organ transplantation.

In 1983 I read an article in *Newsweek* called "The Replaceable Body." It was about how body parts, mostly organs, could be transplanted from one person to another—livers, hearts, kidneys, and more. Before long, I became part of the organ transplant group at the largest organ transplant center in the world: the University of Pittsburgh's Presbyterian-University and Children's hospitals. I embedded myself with surgeons, patients, nurses, and into the transplant milieu, for what became *Many Sleepless Nights*. I scrubbed with surgeons, jetted through the night on organ donor harvests, lived with transplant candidates and their families as they waited, agonized and confused, for someone to die so that they or their loved ones would have a chance to live.

After transplantation, I immersed myself in a children's hospital and subsequently a psychiatric institution, writing books about pediatricians and children with mental health problems, respectively. After that came a book about veterinarians. In many ways, transplant surgeons and veterinarians are outsiders in the medical world—on the fringes of the mainstream. And most recently I wrote about robots by immersing myself in the largest robotics think tank in the world at Carnegie Mellon University. The book that resulted is *Almost Human: Making Robots Think* (2007).

My initial dream of learning more about the world in order to write a novel eluded me, but I found my calling in creative nonfiction. For me, experiencing the lives of other people, watching them in pain, indecision, and triumph, is incredibly rewarding and stimulating—and this intimate knowledge provides the opportunity to have a purpose in life, a goal beyond being a great writer. The creative nonfiction writer with a big issue or idea can wake up the world and make change happen.

These experiences were unique and exciting—and I'll never forget them—but you need to have a spin on the subject. Look at the subtitles of my books: *Many Sleepless Nights: The World of Organ Transplantation; Almost Human: Making Robots Think; The Best Seat in Baseball But You Have to Stand: The World as Umpires See It.*

EXERCISE 6

Try an immersion. It is important for you to learn how to do it— or at least experience it, just once. The immersion is a basic creative nonfiction research technique, most often for "public" rather than "personal" stories, but it can be effective no matter what you are writing. Your first immersion doesn't have to be fancy or excessively demanding, by the way. Do you have a favorite coffee shop to hang out in? Do so for an hour a day, five days in a row, for example. Write sketches of the people you see and excerpts of conversations that you overhear. Where does that lead you?

Spend a half day at the zoo or attend a hockey game. Or, if it's the summer, try little league. Parents interacting with other parents—and other parents' kids—is often interesting to watch. You needn't interview anyone or do any research to start out with. Just watch, listen, take notes (without attracting too much attention), and see what happens. If you can do an immersion that is relevant to something you are writing, then obviously that's the direction you ought to be taking. The important thing is that you experience it—at least once.

The point is that the immersion experience personalizes the nonfiction—gives it the feel of a memoir, but doesn't overwhelm it with the writer's autobiography. Immersion allows you to become intimate with your subject's environment, and it even allows you to write about yourself, to a certain extent. But you need to have a focused nonfiction subject—a reason for the immersion. What will the reader learn? That robots are cute? That baseball is the greatest American game? Maybe. But you must realize you're on a higher mission. Say to yourself, I'm teaching my readers how roboticists work, what they do, how much they sleep, how talented they are—all in the service of making robots think. And fans ought to know that baseball umpires have their own way of looking at the game that differs from players and fans—and that, perhaps, their personalities are flawed.

Conducting a one-on-one interview is helpful to a story, and many interviews, following up on answers given previously, are often very effective. But watching and listening to a person you are writing about or being

---

EXERCISE 7

Choose three newspapers to read each day. The first should be your local paper, since you need to know what's going on in your own backyard. The next should be a national newspaper, like the *New York Times* or the *Wall Street Journal*. (I prefer the *Times*—and I'm not referring to its more liberal orientation. The *Times* covers the country and the world more thoroughly than any other paper. Plus, each day it contains special sections that focus on what's happening in science, business, media, home, sports, and much more.) Then pick a random paper, something different every day, perhaps from a small town—Peoria, Illinois, or Tallahassee, Florida. Scan the headlines and look for interesting features with compelling characters. Today it's as simple as going to your computer and using the Internet to read newspapers. Print out and paste the stories you like—the ones that intrigue you, make you laugh or cry—into your futures file. You'll see how quickly this file grows, and when you're hungry for an idea, look in your futures file to see the trove of information and ideas you've stored there.

When you find a subject that interests you, register for a Google alert. Google will send you anything in its vast database that relates to your subject for as long as you keep the alert active.

---

ensconced in a place you are profiling can be irreplaceable if you are trying to determine the underlying causes and cures of a situation or to analyze and report the motivations of a personality or a group of people. Being there, you see and hear for yourself, and sometimes you observe actions and situations that occur spontaneously—stuff you'd never get from an interview. (As an example, see "Frank Sinatra Has a Cold" on page 109.)

FUTURES OR "IDEA" BOOK

Note that a magazine article initiated my transplant book. Many public and big idea books germinate that way. Writers don't just spontaneously say to themselves, "I think I'll write a book about transportation or field hockey or Michael Jordan. Or astronauts." Something triggers their thoughts—an article, a TV special, a conversation they overhear.

Sometimes these ideas come when you're not ready to follow up on them. Good ideas are rare—and even though you may be occupied by a different project at the moment the lightbulb goes on, you can keep what I call a "futures book." Make a note, write a paragraph, save the newspaper article. This is source material for future projects.

In your futures book, write down what angle interests you and what the bigger idea is—how the experience or the immersion illuminates the public topic. Keep the futures book alive—you never know when another idea will present itself that adds something to an earlier idea, or when you'll be ready to start a new project. You can sometimes have tunnel vision when you're immersed in a project and think you could never write about anything else. But the emptiest experience of all as a writer is to open your eyes one morning after you've finished a book or essay and suddenly realize you have nothing to write about. Talk about panic!

A futures book includes public subjects for immersion, but keep in mind that your life is your own immersion. Many intriguing incidents will come along (or already have) and you'll meet many interesting characters you might at some later time want to share with readers. So, even as you're working on one project, go ahead and jot down incidents and ideas for the future so that you'll always have another story to tell.

Selecting Subjects to Write About

Question: How do I know I've chosen a good immersion subject? What are the parameters?

Answer: Think globally. Remember that you want to reach as many readers as possible. You want to change minds and trigger dialogue. So select subjects that have national or even international roots—or ideas that pique interest in a variety of directions. But act locally. Find a subject with national connections where you live and work. This makes your immersion easier so that you can be available when the action occurs.

For example, for *Many Sleepless Nights*, I knew that the largest and most active organ transplant center in the world was in my home-town—my backyard, almost literally. The University of Pittsburgh Medical Center was at the top of a steep hill, known as Cardiac Hill to locals. My office in the English Department where I was then teaching in the Cathedral of Learning was at the bottom of the hill. I wore a beeper during those days, and whenever there was action in the operating room or an organ harvest was about to take place, it went off. After a breathless ten-minute dash up Cardiac Hill, I was there, ready to observe.

Fifteen years later, I immersed myself in a very different milieu. The Carnegie Mellon University Robotics Institute was a mile from my office and two miles from my home. Although there are few life or death moments (for people at any rate) in the robotics world, there are special experiments and intense debates and dialogues you don't want to miss if you're documenting a process like designing, building, and programming a robot. Be within striking distance of your project, just in case something crucial is about to happen.

There are many terrific writing subjects—juicy immersion opportunities. But unless you have unlimited time and money, you should pick a subject that doesn't force you to "parachute" in. "Think globally, act locally" should be your mantra when you commit yourself to an immersion.

PARACHUTING

"Parachute" is the word Buzz Bissinger uses to describe what he didn't want to do when he was researching his 1990 classic story of Texas high school football, *Friday Night Lights: A Town, a Team, and a Dream*. The book follows the 1988 season of the Permian High School Panthers football team from Odessa, Texas, in its quest for a national high school championship. Bissinger was a sports reporter for the *Philadelphia Inquirer* when he committed himself to writing the book, and although he knew there were areas in his home state of Pennsylvania steeped in high school football tradition, it was Texas where the heat and the action were most intense. Permian High was famous for football.

Although he could have left his family in Philadelphia while he commuted back and forth to Odessa for practices and Friday night games—"parachuting" in and out—Bissinger realized he wouldn't capture the real story and the three-dimensional truth behind it unless he was there, immersed in the life of the town and the Permian football Panthers, for a full season. So he closed up his house in Philadelphia and moved his family to Odessa. His wife shopped in the Odessa supermarket and networked with the neighbors, his children went to the local schools, and Bissinger spent the football season with the players, their families, and coaches, interacting with the townspeople in an effort to understand their bizarre football culture and the madness it created. This was a total immersion.

Had Bissinger parachuted into Odessa, he might have written an excellent football book, but by moving there, he learned a lot more about the community than just football. He discovered "the ugliest racism" he'd ever observed and the misplaced priorities in which football consumed the town's resources. He saw that academics were a distant second in this small town that enshrined football. The immersion led to intimacy and a depth of insight that prompted *Sports Illustrated* to call *Friday Night Lights* the fourth best sports book ever written. *Friday Night Lights* became a successful TV dramatic series for five years on two networks, NBC and Direct TV. Bissinger's immersion paid off.

WHAT THE IMMERSION IS *REALLY* ABOUT: PEOPLE

I've been talking about appealing to readers and broadening the scope of your reading audience, which is what Bissinger and other writers who dig deeply into a subject through immersion attempt to achieve. Had *Friday Night Lights* been a book only about football, the reading audience would have been limited primarily to football fans. But Bissinger's immersion broadened its appeal. It's also about relationships and tensions between minorities in Texas and throughout the South and about high school education. So its readership is expanded to include anyone interested in these broad subjects. And the fact that Bissinger focused on description and character studies of his protagonists made the people in his book real and compelling—and therefore attracted many readers, as well as a prime-time TV audience for five seasons.

MORE ABOUT IMMERSION

Question: How long should I stay immersed with my subject?
Answer: However long it takes.

Often the writer's time frame for the subject defines length. Bissinger wanted to do a season of football, as did I with my umpire book—a season of baseball from spring training through the World Series. Tracy Kidder's brilliant book *House* (1985) begins when property owners decide to build a new house on their land, hire an architect to design it and a contractor to build it, and ends many months later after the house is constructed and the family moves in. "Three Spheres" ends when Lauren Slater, all the while resisting, finally comes face-to-face with her borderline personality patient.

When to end an immersion or a memoir is often an easy question to recognize: when the story you're telling is over. Or when some significant change occurs in the place or within the people you've been observing—or in your own life.

This change doesn't necessarily mean that your immersion or your essay is over—you may decide to follow it forward and capture the change. The change itself is a signal to pay attention—to stop and evaluate. In an afterword, Bissinger updated what happened to the characters he profiled during Permian High's 1988 football season, enough for readers to feel satisfied. Kidder decided to walk out of the immersion once the house was occupied. Both approaches work.

LITERARY SPORTS NOTE

According to *Sports Illustrated*, two of the three best sports books ever were also immersion experiences. The first is Roger Kahn's *The Boys of Summer* (1972), which, among other things, chronicles the Brooklyn Dodgers and their move to Los Angeles in the late 1950s. The second was fading knuckleball pitcher Jim Bouton's memoir, *Ball Four* (1970), about his 1969 season. *Sports Illustrated's* choice for best sports book was A.J. Liebling's collection of personal immersion essays about boxing: *The Sweet Science* (1956).

Roger Kahn's description of the team after it moved from Brooklyn to Los Angeles contains the strongest writing in *Boys of Summer*. In the first part of the book Kahn captures the love affair between Brooklyn and its Dodgers and the local rivalries between the Giants at the Polo Grounds, the Yanks in Yankee Stadium, and the Dodgers. In the second part of the book Kahn profiles some of the heroes of Ebbets Field, where the Dodgers played before they moved west. In the third part of his book, Kahn tells what happened to the players after the move. Hall of Fame catcher Roy Campanella has an auto accident and is now a quadriplegic. Trailblazer Jackie Robinson, the first African American to play in the major leagues, is overwhelmed by the death of his eldest son, Jack Jr., who suffered from drug abuse and died in an auto accident. Superstar third baseman Billy Cox, "the best glove the Dodgers ever had," according to Walter O'Malley, then owner of the club, tends bar in obscurity. What happened to the Dodgers after the move was perhaps more interesting than the move itself.

THE BITTER BETTER END

The best advice is to stop your immersion when you decide the story is complete—when there's a beginning, middle, and end—with drama and action throughout the storytelling. If you realize that you've stopped the immersion prematurely, you can always jump back into the heat of the action and pick up the story where you left off.

Immersions can become addicting. If you do the immersion well, it becomes so much a part of your life that it's hard to leave the story and its characters.

Remember that the people inhabiting the stories you're telling are continuing their lives—the same lives they were leading before you entered their space. You may feel left out in the cold. The story is over, the book or article is complete, the experience has ended. What's next? It's easier to make the transition back to your own life after a short immersion, a day or a week or even a month, writing an essay or article. Withdrawing from book immersions, which can take years, can feel emotionally devastating. It's like being in a witness protection program—moving from one existence to another; when you finish the project, you have to find a new life. That's why you have a futures book. Open it up. Turn the pages. Read your notes. Review the clippings you've saved. Get ready to get excited all over again.

The Tribulations of the Writer at Work

ANXIETY

Whether immersion or memoir, the people you're writing about rarely know how important they have become in your life. Yes, you spend hours with them every day, day after day, sometimes for years, to get their story and understand their dreams and goals. But what they don't understand, can't understand, is that when they go home to their friends and family, *their other lives,* that you're still with them. You take them home with you— memories and reality.

First you're watching them, taking notes, and always thinking about how you'll capture them in words on paper. Then you retire to your office or coffee shop with laptop and keyboard for the year or two years it takes to write the book, and they're on your mind day and night while you're just a fleeting memory to them when the book or article is finished.

And sometimes you never know if your subjects resent or appreciate your work—and why. After the publication of my second memoir, *Truckin' with Sam,* I waited for a response from my son's mother, my family, my friends: not a word. Their silence was painful.

After *One Children's Place: Inside a Children's Hospital* (1990) was published, many of the major characters didn't communicate with me. They received copies of the book but didn't show up at the book launch party. Nor did they write notes, appreciative, angry, or otherwise.

Eventually, months later, I had conversations with two of the people to whom I'd devoted a lot of time and print. The chief of surgery, a self-described "mean dirty bastard" confessed to me he was at first annoyed that I'd captured him in that way. He was embarrassed; so were his wife and family. But I also showed him as a dedicated, talented, obsessed surgeon, which is why he eventually told me, during a chance encounter, that all was forgiven. He was alone in the hospital cafeteria late one night after an emergency surgery on a child when a cafeteria worker, someone he'd seen but never talked to before, approached him. "Doctor," the man said, "I wanted to tell you that I read the book about you."

"And what did you think?" the surgeon asked, gruffly.

"I think you're a great man, a real hero," the cafeteria worker replied.

"But I come off as such a bastard," the surgeon protested.

"But I could understand why you have to be that way," the worker said. "You can't be nice and polite to all your patients. You have to worry most about saving their lives."

This was exactly the point I was making in the book—and that the doctor himself had been trying to make when he confessed that he sometimes acted like a dirty bastard.

Another conversation with one of the pediatricians I profiled, very positively, took place when I finally set up a meeting with him in frustration many months after the publication of the book. I hadn't heard a word from him—not even a "thanks" for the complimentary copy. So when we finally sat face-to-face, I asked him straight out if he hated the book.

He looked at me, shaking his head, surprised. "What're you talking about? I loved it."

"But I never heard a word from you," I protested.

He smiled and blushed: "You said so many wonderful things about me, showed me at my best all the time. I was so flattered I didn't know what to say."

(Note: I had actually met with this doctor months before and reviewed with him, as described previously on page 40, all of the medical and scientific and service or patient-oriented information I used in the book. But for obvious reasons, I never share my personal opinions in these sessions, whether negative or positive. He was probably unaware that I was holding back some "personal" segments of the book, showing him only the factual or informative parts.)

Because they are so often intimate and personal, immersions and memoirs don't always have happy endings for the writer. The umpires I profiled in *The Best Seat in Baseball, But You Have to Stand!* were so angry at the way I portrayed them in the book that two of the four umpires signed affidavits claiming I'd never traveled with them. They contended the immersion was a fraud. One of these two umpires, a man who went on to open a successful umpire school after retiring from the major leagues, telephoned my mother in the middle of the night to tell her what a despicable son she had. Despite the fact that my book focused on his colleagues' racist behavior toward him, a third umpire identified the book as one of the reasons he was fired the following year.

In the end, the lesson is that creative nonfiction writers, whether memoirists or immersionists, sometimes take heat from the people they write about. I can't tell you not to take it personally because, as much as I try to brush it off, the animosity can be hurtful. But it's part of the game—a downside a writer must learn to accept. It's usually worse for the memoirist, of course, because when you're writing memoir, you're playing with your family's and friends' lives—and you have to accept the fact that they and you just might get burned.

Should You Be Part of the Action?

If you *are* part of the action, then *yes.*

Memoir is your story, so of course you're a major character. But the public idea/issue story is usually not about you—or at the least you're not a major character. It's somebody else's story. You may become part of the story because of your immersion, and then the story will not work without you. So, as a rule of thumb, if your presence as a character in this work is required to keep the action going, you should include yourself.

John McPhee often boasts that in the 65,000-plus words of his 1994 book, *The Curve of Binding Energy: A Journey into the Awesome and Alarming*

World of Theodore B. Taylor, he does not use the word "I" in reference to himself until more than halfway through it. He says that's when he became relevant as a character.

McPhee has mellowed regarding his presence in his narratives. In his most recent work, he will include himself from time to time, even if he isn't totally essential. But his general advice should be heeded. Even though you're there on the scene, reporting and observing the action, if you're not involved in the action, if you're there as observer only, then why exist? The reader is aware that the writer was present—otherwise how would you know what's going on?

If it's not a memoir, the reader has probably not purchased your book or decided to read your essay because you've written it; it's most often because the subject intrigues him or he has been seduced by the power of your opening narrative. (That would be excellent.) So stay focused on your subject. The idea or issue is more important than you are.

DOCUMENTING THE IMMERSION

Writers have their own system and their own ideas of how to document their immersion in a project.

Not long ago most immersion reporters tended not to use tape recorders. There were legitimate reasons for this reluctance—sort of. Many people resist technology—or feel that young people have to pay their dues by learning to write the old-fashioned way with pens and pencils and old style reporter's notebooks.

In the early 1980s, the National Endowment for the Arts offered creative writing fellowship recipients free computers. Many writers refused them. The technology frightened or intimidated or annoyed them. Why should they have to develop new ways to compose prose and poetry? If the typewriter was good enough for Hemingway and Fitzgerald, then it was good enough for them. Now, of course, most writers work on computers, at least during part of the writing process. Some writers compose a first draft with pen and paper because it helps them go more slowly and think more carefully about what they want to say. Then they transfer the handwritten text to a computer—and edit and revise from there.

For a long time, veterans like John McPhee and Gay Talese stood staunchly opposed to tape recording. Eighteen years ago, for the first issue of *Creative Nonfiction*, Michael Pearson, a writer from Virginia, went to Princeton where McPhee lives and works to interview him. McPhee refused to grant the interview unless Pearson turned off his tape recorder and took notes. Since then, McPhee has relented and will sometimes use a tape recorder himself while interviewing people for his own stories. He also uses a computer to write. These days, people are more comfortable using and being the subjects of electronic devices, especially now that there are video cameras and recording capabilities in smart phones. Technology has become a familiar part of life.

This is a major consideration. You don't want to do anything during an immersion that will make your subject wary or nervous. For that reason, Talese and many others often try to be as unobtrusive as possible and scribble notes on matchbooks and napkins. Or they don't take notes at all and try to remember everything they can until they're able to slip away to record whatever they have learned. *New Yorker* writer Alec Wilkinson only infrequently takes notes in front of his subjects. After an interview or observation, he retreats as quickly as possible to his car or a nearby coffee shop—whatever quiet place he can find—and records his story on a yellow legal pad. "I can remember almost everything that happened," he once told me.

Working on my own immersions, I'll usually take quick notes with key words to prompt my memory, so that later I can make sense of what I want to remember in great detail. Something like, "Big argument between John and Rachel. John bites his lip. Blood." That's enough to bring back the story. As soon as I'm free and have some time, I'll find a quiet place, take out my tape recorder, and prompted by my key words, pretend I'm telling a friend what happened on that particular day in great detail, one note after another. Sometimes I'll transcribe my monologue because I tend to tell a good story, even if I am talking to myself, or typing up notes from it.

Can I trust my memory without notes? Yes and no. The answer, of course, is to fact-check whenever possible. And as I mentioned earlier, I will often ask characters to listen to me read to them what I've written to be sure I'm remembering the facts and the tenor of our conversation accurately. But let's face it. Exaggeration is quite tempting. And sometimes we really do get carried away and think we see or hear things that we hope for, rather than things that actually happened. Sometimes you knowingly give yourself permission to exaggerate or add missing detail just so you don't interrupt the flow and momentum of your work. But you must always go back at some point and consider what you have written. Because you are well aware of what you can do—and can't do. Have I mentioned this lately?

You can't make stuff up.

SHIRT BOARDS AND FANCY DUDS

Gay Talese, one of the founders of the new journalism and author of books such as *Honor Thy Father* (1971) and the classic profile, published in *Esquire* in 1966, "Frank Sinatra Has a Cold," is a rather eccentric fellow. He typically wears a handsome Italian suit, adorned with a silk tie or an ascot, while collecting the precise details that make up the extraordinarily textured scenes that have made him the preeminent literary journalist of our time.

He doesn't write these details in a reporter's notebook; he takes notes on small pieces of shirt board recycled from the dry cleaner. At night, he goes back to his hotel room, lays out the shirt boards on a desk, and types up the notes on a manual typewriter. He doesn't sleep until every note has been filtered through his typewriter keys. The scribblings on the shirt boards morph into miniscenes in these nightly no-taping sessions, and it's with these typed notes, these developing narratives, that Talese works out the direction of his stories.

It's the Story, Stupid

When Bill Clinton was running for the presidency in 1992, he was a long shot. His opponent, George H.W. Bush, was considered unbeatable because of his extensive foreign policy experience at a time when the cold war with the Soviet Union and the Persian Gulf War were ending. Bush had championed the successful coalition that had defeated Saddam Hussein after Hussein had invaded Iraq.

But James Carville, Clinton's top strategist, had new ideas and a catchy, blunt war cry, which he peppered in posters and Post-it notes around Clinton's campaign headquarters: "It's the economy, stupid!"

What he was saying was that Clinton, a not-very-well-known governor from a not-too-progressive-state, Arkansas, could take the election from Bush by focusing on the fact that there was a recession going on, Bush's recession, and Bush had been unable to do anything about it. Focus on the money and win the election Carville said—money, the economy, is what the American public cares about the most.

Now twenty years later, as I write this, we're slowly emerging from a much deeper recession precipitated by another Bush who was president during wartime. But now I'm adapting the message of the winning Clinton campaign to your campaign to reach readers and make them appreciate you as a writer, to entice editors to want to publish you, and to write the best creative nonfiction you are capable of—a message that should be plastered around your writing space and reverberate in your brain every time you begin to write or even think about writing. This is the secret to creative nonfiction success: "It's the story, stupid!"

Story is what creative nonfiction is all about.

THOMAS AND LINDA AND THE POWER OF THE STORY

I'm a long distance runner. I've been running for maybe thirty-five years. And when I'm in Pittsburgh, I'll frequently run from my house in Shadyside, my neighborhood, through Oakland, Pittsburgh's academic district (where the Cathedral of Learning is located) and into Schenley Park. It's a beautiful little park with five miles of wooded trails to walk or run or bike—a quiet respite from the noisy, crowded academic and medical center of the city.

When I'm running, there's a spot on one of the trails I always look forward to reaching. You run up a long, graveled grade between a hillside filled with shrubs and trees on your right and a shallow canyon with a narrow creek meandering to the bottom on your left. At the top of this grade is a crossroad. To the right you can exit the park through a playground, and to the left you can go down a trail into the canyon, paralleling the creek. If you choose to go left into the canyon, you must cross a bridge made of large gray stones. Carved into one of the stones is a date—1939—which is when President Franklin Delano Roosevelt's Civilian Conservation Corps, formed during the Depression to provide jobs for the jobless and expand our nation's infrastructure, built and dedicated the bridge.

At this stone bridge, near where 1939 is carved into one of the large stones, I learned that Thomas, my best friend at the time, and Linda, also a friend and a colleague, were having an affair.

Both Thomas and Linda were married (to other people), and the two couples were good friends. Thomas broke the news to me one day at that bridge—more than three decades ago. Not too many years later Thomas got divorced and our friendship gradually faded. Linda and her husband and I grew apart as well. And then I left the University of Pittsburgh and moved to Arizona State University. I'd wager that over the past two decades

I haven't seen Thomas more than a half dozen times, mostly in passing, and I haven't had a conversation lasting five minutes with him. I've seen Linda around more often. We greet each other with a smile or a nod, but we rarely pass the time of day. These things happen.

So why is it then that every time I jog through Schenley Park, run up the grade paralleling the creek, I begin to think of them? Why is it that when I make my turn and head down into the canyon, crossing the 1939 bridge, I hear Thomas's words confessing his affair with Linda? Why do I see his face, smirking and shameful, and remember the surprise that shuddered through me when he broke the news? From that moment on, I viewed Thomas differently—as a person who was less trustworthy than I'd previously imagined. Why, then, do I devote time, sometimes only a few seconds, but other times maybe five or ten minutes, remembering the experiences I shared with Thomas and his family, not to mention his fine work as a writer and a scholar?

It's because of the power of story, which is often triggered by evocative events or pictures or scenes. Stories are usually not lost to the past. Most powerful stories can't be eradicated by time. In fact, stories can grow stronger and become more vivid as time passes. This is why so many powerful memories can be recreated by memoirists years after the events occurred. Story, or narrative, is the bone and sinew of creative nonfiction.

THE STORY BEHIND THE STORY

Over many years, researchers have confirmed the vital importance of story in making an impact on people and communicating fact. Frank Rose, writing for Wired.com, discusses a 1944 study involving thirty-four Massachusetts college students who were shown a short film in which two triangles, one small, the other larger, and a circle moved across a two-dimensional surface. A rectangle was on the screen as well—but it didn't move. The subjects were asked to describe what happened in the film.

Thirty-three of the thirty-four students invented elaborate narratives to explain the movement on the screen. The students envisioned the triangles as two men fighting; they saw the circle as a woman trying to escape the bigger triangle, which was bullying and intimidating. Many participants imagined that the circle and the smaller triangle were "innocent young things," while the big triangle was "blinded by rage and frustration." Almost all the students found a story with characters in the film. Only one test subject described the film exactly as what it was—several geometric shapes moving across a flat plane.

This experiment demonstrates our propensity to see or interpret all aspects of life as a story. We weigh characters and situations, imagine multiple conflicting endings, and recreate alterative scenarios in our attempts to understand and relate to the world. The power of story helps individuals connect and make sense of the larger and exceedingly complicated world.

Recent research confirms this study and expands on it. Dan P. McAdams, a professor of psychology at Northwestern University and author of *The Redemptive Self* (2005), has conducted studies and experiments that make three significant points about the power of story:

- People remember facts longer and more completely when they are part of a story. This is especially significant for the creative nonfiction writer, whose objective is to communicate information in the most compelling and memorable way possible.
- People are persuaded more quickly and effectively when information and ideas are presented in story form. Remember, creative nonfiction is not necessarily balanced and objective; most creative nonfiction writers have an agenda. They have something to prove.
- When asked to relate their life stories, people usually isolate and recreate selected events, like "the day I failed chemistry in high school" or "the year of my cancer scare" or "my parents' struggle over assets during their divorce," and the like. Just like chapters in a memoir or a novel, these situations lead to traumatic experiences and life lessons. McAdams points out that his interview subjects usually describe several crucial scenes from their life stories in minute detail, complete with a list of characters and suspenseful and surprising turning points. He concludes that people use these

stories to decide who to marry, whether to take a certain job, and other important life decisions based on memory and their vivid recreation of a scene.

The scene is the foundation and the anchoring element of creative nonfiction.

It's the Information, Stupid!

As I've said, the general tenet of creative nonfiction is that the writer is permitted and encouraged to use the techniques of the fiction writer in order to communicate facts and ideas. We can also call this "information transfer" or the "teaching element." We are teaching/educating/informing our readers through story. This is exactly what television producer Neal Baer tries to do in his popular TV show *Law and Order Special Victims Unit (SVU)*.

Baer is a pediatrician by training, and he frequently embeds important messages about medical issues in *SVU* episodes. He once produced an episode with a story line about HPV (human papillomavirus) infection, including the fact that HPV infections are a leading cause of cervical cancer. To judge the effectiveness of the message embedded in story, Baer collaborated with Kaiser Permanente, a managed care consortium, to survey a sampling of viewers before and after the show was aired. The subjects were interviewed twice more—after one week and after six weeks. The results were impressive.

After one week nearly three times as many viewers could define HPV and explain its connection to cervical cancer. Six weeks later, that number had declined, which was not unexpected. But many people were still more informed about HPV than they'd been before watching the show.

As we move on to Part II, "The Writing and Revising and Writing and Revising Part: How to Do It," continuing to put pen to paper, fingers to keyboard, writing, rewriting, and revising, you'll see that creative nonfiction is an amalgam of style and substance. Whether you are writing memoir or immersion or a combination, remember that dark horse Bill Clinton won the presidency by remembering the money; you can write successfully by writing smart and writing story. This is a fact.

EXERCISE 8

By this time, I am hoping that you have started two writing projects. The first, a memoir/personal essay that captures vividly something that has happened to you or a friend. You have been able to take that incident and expand on it by adding research or triggering discussion. The second piece should be more public—an idea that focuses on substance rather than style but at the same time incorporates story—yours or someone else's.

Go back now, considering all that we have covered in these pages, and revise both of your projects one more time—or more than once—before moving forward. The more you rewrite, the stronger your writing will be—and the more marketable. Remember that writing is part of a long process that can be spiritual, passionate, and provocative, and sometimes painful and tedious—and not a single instance or event.

And Finally, a Gentle Reminder

Every morning between 9:00 and 12:00 pm I go to my room for a piece of paper. Many times I just sit there with no ideas coming to me. But I know one thing. If an idea comes between 9:00 and 12:00, I am ready for it.

—FLANNERY O'CONNOR

THE
WRITING
AND
REVISING
AND
WRITING
AND
REVISING
PART:
HOW TO DO IT

Introduction to Part II

The title of Part II is not a typo or an editing oversight. It is meant to send a message. Initially, I was going to structure this book in three parts, the last two parts being "Writing" and "Revising." But the more I played around with this structure, the less sense it made. You can't divide or separate writing and revision. Even as I write these words, I revise. I have started this introduction three times—and God knows how many more times I will try to write it (or rewrite it) until it works. And then, even though I will think or assume it works for me today, tomorrow I may change it—and then I may change it again and again in the coming weeks.

From time to time people ask me, What do writers do every day? I used to answer, "What do you think? We write!" But these days I have a different answer: "We rewrite!"

Almost anybody can sit down and write something—once. But the real writer, the committed and potentially successful writer, will write and revise and write and revise until whatever she is writing . . . works.

All of the chapters in Part II, the readings and the exercises and the craft profiles, are devoted to the writing and the revising, which to me are pretty much the same thing.

How to Read

_____

The exercises in this book are designed to help you to get started writing, either with a personal essay/memoir or a public or big idea/big issue piece—or both. I hope that you've been using the exercises as guidelines and are writing regularly. If you are still on the sidelines contemplating rather than doing, maybe it's time to commit. Or maybe you will just keep reading for a while—and thinking. That's okay too. A lot of writing and rewriting begins with contemplation. We are all not ready to jump in and put pen to paper or pound on keyboards on the same time frame. So don't worry. Keep reading and thinking until you are ready to write or to rewrite. Part II will be helpful either way. It will tell you more about the writing life, the act of writing, and focus your attention on the vital importance of revision.

You will have plenty of reading to do, by the way—much more than in Part I. Up to now there have been reading excerpts, snatches of what writers write, but Part II includes a half dozen essays, published in totality. These essays were selected to introduce and showcase structure and technique; they are successful and effective examples of the work we are striving to produce. Some of the writings are well-known, like Rebecca Skloot's bestselling story of Henrietta Lack's cells, Gay Talese's classic profile of Frank Sinatra, and Lauren Slater's memoir. There's also work from emerging writers, like Eve Joseph, whose profession as a former hospice worker led to this lyrical essay.

If this seems like a lot of reading, it's for a good purpose. We are going to deconstruct each of these pieces so that we understand and appreciate the heart and soul of creative nonfiction from overall structure to bottom line basic craft and techniques.

It is impossible to exaggerate how important reading can be to help you become a better writer. To know if your writing project works, you must know how to read it. Reading is the first best way to evaluate your writing—to know when and if it's working and when you need to revise it.

Writers must learn two things about reading: how to read like a reader and how to read like a writer. The process and the result are different for each viewpoint, as I will explain.

READING OVER YOUR READER'S SHOULDER

Why do we write? Because we hope to send a message, connect with a constituency, make a point, change a life. The worst thing that can happen to a writer is to write a book or essay that goes unread or doesn't elicit a ripple of response. It doesn't actually matter so much whether the ripple is positive or negative (of course we all want praise); what's important is that you've made a connection with your prose and your ideas, triggered some energy.

So love and honor and understand your readers. Think about who they are. You need to know if you're writing for *Scientific American* or *Esquire* readers or CNN viewers. You may need to appeal to those audiences somewhat differently, not only through content but also style. Here's what to do:

After you finish a draft of an essay or article, a chapter or a book, put yourself in the reader's place. Imagine that you walk around behind the reader and peer over his or her shoulder. Pretend that you're Mr. Spock from *Star Trek* and do a "mind meld" so that you and your reader will, for the moment, be one.

Read what you've written from your readers' perspective. Decide if it works for *them*—not you. Have you written something readers won't understand or will find objectionable on moral grounds? Is the story hard to

follow? Can readers visualize the characters and can they empathize with
them? What's the take-home message of this piece of prose for the reader?

If reading over your reader's shoulder isn't a smooth, positive, experience, if it doesn't evoke the emotions you are expecting and/or communicate the ideas you feel are essential, then you should assume a red flag, a
warning sign that all isn't well with what you have written. Stop at the moment you fear the reader may be disconnecting and try to determine how
to fix the problem so that your next reader won't be similarly annoyed or
discouraged. These revisions can be crucial.

I Remember Mama

That's the title of an old 1950s TV show in black and white, starring the
then famous actress Peggy Woods, but "Mama" is also a theoretical target
reader for all of writer Joel Garreau's books and articles. Garreau, author
of the best-selling book *Radical Evolution, the Promise and Peril of Enhancing
Our Minds and Bodies and What It Means to be Human* (2005), who also

wrote and edited the "Outlook" section of the *Washington Post*, explained in a recent presentation at Arizona State University that no matter how complicated and esoteric the subjects of his books are, he always uses his mom as representative of a target audience. Here's his explanation in his own words:

> Now, let me explain what I mean by my mother. For me, that's code for somebody who is bright and interested but has no idea what my subject matter is about. This person is also somebody who has no patience for stories about boys and their toys. They care about humans, their families, their friends, who they are, how they got that way, where they're headed, what makes them tick.
>
> In other words, whether they know it or not, they care about culture and values as they recognize it and live it. So that's the reason why I tell stories about people. If you do that, I've found, if you can talk about people you can slip in all that other stuff that I think of as spinach. That's the stuff at Outlook we used to call DBI (Dull But Important).
>
> You really have to work at pulling the reader through that DBI. You have to give the reader tasty nuggets in between and you have to do it at a regular pace. An anecdote, a joke, a description, a human being talking like a human being. You have to keep up the rhythm and the momentum or else you'll lose them.
>
> I once had a great editor, Deborah Heard. She never actually changed any words. All she would do is draw a line down the side of my pages when she found her mind wandered. That was terrific.
>
> That's all I needed. I mean, I obviously thought that everything I've written was sterling prose, you know, or I would not have handed it in. But she told where I had gone wrong simply by showing me where I was losing her. What a terrific editor she was. By the way, speaking of showing, that's an important thing. Never tell somebody when you can show them.

So Joel Garreau is reading over his mother's shoulder—and his editor's.

READING WITH A WRITER'S EYE

When you've finished reading your work with the eye of a reader (or your mother), then you can move on to the second vital way to learn to read your work—with the eye of a writer—which is an entirely different experience.

The tendency when revising or editing is to worry about words. I've been involved in hundreds of workshops over the years, listening to people praise (and criticize) one another: *What a great sentence! What a wonderful metaphor! An evocative image!*

We all appreciate feedback. But such responses can be premature. Writers need to worry about the shape and structure of a piece of writing before honing in on phrases and sentences. So let's do another mind meld and study the architecture of the creative nonfiction essay, chapter, or book.

When architects view bridges and buildings, they first try to see them the way a pedestrian might. This is like reading over the reader's shoulder—looking at your work through the consumer's or pedestrian's eye. But the architect also looks at a structure on another level, picturing the blueprints of the bridge, its design, the way its various parts came together.

A writer works in a similar manner, examining the many parts of the creative nonfiction essay, chapter, or book, looking for the various elements that give the writing its structure.

Editing takes place in several phases, but it almost never starts with the line of prose, the sentence, or word choice. You may write gorgeous, exciting prose line by line, but if it doesn't become a compelling whole, your readers may not have the opportunity to appreciate your linguistic talents.

So consider the blueprint, the structure and shape of your piece of writing first. You'll see that the words, images, and ideas will change as you reshape the structure of your piece, so there's no point in addressing them early on in the revision process.

You are a sculptor with words. Once you've established the shape of your writing project, you'll begin to concern yourself with sentence structure, diction, and the many specificities of prose.

The Building Blocks

In Exercise 1, I asked you to write a scene—to recreate an experience, a happening, an incident—in a cinematic, descriptive way. A little story. Like the incident I experienced at St. Edwards University: the woman—the creative nonfiction police person—jumped up with her badge and bare feet and startled me and everyone else in the audience. Or remember the rope test? My boot camp triumph—and what I learned from it? The exercises leading up to this point in the book have mostly relied on scenes.

The scenes have been the jumping-off points for you to present relevant and important ideas and information related to these scenes or little stories. I can't overstress the importance of scenes in creative nonfiction and how they will allow you to introduce and educate your readers in related subject matter.

Scenes are the building blocks of creative nonfiction, the foundation and anchoring elements of what we do. This is what I tell people who want to write but have no experience writing. And I tell the same thing to the graduate students in my writing classes—and PhD students. Writing in scenes is one of the most important lessons for you to take from this book—and to learn.

The idea of scenes as building blocks is an easy concept to understand, but it's not easy to put into practice. The stories or scenes not only have to be factual and true (You can't make them up!), they have to make a point or communicate information, as I have said, and they have to fit into the overall structure of the essay or chapter or book. It is often a daunting task. But it's essential.

Writing in scenes represents the difference between showing and telling. The lazy, uninspired writer will *tell* the reader about a subject, place, or personality, but the creative nonfiction writer will *show* that subject, place, or personality, vividly, memorably—and in action. In scenes.

The Yellow (or Highlighting) Test

When I give my creative nonfiction lectures or workshops, I always pass out creative nonfiction readings, such as those printed in this book, and I ask participants to do something really important, what I call "the yellow test."

Here's how it works:

You take a yellow highlighter and leaf through your favorite magazines—*Vanity Fair, Esquire,* the *New Yorker,* or *Creative Nonfiction.* Or return to favorite books and authors, writers I've mentioned here, like Talese, Dillard, Hemingway. Don't forget James Baldwin, George Orwell, Truman Capote, Susan Orlean—any respected, major writer will pass the test.

Then I tell my students, "Highlight the scenes with yellow, just the scenes, large and small, from start to finish. Then return to the beginning and review your handiwork. Chances are, anywhere from 50 to 70 percent of each essay, chapter, or book excerpt you selected will be full of yellow blocks. "Bright yellow," I say to my students, "will be blaring and glaring back at you!"

And why is that? Because the building blocks of creative nonfiction are little scenes or stories. The best and most successful work is constructed that way. "Look at all of that yellow!" I announce at the end of the yellow test exercise. This makes a memorable and impressive point.

That having been said, if you leaf forward a couple of pages, you will notice that there's no yellow in this book. No red, green, or blue, either. No color whatsoever. A second color wasn't in the budget for this book, my publisher informed me. A second color would push the project into the red, so to speak. After debating the options for a couple of weeks and experimenting with alternatives, we settled on underlining. So we have to resign ourselves to the idea that in this book underlining means yellow.

"Use the word 'highlight,'" my editor advised me. "'Highlight' will mean yellow—or any other color or method of calling attention to the scene, including underlining."

Okay. Highlight. But please understand me. From this point on, I will use the word "highlight." But what I really mean is yellow—or any other color that will help you notice and understand the design, shape, and importance of scenes.

So after you finish writing a draft of your essay, chapter, or book, give it the . . . highlight test. If you don't see a lot of highlighted color in the pages of your own prose, meaning not a lot of scenes, it's not wrong or right—but a warning that you need to look more carefully at your work and determine why it failed the test. Maybe there's a good reason. Or maybe you'll have to return to the drawing board and rethink the piece. Where are the building blocks?

Not to worry. This is all part of that dance writers enter into—nothing is ever perfect, but you need to try to make things better with every draft, for revision is always part of the creative process—no matter what color or method you use.

A Famous and Memorable Scene

The scenes that you write may not be as powerful or bristling with immediacy as the one excerpted below. But it's an ideal example of what we creative nonfiction writers should be attempting to achieve. This scene comes from the classic profile I mentioned previously, "Frank Sinatra Has a Cold" by Gay Talese, published in 1966 in *Esquire*. Not long ago, in celebration of the seventieth anniversary of its founding, *Esquire* editors decided to reprint the best story *Esquire* ever published. This distinction went to "Frank Sinatra Has a Cold."

The following scene took place about one-third of the way through this very long profile (about 22,000 words, a third of the length of the average book). Sinatra is at a private club. He's not feeling well. This is the way the profile begins, giving readers their first glimpse of Sinatra:

> Frank Sinatra, holding a glass of bourbon in one hand and a cigarette in the other, stood in a dark corner of the bar between two attractive but fading blondes who sat waiting for him to say something. But he said nothing; he had been silent during much of the evening, except now in this private club in Beverly Hills, he seemed even more distant, staring out through the smoke and semi darkness into a large room behind a bar where dozens of young couples sat huddled around small tables or twisted in the center of the floor to the clamorous clang of folk rock music blaring from the stereo. The two

blondes knew, as did Sinatra's four male friends who stood nearby, that it was a bad idea to force conversation on him when he was in this mood of sullen silence, a mood that had hardly been uncommon during this first week of November, a month before his fiftieth birthday.

This first glimpse goes on to explain why Sinatra is in such a bad mood, in addition to the looming awfulness of his fiftieth birthday. He is currently starring in a film he dislikes and can't wait to complete; he was getting a lot of negative publicity because he was dating a twenty-year-old actress, Mia Farrow, who was unable to see him that night; he was worried that an upcoming CBS television documentary of his life might reveal his alleged Mafia connections; and he was concerned that the NBC television special he would soon be taping would require him to sing eighteen songs—"and this was the crux of the situation"—because his voice was not sounding right. It was weak and sore and uncertain because, Talese writes, "he was the victim of an ailment so common that most people would consider it trivial. But when it gets to Sinatra, it can plunge him into a state of anguish, deep depression, panic, even rage. Frank Sinatra had a cold."

Talese then explains in more detail why Sinatra is so down in the dumps, and provides the readers with a riveting portrait of the star and his two blonde companions. Notice that Talese describes Sinatra in the context of an action, a miniscene in itself.

> The two blondes, who seemed to be in their middle thirties, were preened and polished, their matured bodies softly molded within tight dark suits. They sat, legs crossed, perched on the high bar stools. They listened to the music. Then one of them pulled out a Kent and Sinatra quickly placed his gold lighter under it and she held his hand, looked at his fingers: they were nubby and raw, and the pinkies protruded, being so stiff from arthritis that he could barely bend them.

Eventually Sinatra's depression and boredom, unrelieved by his two blonde companions, become too much for him, and so he decides to go into the club's billiard room. The scene that follows, unplanned and totally spontaneous, was recorded in a notebook by Talese as it happened.

Now Sinatra says a few words to the blondes. Then he turned from the bar and began to walk toward the poolroom. One of Sinatra's other men friends moved in to keep the girls company. Brad Dexter, who had been standing in the corner talking to some other people, now followed Sinatra.

The room cracked with the clack of billiard balls. There were about a dozen spectators in the room, most of them young men who were watching Leo Durocher shoot against two other aspiring hustlers who were not very good. This private drinking club has among its membership many actors, directors, writers, models, nearly all of them a good deal younger than Sinatra or Durocher and much more casual in the way they dress for the evening. Many of the young women, their long hair flowing loosely below their shoulders, wore tight, fanny-fitting Jax pants and very expensive sweaters; and a few of the young men wore blue or green velour shirts with high collars and narrow tight pants, and Italian loafers.

It was obvious from the way Sinatra looked at these people in the poolroom that they were not his style, but he leaned back against a high stool that was against the wall, holding his drink in his right hand, and said nothing, just watched Durocher slam the billiard balls back and forth. The younger men in the room, accustomed to seeing Sinatra at this club, treated him without deference, although they said nothing offensive. They were a cool young group, very California-cool and casual, and one of the coolest seemed to be a little guy, very quick of movement, who had a sharp profile, pale blue eyes, blondish hair, and squared eyeglasses. He wore a pair of brown corduroy slacks, a green shaggy-dog Shetland sweater, a tan suede jacket, and Game Warden boots, for which he had recently paid $60.

Frank Sinatra, leaning against the stool, sniffling a bit from his cold, could not take his eyes off the Game Warden boots. Once, after gazing at them for a few moments, he turned away; but now he was focused on them again. The owner of the boots, who was just standing in them watching the pool game, was named Harlan Ellison, a writer who had just completed work on a screenplay, The Oscar.

Finally Sinatra could not contain himself.

"Hey," he yelled in his slightly harsh voice that still had a soft, sharp edge. "Those Italian boots?"

"No," Ellison said.

"Spanish?"

"No."

"Are they English boots?"

"Look, I dunno man," Ellison shot back, frowning at Sinatra, then turning away again.

Now the poolroom was suddenly silent. Leo Durocher who had been poised behind his cue stick and was bent low just froze in that position for a second. Nobody moved. Then Sinatra moved away from the stool and walked with that slow, arrogant swagger of his toward Ellison, the hard tap of Sinatra's shoes the only sound in the room. Then, looking down at Ellison with a slightly raised eyebrow and a tricky little smile, Sinatra asked: "You expecting a storm?"

Harlan Ellison moved a step to the side. "Look, is there any reason why you're talking to me?"

"I don't like the way you're dressed," Sinatra said.

"Hate to shake you up," Ellison said, "but I dress to suit myself."

Now there was some rumbling in the room, and somebody said "c'mon Harlan, let's get out of here," and Leo Durocher made his pool shot and said, "Yeah, c'mon."

But Ellison stood his ground.

Sinatra said, "What do you do?"

"I'm a plumber," Ellison said.

"No, no, he's not," another young man quickly yelled from across the table. "He wrote The Oscar"

"Oh, yeah," Sinatra said, "well I've seen it, and it's a piece of crap."

"That's strange," Ellison said, "because they haven't even released it yet."

"Well, I've seen it," Sinatra repeated, "and it's a piece of crap."

Now Brad Dexter, very anxious, very big opposite the small figure of Ellison, said, "C'mon, kid, I don't want you in this room."

"Hey," Sinatra interrupted Dexter, "can't you see I'm talking to this guy?"

Dexter was confused. Then his whole attitude changed, and his voice went soft and he said to Ellison, almost with a plea, "Why do you persist in tormenting me?"

The whole scene was becoming ridiculous, and it seemed that Sinatra was only half-serious, perhaps just reacting out of sheer boredom or inner despair; at any rate, after a few more exchanges Harlan Ellison left the room. By this time the word had gotten out to those on the dance floor about the Sinatra-Ellison exchange, and somebody went to look for the manager of the club. But somebody else said that the manager had already heard about it—and had quickly gone out the door, hopped in his car and drove home. So the assistant manager went into the poolroom.

"I don't want anybody in here without coats and ties," Sinatra snapped.

The assistant manager nodded, and walked back to his office.

This vivid confrontation is not only exciting and action-driven, but it tells readers all they need to know about Sinatra, the man, especially when he is down in the dumps with the common everyday cold. Just like the old cliché, "a picture speaks a thousand words," a good real-life scene can show readers an aspect of character and personality that a writer could never achieve by telling it. The scene is also structured so that it bristles with suspense. The reader must guess what Sinatra, his adversary Harlan Ellison, and the many bystanders will say or do to make the situation even more uncomfortable—or worse!

To Highlight or Not to Highlight:
That Is the Question

If the building blocks of creative nonfiction are scenes or little stories, and if a good way to find out whether you're writing in scenes is by applying the highlighting test, then let's examine the elements of a scene so you know what to highlight with your marker.

SOMETHING ALWAYS HAPPENS

First, a scene must contain action. Something happens. It certainly does in the Sinatra-Ellison confrontation. Now let's consider two scenes from my memoir *Truckin' with Sam*. It's early July, and I jump on my motorcycle and cruise through Yellowstone National Park with my friend Burt. It's a gorgeous day—at least it begins that way. Lots of sun and a cool breeze. We see steaming geysers, bears, and deer as we wend our way through the park until, suddenly, the weather changes. It gets colder and colder and then it begins to snow, and we know we're in trouble. Something's happening:

> I was leading and the snow was getting ever deeper and more treacherous, yet I rode progressively faster as we wound up and down the mountains. I watched the road ahead, fascinated by the way my front tire cut a narrow black line in the white powder, like a crayon in cotton. The harder the snow came, the faster I pressed along the

highway. The sheets of snow caked on my face shield. I rode with one hand and gloved the shield with the other—back and forth—like a car's windshield wipers, pushing away the snow to see, seeing to go ever faster. I rode the white line, squeezing between the cars that were ahead, and the cars that came toward me from the opposite lane. Burt was somewhere behind, although I could not see through the ice that froze away his reflection in my rearview mirror.

At one point, we stopped at an outhouse, an old shack sagging under the weight of the snow. Burt pulled in beside me, but we didn't talk. We walked down the hill from the road toward the building, went inside, took off our shirts and wrung them out. We smoked cigarettes, inhaling the foulness of the outhouse, trembling in the cold corner of the hut, laughing as if we were crazed. Later, plunging into the Tetons, the snow dissolved to rain. The roads were black and shiny, spiraling up and down the mountains. Forgetting caution, we ran from the cold, searching for the sun, leaning drunkenly into semi-circular bends, when Burt lost control and dumped head-on into the side of a rocky hill.

I heard the metal of Burt's machine scrape against the asphalt. In my rearview mirror, I saw the bike, with Burt riding the side of it, shooting a stream of golden sparks along the asphalt, smashing against a wall of rocks against a hill. Then I dropped my bike. I was running before the bike hit the ground. It caught my leg and I went down. I scrambled up and fell down again. I pawed at the ground until I pulled my leg out. Burt was wedged between the rocks and his machine and he was bleeding. The road had ripped through his rain suit and the Levi's under them, and scraped away his skin. He was covered with mud, and there were cinders stuck in the flesh of his leg.

So consider the situation. It is snowing in Yellowstone and we are on two wheels, and certainly not dressed appropriately for this experience. What will happen to us? There are two smaller scenes or events in this story—we're in an outhouse, smoking and shivering, and then Burt's in trouble.

There's action and a bit of suspense. If readers care about these characters, they will keep reading in order to find out what happens to them. In the next scene I am with my mother at Radio Shack. Something happens, and it's complicated; you can count more than one situation in this scene:

Not too long ago, I took my mother to a nearby Radio Shack so that she could purchase a new cell phone and choose a new service provider. While the transaction was still in process—we were transferring from her current service provider to a competitor—my mother was at the cash register purchasing, separately, for cash, a 9-volt battery for her smoke alarm. I wasn't paying a lot of attention, nor was Sam, who was occupied with his own battery needs. The store was bustling with browsing customers, like Sam, examining gadgets, reading product descriptions, and asking questions. My thoughts were drifting, wondering why Sam has had such a long and ongoing fascination with batteries and his continuous comparison and dialogue about disposables vs. rechargeables when, suddenly, I heard my mother's voice, and when I looked, she was shaking her finger and yelling, "You stole from me! I want my money back!"

Her anger and her finger were directed at the Radio Shack sales clerk, a plump, baby-faced young man in his early twenties named Caleb, who was standing behind the cash register holding a five-dollar bill in his hand. Caleb was new on the job—still in training, judging by the slow and methodical way in which he had handled the cell phone transaction. Now at the cash register, he seemed taken aback by my mother's outburst. "This is the bill that you gave me," he said, waving the greenback like a handkerchief, "and I gave you ninety-eight cents change." He pointed to the money on the counter. The battery was $4.02.

"But I gave you a ten-dollar bill," my mother said. "And that five dollars is what you owe me—not what I gave you. You can keep this change." She pushed the coins toward him across the counter. "But I want the cash."

My mother is 89 years old—and a miracle, some might say. She's healthy, articulate, and although hard of hearing and somewhat forgetful, basically self-sufficient. She lives in our family home, alone—which was actually her father's house, and then, when my grandfather died, the house she shared with my dad—and, as long as the weather is mild, she walks twice a week to the supermarket a few blocks away and carries her groceries, including cans and bottles, back home. She doesn't drive, never has, but she's lucky enough to have a few remaining friends her age who are still driving. They'll take her to restaurants for those late-afternoon early bird specials once or twice a week, and she'll usually take leftovers home so that she has lunch or dinner the following day. She'll also use public transportation for her weekly visit to the beauty shop or to one of her numerous doctors' appointments.

Sometimes she gets scared, though. Recently, there was a series of incidents in which she thought she couldn't breathe—until the paramedics wanted to take her to the Emergency Room, at which point she miraculously, in the blink of an eye, recovered. In response to that incident, I convinced her to undergo an intensive examination—every conceivable test Medicare would pay for. She passed with flying colors and has not experienced any panic attacks since—unless you want to count this incident at Radio Shack. Actually, Caleb, facing this old blue-haired lady with the wagging finger demanding money and yelling "I've been cheated!" so that everyone in the store could hear her and look at him with suspicion for trying to cheat a defenseless old lady, may have been experiencing his own panic attack.

"You gave me five dollars," he said again, talking slowly to accentuate his patience and professionalism. "We only have one ten dollar bill in the register," he pointed down at his open cash drawer, "and that has been there all day."

But my mother, unimpressed by his polite approach, was still yelling and wagging her finger: "I don't care what you have in the cash register—I know how much money I had in my wallet—This is something I always know," she stressed, "and how much I gave you; I won't be cheated or taken advantage of."

By this time, I was back at the scene of the crime at the cash register. I took the receipt from the sales clerk's hand; he had been about to put the receipt in the bag with the battery, as was his routine. "It says here," I said to my mother, "that you gave him five dollars. It is clearly marked. He gave you ninety-eight cents change."

"I don't care what it says," my mother told me, "I know how much money I had in my wallet—there was a ten dollar bill and eight ones—and now," she opened the flap of her wallet and motioned for me to look inside, "the ten is gone because that is what I gave him. The eight ones are still here."

I nodded and hesitated, taking stock. Just a few minutes ago, she was whispering in a very conspiratorial tone to Caleb about how much she hates cell phones and doesn't really want one because it is such a waste of money since she never uses it, and she is only getting it for emergency purposes because, basically, her children insisted that she have one, despite the cost, especially if you consider her previous cell phone, which didn't work too well inside her house—she had to go out onto the front porch in order to take advantage of the free minutes, very inconvenient, especially in the middle of the winter—and so on.

"The receipt says," I repeated, "that you only gave him a five." I tapped my finger on the item marked on the smooth white strip of paper, but she refused to even look.

"Anybody can say what they want on a receipt." She looked at Caleb. "I wasn't born yesterday," she said.

By this time, there were a number of customers waiting in line behind her to pay for purchases and those around the store, browsing, were all turned in our direction, watching the action. There was a woman waiting in the line who was being helped by the other clerk, an older man, to whom she said, motioning to my mother, "Why don't you check your receipts at the end of the day, and then you will know the truth? You can call her if the register is five dollars over and you can return the money."

"Let them check their receipts at the end of the day and see if the register is five dollars over," I said to my mother. "It's only five dollars, and you'll have it back tomorrow or tonight if you're right—you don't need it now."

"Five dollars may not be important to you—you're a big shot—but to me, it's a lot of money." Her hand was in the air, her finger still wagging. My mother's face is relatively youthful; you'd never guess she was eighty-nine. But you can read her age in her hands, blemished with liver marks and scarred with gnarled blue veins. "Let them give me the five dollars they owe me and then they can check their register at the end of the day and if it's five dollars short, they can call me and tell me."

"Would you give it back if it was?" Caleb said to my mother.

"I'll have to think about it," she replied.

ENDINGS

The excerpts in this chapter and the Frank Sinatra profile lead to (and contain) other stories and scenes. By "endings," I mean the end of an incident, which is a scene, not necessarily the end of a story. The following day there were reverberations in the Sinatra camp about Frank's confrontation the night before. Burt fell from his motorcycle and slid to a stop on the pavement. Was he hurt? Did he go to the hospital? That's all up in the air. The writer can choose to continue to tell the reader what happened next in the story—or end of the scene at that point.

My mother was considering the option of returning the money if she was proved wrong. I decided to end the scene at that juncture and resume it later in the book. This enhances suspense, kind of like a cutaway in a movie. But make no mistake about it. These scenes have a start and a finish, a beginning and an end. They are building blocks, and thus properly highlighted. Things happen, actions take place, although they are concluded.

Picture a football field. A quarterback takes the ball from the center, fades back to pass. He's pursued by a four-hundred-pound defender—and he's tackled. A beginning and an ending to an incident. An action but not the end of the game, or even the end of his team's set of downs. There's more football and more action to come.

EXERCISE 10

Here's an excerpt from Rebecca Skloot's *The Immortal Life of Henrietta Lacks*. It is linear in the sense that it follows logically from one event to another. Yet there are really two scenes here—two highlighted blocks—contained in one. This entire chapter is reprinted later in this book (page 189), so you can see how it all ends. But now I want to focus on these two building blocks. Can you see them? There's a scene—one block—and then a flashback scene—and second block. Please highlight both of them.

On January 29, 1951, David Lacks sat behind the wheel of his old Buick, watching the rain fall. He was parked under a towering oak tree outside Johns Hopkins Hospital with three of his children—two still in diapers—waiting for their mother, Henrietta. A few minutes earlier she'd jumped out of the car, pulled her jacket over her head, and scurried into the hospital, past the "colored" bathroom, the only one she was allowed to use. In the next building, under an elegant domed copper roof, a ten-and-a-half-foot marble statue of Jesus stood, arms spread wide, holding court over what was once the main entrance of Hopkins. No one in Henrietta's family ever saw a Hopkins doctor without visiting the Jesus statue, laying flowers at his feet, saying a prayer, and rubbing his big toe for good luck. But that day Henrietta didn't stop.

She went straight to the waiting room of the gynecology clinic, a wide-open space, empty but for rows of long, straight-backed benches that looked like church pews.

"I got a knot on my womb," she told the receptionist. "The doctor need to have a look."

For more than a year Henrietta had been telling her closest girlfriends that something didn't feel right. One night after dinner,

Action needn't be wild, sexy, bizarre, or death defying. There are many subtle actions during a family dinner or in the classroom, for example. A student asks a question, which requires an answer, which necessitates a dialogue, which is a marvelously effective tool to trigger or record action that ends the scene. But then the class continues.

---

she sat on her bed with her cousins Margaret and Sadie and told them, "I got a knot inside me."

"A what?" Sadie asked.

"A knot," she said. "It hurt somethin' awful—when that man want to get with me, Sweet Jesus aren't them but some pains."

When sex first started hurting, she thought it had something to do with baby Deborah, who she'd just given birth to a few weeks earlier, or the bad blood David sometimes brought home after nights with other women—the kind doctors treated with shots of penicillin and heavy metals.

About a week after telling her cousins she thought something was wrong, at the age of 29, Henrietta turned up pregnant with Joe, her fifth child. Sadie and Margaret told Henrietta that the pain probably had something to do with a baby after all. But Henrietta still said no.

"It was there before the baby," she told them. "It's somethin' else."

They all stopped talking about the knot, and no one told Henrietta's husband anything about it. Then, four and a half months after baby Joseph was born, Henrietta went to the bathroom and found blood spotting her underwear when it wasn't her time of the month.

She filled her bathtub, lowered herself into the warm water, and slowly spread her legs. With the door closed to her children, husband, and cousins, Henrietta slid a finger inside herself and rubbed it across her cervix until she found what she somehow knew she'd find: a hard lump, deep inside, as though someone had lodged a marble the size of her pinkie tip just to the left of the opening to her womb.

Henrietta climbed out of the bathtub, dried herself off, and dressed. Then she told her husband, "You better take me to the doctor. I'm bleeding and it ain't my time."

Your mother comes into your bedroom. It's late at night and she stares into the dark for a long minute when you pretend you're sleeping, then backs out into the hallway. Something happened, even though we don't know what or why. But a movement has occurred, with a start and a finish that advances the story—and often leads to another action.

Back to Gay Talese.

Sinatra has a confrontation with Harlan Ellison. And then he has a mini confrontation with Brad Dexter. There's tension in the air, suspense: how will this be resolved? That's what the reader is waiting for. The confrontation ends somewhat ambiguously with Ellison, but Sinatra snaps an order to the assistant manager to take a message to the manager—who escapes out the back door. So in this instance it begins in one way and ends in another way, but it allows the reader to move on.

Always remember that a scene isn't a scene—it doesn't pass the highlighting marker test—unless something, however big or small, happens. And it is best that whatever happens inherently promises that something else will happen. You always want to keep your reader engaged—and wanting more. Which is exactly the point and the case in the scenes discussed above.

Dialogue and Description

Since creative nonfiction should read like fiction—it should be dramatic and cinematic—what techniques do fiction writers use in creating scenes and stories that require dialogue and description, two of the primary anchoring elements of fiction?

In creative nonfiction people talk to one another. Dialogue represents people expressing themselves and communicating information in an easy to understand, realistic manner. Discovering realistic dialogue is one of the reasons we writers immerse ourselves at police stations, bagel shops, or zoos, with roboticists, baseball umpires, or schizophrenics: to discover what people say to one another and about one another—not in response to prepared questions. To capture people as they are, spontaneously and sometimes unaware, real and authentic, you listen to them talking, observe them in conversation, and study their interactions with other people.

In "Frank Sinatra," Talese has masterfully captured the back-and-forth interaction between Sinatra, Ellison, and even Dexter. You can hear them snapping at one another—and you can feel the disdain and trepidation in the air.

And take a look at the fast-paced, realistic back-and-forth banter between Sadie, Margaret, and Henrietta. The reader is there, eavesdropping on it all, along with Skloot whom we cannot see but whose presence is definitely felt, as is Talese's.

Dialogue is not only a tool for writers of immersion. Dialogue is an equally essential tool for writing memoir. You don't want to *tell* your reader about your wife, mother, boss, or neighbor. At the least, you want to minimize telling and maximize showing. Such as in the back-and-forth conversation that occurs as my mother frustrates, embarrasses, and debates poor Caleb at Radio Shack.

You want to show your characters to your readers so that they become unforgettable and so that readers can identify with them. Dialogue demonstrates what kind of people your characters are and how they express themselves when they speak.

And as you can see in the Radio Shack scene and in Talese, description and dialogue go hand in hand. Reading good creative nonfiction is like watching a nonfiction movie; it is real and vivid. When you're writing description, you don't want to lean on adjectives. The key to effective and evocative description is choosing intimate and specific details.

Intimate Details

In October 2001 I was returning to Pittsburgh through New York's La-Guardia airport—my first visit to the city since the September 11 terrorist attacks. It was my first brush with the enhanced security regulations we're now, more than a decade later, so familiar with and annoyed by.

The security guard on this trip, a short, slender Latino in his late twenties, quickly rifled through my clothes and papers, but it was my shaving kit that attracted his attention. I'd arrived an hour and a half before my flight, hoping to go standby on an earlier flight scheduled to leave in twenty-five minutes. So I was conscious of the seconds ticking away.

This man was intense and meticulous. He opened the top of my water-resistant, metallic blue Mini Maglite and examined the batteries. This is an emergency item I carry wherever I go, in response to being trapped one summer night in the Georgetown Inn in Washington, DC, during a twenty-six-hour blackout and almost killing myself in the pitch black trying to find the emergency exit. But the guard found a second flashlight I didn't know I had, a white plastic rectangular miniature from the Western Pennsylvania Cardiovascular Institute—a place I'd never heard of. The batteries were corroded and had leaked onto the case, so I threw it away in the nearby trashcan. I don't know how it got in my bag.

He also discovered two nail clippers with miniature nail files about an inch long with moderately sharp points. If I intended to keep the nail files, he said, he'd have to check my shaving kit, tag it, and send it separately as baggage. I suggested he break the files off from the clippers and discard them. We also trashed the cuticle scissors I use to trim my mustache.

Next he unscrewed the top from my After Bite Itch Eraser, housed in a plastic tube the size of a ballpoint pen. It had a metal clip to attach to a pocket. He touched the tip of his finger to the rollerball applicator and glanced up at me suspiciously. I turned away. No event in my past had precipitated the use of After Bite, but I like being prepared for the unexpected.

The guard opened my cinnamon-flavored Blistex, my Advanced Formula Krazy Glue, my waxed CVS dental tape, and my septic stick. He sniffed my prescription-strength Cruex cream (for jock itch). I also had a small bottle of Listerine in the bag, as well as an Arrid XX Ultra Clear antiperspirant.

He didn't open the Tic Tac box in which I store my emergency medications—aspirin, Motrin, sinus pills, and laxatives—and didn't ask me why I had three half-used toothpaste tubes, two travel toothbrushes, two Gillette Mac 3 razors, and one Schick disposable razor. I just put things in this kit whenever it occurs to me I might need them.

Not that this man cared about the reasons behind its contents. But I couldn't help feeling, as I stood at the table near the security area with people waiting behind me to have their own bags checked, observing what I had in mine, that my life was now an open book and that I'd lost a significant measure of my privacy and dignity. There was nowhere to hide; we were all exposed to each other.

Of course we've all been faced with foreboding and a growing sense of loss since the horror of September 11, and I don't intend to compare the minor indignity I suffered at LaGuardia that October day to the devastation of those who lost lives, loved ones, or livelihoods. But every day since September 11, 2001, more than a decade later, we continue to discover new ways our daily routines and the freedoms we once took for granted have been substantially altered by those horrific events.

I knew two people directly affected by the tragedy of September 11. Fred is a high-ranking executive in a major international financial institution with a large Wall Street facility. Lynn, his wife, is an artist whose bold canvases electrify their sprawling, high-tech Tribeca loft. On September 11 the first plane literally buzzed their loft before crashing into the World Trade Center. Lynn was in the shower and heard the sickening sound of a collision. She said to her husband, "Something terrible must have happened down in the street." He went to the window and then shouted for her to come see the awful sight.

They sat on their living room sofa, screaming and weeping and watching tiny figures—real people—leaping out of windows sixty stories above the street, the remains of the Boeing 767 hanging precariously from the WTC, piercing the heart of the financial district. Friends from neighboring lofts joined them. Later, as ash-covered survivors fled the devastation, Lynn and Fred rushed into the street and escorted the dazed victims into their apartment so they could clean up and call their families. Soon after the buildings collapsed, their tap water turned brown.

In the *New York Times* nearly three weeks afterward, N. R. Kleinfield described the aroma of the ash and of the smoldering buildings. "It's the odor of a burning computer. Or a burning tire. Or burning paper." One person said it was the scent of unsettled souls. Kleinfield went on: "A few people had their jacket collars pressed against their noses. A few others had tied handkerchiefs around their faces, bandit style. One young man simply pinched his nose with his fingers as he walked. A middle-aged woman had folded an American flag over her mouth." When I visited Ground Zero that week, the smell still pervaded the air. It clung to my lungs like a living organism. I can still feel it, a scratching, haunting residue of those innocent victims whose lives were stolen from their children, families, and countries.

Earlier that day at Café Europa, one of my favorite midtown morning haunts across from Carnegie Hall, the wait staff was unusually friendly, greeting me like an old friend, though I'm certain they hardly remembered me. They presented a free chocolate cookie with my portobello sandwich. A man in a purple sweater, yellow jacket, and silk scarf sang Karaoke-style to the music piped in over the speakers, smiling warmly over his tuna salad sandwich. I'd never heard music at Café Europa before, perhaps because the place was usually mobbed at breakfast and lunch. Now, at 11:45 AM, there were just six patrons. I won't soon forget the scene at Europa, the odor Kleinfield described, the water turning brown in Lynn and Fred's loft, or the images of crusts of ash clinging to the people stumbling·from the wreckage—not only because the reality of the experience is so stark, but also because these details are so specific and intimate.

This is a lesson writers of all genres need to know—the secret to making prose and poetry memorable and therefore vital and important is to catalog with specificity the most intimate details. By this I mean ideas and images readers can't easily visualize on their own—ideas and images that symbolize a memorable truth about the characters or the situations you're writing about.

In the introduction to his 1973 anthology *The New Journalism* (1973), Tom Wolfe writes about how Jimmy Breslin, a columnist for the *New York Herald Tribune*, captured the essence of experiences by noticing details that could act as metaphors for something larger and more all-encompassing he wanted to say. Wolfe describes Breslin's coverage of the trial of Anthony Provenzano, a union boss charged with extortion. At the beginning, Breslin introduces the image of the bright morning sun bursting through the windows of the courtroom and reflecting off the large diamond ring on Provenzano's chubby pinky finger. Later, during a recess, Provenzano, flicking a silver cigarette holder, paces the halls, sparring with a friend who came to support him, the sun still glinting off the pinky ring.

Wolfe writes: "The story went on in that vein with Provenzano's Jersey courtiers circling around him and fawning while the sun explodes off his pinky ring. Inside the courtroom itself, however, Provenzano starts getting his. The judge starts lecturing him and the sweat starts breaking out on Provenzano's upper lip. Then the judge sentences him to seven years, and Provenzano starts twisting his pinky finger with his right hand."

The ring is a symbol for Provenzano's ill-gotten gain, his arrogance, and his eventual vulnerability and resounding defeat.

Although we can't achieve such symbolism each time we write about an incident, writers who want their words to be remembered will try to capture the detailed observations that symbolize the heart of the story. The details the security guard revealed about me by unpacking my shaving kit in front of a half dozen strangers were not shockingly intimate, but they were specific and telling. You can piece together snatches of who I am and the way I think from my flashlight, my Itch Eraser, my Cruex, my triple toothbrushes, and razors.

It's true I'm absentminded and cautious. I back myself up with flashlights and salves to avoid situations that might annoy me or curtail my activities. If I confessed these traits in an essay, you probably wouldn't find them memorable, but in the context of an airport security search, the specifics of my shaving kit provided a porthole into my personality.

Why did I go to New York in the first place? Because I felt compelled to get on a plane to break the spell of hesitation and alienation September 11 cast for me. Normally I'm on the road for a day nearly every week, but after September 11, I remained in my neighborhood for more than a month. After that month, I felt compelled to experience New York, to understand that in almost every respect it was the same city as before—more sober, wounded, and scarred, perhaps, but inherently unbreakable. And I wanted to prove myself unbreakable as well. I want my willingness to confront adversity to be a metaphor of my life. By "confront," I don't mean to say "fight." Confronting adversity can and should mean understanding your strengths and vulnerabilities and learning to work within them—and reaching, gradually, beyond them.

A FAMOUS INTIMATE DETAIL

Through the use of intimate detail, we allow the reader to hear and see how the people we are writing about reveal what's on their minds; we note the inflections in their voices, their characteristic hand movements, and any other eccentricities. "Intimate" is a key distinction in the use of detail when crafting good scenes. "Intimate" means noting details the reader might not see or imagine without your insight. Sometimes intimate detail can be so specific and telling that the reader never forgets it. Gay Talese uses what became a famous "intimate" detail in "Frank Sinatra Has a Cold."

Talese leads his readers on a whirlwind cross-country tour, showing Sinatra and his entourage interacting with one another and with the rest of the world, demonstrating how Sinatra's world often collided with everyone else's. These scenes are action-oriented; they contain dialogue and evocative description with great specificity and intimacy. One such detail—a gray-haired lady spotted in the shadows of the Sinatra entourage who guarded Sinatra's toupees—remains so vivid in my mind that even now, thirty-five years later, anytime I see reruns of Sinatra on TV or spot his photo in a magazine, I find myself searching the background for the lady with the hatbox.

Note also how Talese describes the blondes and Sinatra in the billiard room scene:

> The two blondes . . . were preened and polished, their matured bodies softly molded within tight dark suits. They sat, legs crossed, perched on the high bar stools . . . Sinatra's fingers were nubby and raw, and the pinkies protruded, being so stiff from arthritis that he could barely bend them.

MORE EXAMPLES OF INTIMATE OR SPECIFIC DETAIL

Some really terrific intimate and specific detail was captured in a wonderful scene in a *New York Times* article, "Shared Prayers, Mixed Blessings," focusing on how integration saved a church. It's masterfully written and highly accurate. (The *Times* staff won a George Polk Award and a Pulitzer Prize for National Reporting in 2001 for a series of stories titled "How Race is Lived in America.") The article begins with a scene in which head usher Howard Pugh, "on patrol," is looking for parishioners who violate the no food and beverage rule. When Pugh catches a violator, he not only glares at him but wags his finger, as Sacks describes it, "the slightly palsied shake of the left index finger." Specific yet intimate detail at its most memorable and incisive. Later, Pugh is described as "a white man with a bulbous pink nose," another vivid image, unique and unforgettable. You know that Sack was on the scene, watching and listening and taking notes. This is not ordinary journalism; it is deep and evocative.

Look at how precisely, colorfully, and expressively Kevin Sack nails the description of some of the other parishioners taking part in the service on that Sunday morning:

Robert Lawson, "a soulful tenor with a fondness for canary-yellow suits."
Rueben Burch, "a 6-foot-7 black man whose blue usher's blazer is a
    tad short in the sleeves."
Madge Mayo, "the spry 85-year-old widow, stands 4-foot-9 and keeps
    her luminescent white hair in a tight bun."

In a few carefully selected words, he's said something about these characters that not only helps readers visualize them but also communicates an idea of their character or personality. Lawson isn't just a "singer," but more specifically, a "tenor," and his suits aren't "yellow" but "canary" yellow. Specificity packs a memorable punch.

An Important Note About Interviewing

Remember that you're seeking scenes and little stories, details and dialogue. Writers sometimes lose sight of this goal when they're interviewing people because they want to get the information—the facts—straight. Keep in mind that there are facts related to the subject and facts related to the people communicating the subject—which is the story.

You know you're going to have to recreate the story at some point, so ask your subjects to help you. When you interview them, ask for the details you know you'll need to craft your scene. Imagine that you're a fiction writer, making up the scene. What would you want to show your readers? How can you recreate vividly?

You can ask these key questions:

What happened? What happened next? What happened after that?
    (That's the plot.)
What did he/she/they say to one another? Can you recall the con-
    versation? (Dialogue.)

What were you thinking? (Inner point of view. See page 135.)

What were people wearing? What did the room or the house or the neighborhood look like? What was the weather that day? (Specificity and intimacy of detail.)

DOES ABSENCE OF THE WRITER MEAN ABSENCE OF DETAIL—OR A WEAKNESS IN THE STORY?

The fact that Sack, Talese, and Skloot were on the scene, listening, taking notes, and watching, represents the best way to practice creative nonfiction. Sometimes we cannot be there, but this doesn't mean that we can't write colorful and realistic scenes.

Here are a couple of brief excerpts from an article published in a journal that never before published creative nonfiction—*Issues in Science & Technology*. The piece, published in the winter 2011 issue, was co-written by a scholar, Adam Briggle, and a writer, Meera Lee Sethi, who were paired in an experiment the National Science Foundation funded through Arizona State University to see if the writer could help the researcher communicate his ideas in a more accessible way, and the researcher could help the writer think more deeply about serious subjects through use of creative nonfiction techniques.

Entitled "Making Stories Visible: The Task for Bioethics Commissions," a rather geeky, wonky title, the article features a talk by scientist David Rejeski, who directs the Project on Emerging Nanotechnologies and the Foresight and Governance Project at the Woodrow Wilson International Center for Scholars in Washington, DC. Though the article doesn't include much action, the writers provide a strong representation of Rejeski's physical appearance and his manner. And considering the fact that neither Briggle nor Sethi was in the room, or even in town at the time of Rejeski's talk, this is an accomplishment—and an important lesson for you as a writer:

> At about 9 a.m. on July 9, Rejeski, dignified in a dark gray suit that hung just a hair too large on his shoulders and a striped tie that he reached up to smooth several times as he began to speak, took the

place assigned to him in the cool carpeted conference room of the Ritz-Carlton hotel in downtown Washington, DC, where the PCSBI had chosen to hold its first round of meetings. To his front and sides were the 13 members of the commission and two fellow panelists; together, these central attendees were seated at tables that formed a closed square. Behind them, and out of Rejeski's sight, about a half dozen rows of chairs were slowly filling up with members of the public. He didn't need a good view to know that these probably weren't teachers or electricians or firemen who just happened to have a personal fascination with genetics; instead, the audience was made up of a small and very specific set of people with a vested interest (money, mostly) in synthetic biology . . .

. . . He was the first speaker of the day, and he began simply enough. "Let me start," he opened, "by saying that we have devoted about six years of our time . . . trying to bring the voice, or voices, of the public into the conversation about science policy on emerging technologies." If you weren't paying attention, you might have missed his next sentence, delivered almost as a throwaway as he searched on the table for the clicker he would need to control the rest of his presentation. It didn't draw a laugh from the crowd but was obviously charged with a deeply dry humor that emerged from Rejeski's sense of how little attention is paid to this kind of work. "In terms of how we do this?" he said, "It's pretty easy: We talk to them."

Later the physical picture of Rejeski is expanded:

David Rejeski has grown basketball-player tall and cultivated a rumpled shock of salt-and-pepper hair that brushes over his ears; together with a matching mustache, it gives him a little of the look of a leggy Einstein. He has big, graceful hands that he still doesn't shy away from getting dirty. The first degree Rejeski earned was a B.F.A., and in one of his lives he dreams up and sculpts beautiful pieces of handcrafted furniture, like smooth hardwood tables whose tapering legs are inspired by the shape of chopsticks or whose surfaces bear the intricate texture of thousands of individually chiseled facets. In his work life, though, the one in which he finds himself wearing the uniform of suits and ties and uses those wood-calloused hands to gesture with broadly as he speaks before government officials, Rejeski grew up to be a scholar of science, policy, and technology.

How have the collaborators helped Rejeski come alive? The action and the details in the article are all reconstructed. In Sethi's own words, here's how they did it, beginning with a telephone interview with Rejeski months after the talk. Notice Sethi's focused and persistent questions:

> When I asked about the day of the testimony I didn't really get anywhere. He was feeling pretty relaxed that day, he said; yes, it was an important presentation but he did this kind of thing all the time so he wasn't especially nervous. He couldn't really remember anything particularly striking about the atmosphere or mood in the room; yes, he was comfortable in his seat; no, no one talked to him beforehand; no, he didn't really look around at the audience or recall making eye contact with any of the commission members in particular when he was speaking. Really, he was just focused on going through his slides. Fortunately, I was lucky enough to have access to video of the testimony itself, which is how I was able to say anything at all about what he was wearing, whether he smoothed his tie, when he paused, the pace of his speech and when it changed, etc. The video didn't show the audience in any great detail, so I didn't try to describe them. Instead I used their facelessness to my advantage:
>
> . . . Because I was so very short on details I didn't hesitate to include anything that I noticed even if there was a chance it might sound undiplomatic (like saying his suit looked a hair too big for him). When I ran out of descriptors I decided that I would compare him to someone (Einstein), because beyond the genuine resemblance I thought it would be a quick and dirty way to flash a clear image of him in the reader's mind. Finally, I learned about his other life— the one in which he makes such amazingly cool furniture—from a

personal site he is kind enough to keep on the web for snoopy writers to find. There wasn't a lot of information about him on the Internet, but what there was, I used.

Sethi and Briggle demonstrate that the "creative" in creative nonfiction often means being proactive and imaginative in how you seek, gather, and utilize information. You don't need to make stuff up.

Inner Point of View

It's a leap, for sure—a new orientation. But just because you're writing nonfiction doesn't mean that you can't get into your characters' heads and show your readers the world through their eyes. Truman Capote did this masterfully in *In Cold Blood* (1965).

Remember the book, or the movie? It's about the savage shotgun murders of four members of the Clutter family in the small town of Holcomb, Kansas. There was no motive for the crime and few clues, but eventually two young drifters, Dick (Richard Eugene Hickock) and Perry (Perry Edward Smith), were captured and confessed to the crimes. Capote, then known as a short story writer and novelist, traveled to Kansas and remained there for many months, reconstructing the murder, the investigation, the capture of the two murderers, and their trial and execution. He conducted more than four hundred interviews, talking to everyone who knew the family or was involved in any way in any aspect of the crime and punishment. He put special emphasis on the two killers, Dick and Perry, to whom Capote had nearly unfettered jail cell access. He knew his subjects so well he could make the leap and view certain situations from his protagonists' point of view.

This reconstructed scene takes place in the Mojave Desert. Dick and Perry have murdered the Clutters and are now wandering around and looking for illicit ways to finance their travels. They're desperate and cavalier. They're sitting on the side of the road waiting for the right opportunity—looking for a solitary traveler with money in his pocket in a nice car, "a stranger to rob, strangle, discard on the desert," writes Capote. They wait patiently while Perry plays his harmonica:

> Dick heard the grim vibrations of an oncoming not yet visible car. Perry heard it, too; he put the harmonica in his pocket . . . and joined Dick at the side of the road. They watched. Now the car appeared and grew until it became a blue Dodge sedan with a single passenger, a bald skinny man. Perfect. Dick raised his hand and waved. The Dodge slowed down and Dick gave the man a sumptuous smile. The car almost but not quite came to a stop, and the driver leaned out the window, looking them up and down. The impression they made was evidently alarming. The car leaped forward and sped on. Dick cupped his hands around his mouth and called out, "You're a lucky bastard!"

Here we see the world through the eyes of Dick and Perry and even, for a brief moment, through the eyes of the driver, the "lucky bastard." Capote wasn't there—he didn't even know the event had taken place until much later. But his research was flawless and intensely deep. After devoting so much time to interviewing Dick and Perry he could get inside their heads.

Remember that Capote had terrific access to Dick and Perry. Unfettered. He could talk with them night and day, for as long as they all wanted to hang together. So Capote could dig deep and repeatedly ask them to go over their experiences, thus allowing him to see the world through their eyes. Using inner point of view as a technique is fun and effective, but you must make certain that you, like Capote, are not pushing way past the line of reality. It is easy to go overboard when assuming what others are thinking.

Kevin Sack's "Shared Prayers, Mixed Blessings" presents another example of an inner point of view. While patrolling the church, Howard Pugh sees an eighty-one-year-old white man sitting in the sanctuary who is getting increasingly agitated by the minute. This is Roy Denson, to whom Mr. Lawson's "improvisational riffs sound like so much screeching and hollering." Denson tries to control himself and not lose his patience or his temper,

EXERCISE 11

Now it is time for you to put the techniques we've discussed into practice. Look at the pieces you have been writing. Do you have dialogue, specific and intimate detail? Inner point of view? Do the incidents you are capturing have a definite starting and stopping point? If so, then terrific. They are real building blocks—scenes. And if not, look for opportunities to turn telling into showing through all of the techniques we have been considering, beginning with dialogue. Are your characters described in such a way that your readers can actually see them? The descriptions don't have to be long or detailed. Go back and see how Sack captures his characters in a few pointed and vivid words. Maybe you even want to attempt to inject an inner point of view—showing your readers the world through your characters' eyes. You might know enough to make this possible.

When you think you have used these techniques or at the very least tried them out in your scenes and stories, then move forward—and start to dance!

but he's been a member of this church for more than half a century—he helped hang the Sheetrock with his own sweat and muscle—and it is driving him crazy that the blacks are taking over, with the whites not only letting it happen but helping it along.

> He gets angrier and angrier, listening to these boisterous black folks desecrate his music, until he simply cannot bear it. "I ain't sitting there and listening to that," he mutters on his way out. "They're not going to take over my church."

Mr. Denson eventually departs, castigated by Howard Pugh:

> "Now, Roy," Mr. Pugh begins, stroking his seafarer's beard, "what are you going to do when you get to heaven? Walk out of there, too?"

THE CREATIVE NONFICTION DANCE

As I've said, creative nonfiction is an amalgam of style and substance, information and story. Whether it's personal information, as in memoir, or public information as in immersion, you're using the building blocks, scenes, and/or little stories to communicate ideas and information as compellingly as possible.

I'm not an artist, but I'm now attempting to show, visually, the classic structure of the creative nonfiction essay, chapter, or book. So here we have a rectangle with nine blocks. (Nine is arbitrary; it could be five or fifteen—or any number.)

The first block represents story or action because it's usually best to start with a scene to draw readers in and get them involved. After you've captured your readers, you can provide any information you want or need to tell them. But you don't want to provide too much information all at once because you'll bore them or they'll lose the thread of the story. So the third block continues the scene or story or starts another story. That's the rhythm, what I call the creative nonfiction dance. Information and story—back and forth—repeatedly.

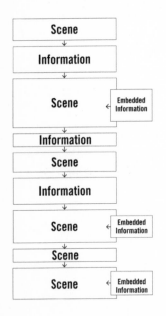

The objective of the dance is to embed information inside the scene or story so that the movement between blocks is seamless. Each scene or little story should simultaneously excite with action and teach with precision. In the perfect world, information will also be embedded inside each scene. As you can see, that is happening here.

Let me say a little more about the structure of the creative nonfiction essay—or book. Creative nonfiction, as I have pointed out, is an amalgam of style and substance. The scene and story, the characters and the inherent suspense get people interested and involved, allowing the writer to communicate the information—or the nonfiction part of the genre—and keep readers interested. This is especially the case for readers who might not have an inherent interest in the subject.

So here's the dance that is diagrammed. The scene gets the reader interested and involved, so you can then provide information, nonfiction, to the reader. But sooner or later, a reader will get distracted or overloaded with information, and you will lose him. But before you allow that to happen you go back to the scene—or introduce a new scene—and reengage. And it is really terrific when you can embed information inside the scene. This, as you can see in the dance diagram, allows you to go from scene to scene—without a break.

REMINDER: WRITING IS REVISION

Question: I don't understand why you are telling me all of this now. I have been writing, as you have suggested in the exercises, and not paying attention to structure. But now I know the dance—the highlighting test. Why couldn't you tell me before, at the beginning?

Answer: I am glad you know more about structure and technique now. But writing should be a spontaneous experience. Explaining structure and technique at the outset might have caused you to try to mimic the structure, as if a formula. This would not be good. I'd like you to keep all of this information in mind, but don't allow it to get in the way of your creative bursts of inspiration. So write expansively, follow your instincts, go off on tangents—and don't worry that you won't be doing the creative nonfiction dance, following rules or guidelines. Once you have a draft, then you can look at it and see how well it falls into the classic structure—the dance. And then you can decide how to proceed. You can alter your work to fit the structure or dance—or you can ignore some of it or all of it. If you are going to break the rules (I actually like the word "guidelines" better than "rules"), then you ought to know what they are.

NOW LET'S DANCE

Let's give two essays, my "Difficult Decisions" and Lauren Slater's "Three Spheres," the highlighting test to see how closely they reflect or follow the guidelines. We'll start with "Difficult Decisions." I count nine scenes—or blocks in highlight—in this 3,700-word essay.

First I will mark this up with explanatory notes in brackets, and then I will add commentary at the end of the essay, so you can clearly see and understand what is happening.

"Difficult Decisions," by Lee Gutkind

Scene 1 is not a great scene, but it involves the reader and is a part of the frame, which we will discuss later.

The veterinarian guns the accelerator of her mobile clinic—a large pickup truck with a double cab, outfitted with a Fiberglas shell with drawers and compartments designed specifically for practicing veterinary medicine. She thunders out of the parking lot and down the road, her rear tires spitting gravel. As she drives, she fingers the stethoscope draped around her steering wheel and frequently turns to make eye contact. At first, her lack of attention to driving makes me nervous,

Intimate detail; the stethoscope.

but I soon note her uncanny ability to sense dips and turns in the road. Luckily there are only occasional oncoming vehicles, controlled primarily by people who seem to regard driving as an afterthought.

Although the veterinarian will treat a variety of animals on the many farms that dot this fertile valley, her specialty is ruminants, sheep and goats especially, for which she possesses a special passion. A ruminant is a cloven-hoofed animal, with four compartments in their stomachs; they ruminate, meaning they eat food, regurgitate it back up, and eat again.

Information; the veterinarian is speaking, though, not the writer.

"From a treatment point of view, goats are pretty easy to handle. You can knock them down and flip them over. They're not going to kill you; they don't require a lot of equipment. Mostly, the diseases they get are straightforward and simple. If they end up having a serious enough disease, you euthanize them, because they're not worth a lot of money. It boils down to economics; a farmer looks at a sick animal and says, 'I can replace her for $50, why spend $500 trying to make her better?'"

She shrugs and turns toward me, as if she has said something that might offend. The veterinarian—her name is Wendy Freeman—has a well-scrubbed look: tall, slender, plain. Wearing faded, almost-white khakis, she is lean, freckled and boyish. I take off my baseball cap and toy with the brim while nodding in a reassuring manner, hoping she will not feel self-conscious. Working with animals, God's creatures, intrigues me. In fact, I am writing a book about veterinarians and how they interact with animals and people. Without the luxury of words, veterinarians mostly communicate with their patients in the special, silent language of touch. As any doctor, they may often save lives through technology and perseverance. But veterinarians also possess an invaluable escape clause. The ability to legally end life is perhaps the supreme privilege and the overwhelming psychic burden of their work and mission.

Continuation of scene, with embedded information.

Euthanasia, the veterinarian says, is often difficult for clients to accept. Horses, such as the one she will be examining on her first stop that day, seem to generate an emotional attachment that makes an owner more sentimental than responsible. Ricki, who lives in a rambling brick ranch house on the edge of a lime green field dotted with a rainbow of summer wild flowers, is clearly perplexed over the fate of a thickset, whiskered 28-year-old mare named Honey, who is slowly and painfully dying from old age and arthritis.

Space break; sometimes used instead of a transition.

More information. Begin scene #2.

Listening to Ricki talk about her daughter's unwillingness to even so much as discuss euthanasia and nodding frequently, the veterinarian removes the plastic cap of a needle by yanking it with her teeth and proceeds to vaccinate the horse for botulism and rabies. Because one hand is always holding down or caressing an animal, veterinarians, as a matter of course, employ their teeth as a third hand.

Intimate detail; the cap yanked by her teeth.

"Sometimes an old or sick horse like Honey will be 'cast,' that is, fall or lie down to sleep and be unable to lift themselves back up," the veterinarian tells me.

"We do sometimes find her wedged under the pasture gates or the stall door," Ricki replies. "But my daughter is 25 years old and has never known life without Honey. She won't come outside when the veterinarian is here because she refuses to enter into a discussion." Ricki throws up her hands and rolls her eyes. She is short, stocky, well-tanned, with Levi's, white sandals, and painted toes. "Do you ride?" she asks, motioning down at my boots.

Notice dialogue.
Notice information
embedded in the
scene, as they
speak.

"Motorcycles," I tell her. "Not horses."

The veterinarian continues down the line of Ricki's three other horses, yanking off the caps of needles with her teeth, patting and caressing each animal with gentle assurance before sinking the needle into a fleshy area at the nape of the neck.

"What do you think we should do about Honey?" Ricki asks. She gazes toward the silent house where her daughter is hiding, as if the question itself will bring her to the window.

"It's a quality of life issue," says the veterinarian. "Is Honey eating well, maintaining her weight? Ambulatory? I've seen some very lame horses that still had life quality; they're hobbling, but happy. When small animals are so sick they can't make it outside to go to the bathroom, they get upset, they have anxiety attacks. It is very painful and embarrassing."

"So do you think it is time this horse be put to sleep?" she asks, once more glancing toward the house.

"When you think the time has come, I'll support you. I'll do it here in Honey's home where she feels comfortable or I'll take her away and put her to sleep in the hospital, whatever is easier for you or your daughter."

"I don't want my horse to become a pasture potato," Ricki says.

"I understand," says the veterinarian. "It's a difficult decision."

"So then, what should we do?"

Scene 2 ends.
Another space
break—used when
you want your read-
ers to take a
breath.

"I wish I had ten dollars for every person who wants me to make that decision for them."

On the average, Wendy Freeman will see eight cases a day, treating horses, goats, sheep, cows and an occasional llama. On an emergency basis, she'll see dystocias, which are difficult births, and preg-

nancy toxemia, common in ewes close to lambing—and the walking
wounded from dog attacks. For horses, lameness and foot abscesses
are common, as is colic—stomach pain. Cows get "milk fever," and
when they get into the grain they will often overload, like a child
with a stomachache after eating a package of cookies. Overeating
could kill any farm animal.

    Difficult pregnancies and deliveries are routine and troublesome.
"I once chased a beef cow with a newborn calf hanging out of her by
its feet. She was running wild in a 2 acre field. The farmer and I tried
to round her up with our trucks and push her into a shed. We gave up
that idea when she smashed in the doors of both trucks with head
butts. So we decided to rope her; took us an hour before we got the
rope around her. We tied her leg to the bumper of my truck, stretched
her out, knocked her down, pulled the calf out. It was rough work."

    "Rough work" is an understatement in this particular instance
and in calving generally, which is one of the most grueling aspects
of her job, especially for a spare, slight woman like this veterinarian,
who weighs all of 120 pounds. Sometimes even catching a wild and
frightened cow in this bizarre drama is only the beginning. Sometimes a cow is so swollen with pregnancy and the calf wedged so
deeply inside the womb that the struggling veterinarian, reaching
and groping vainly for hour upon exhausting and frustrating hour
on end, will lose her sense of time and grip on reality, and eventually
begin to imagine the nightmarish possibility of literally losing herself—drowning inside the mother. Or inadvertently pushing rather
than pulling and suffocating the almost born infant. Sometimes the
veterinarian, shivering violently in the freezing night air, drained of
all energy and spirit, will begin to envision the unmentionable but
tempting notion of failure—of giving up—and the alluring rewards
such a decision might bring: warmth, food, coffee, sleep.

    But even in triumph, when the calf is finally pulled out, she will
often experience a momentary and panicky feeling of failure. Calves
in difficult births frequently look dead when they are first born.
Their eyes are glassy; their tongues are bloated. The veterinarian

Information.

Transition and scene 3.

Information.

Inner point of view: seeing the birthing event through the veterinarian's eyes.

knows she must encourage and coax life back, clear throats of possible obstructions, initiate artificial respiration—and pray through agonizingly long seconds until the animals can wrench their sticky eyes open and begin their tentative jerky attempts to communicate with the body and instigate control. In the end, the veterinarian says, she always experiences simultaneously fear, exhaustion, and frustration, along with an exhilarating feeling of triumph, which she carries with her—until the next long and endless night.

Scene 4.

Recently, a cow decided to calf in a swamp two miles away from the nearest barn and in a pouring rain. The farmer, a stubborn and money-minded businessman, waited until 10:30 PM to telephone her. The veterinarian arrived within thirty minutes, helped hitch the cow to a tractor and drug her to solid ground. "I should say solid mud. We were covered in guck. Our rain gear was useless." She tried to deliver the calf, but it was breech, necessitating surgery.

The farmer wanted her to perform surgery in the field. It was the most economical approach, but not the safest for either mother or calf. When the veterinarian pointed out that it was pouring down rain, the farmer suggested pitching a tent. But she countered by stressing the need for electricity, so the farmer said he'd make a skid with the tractor—tomorrow—and take the mother down to the barn. The veterinarian refused to wait a day for the skid and persisted until the farmer agreed to call for the ambulance from a nearby animal clinic where the delivery could be made under safer conditions. In the end, her client—the farmer—had been cooperative, but some farmers are more difficult to deal with than their animals. Sometimes their eyes reflect dollar signs, their ears listen to the grunts and groans of the struggling vet, but hear only cash registers ringing. Farmers often think that they know more about their animals than veterinarians do.

Space break is unnecessary—the two scenes flow together

Scene 5.

A farmer telephoned one night and asked her to do a caesarean section on a pregnant mare who was toxic and dying, in order to save the foal. The surgery took place in the field, lighted by the headlights from two pickup trucks. They put a catheter in the mare's neck so that the euthanization could come immediately after delivery, blocked out an area on her stomach, and cut her open. The foal came out easily, but the mare was dead. "It's pouring down rain," says the veterinarian, "lightning and thunder cracking everywhere. The mare's lying right along a major highway, and I said, 'You have to get this horse out of here. Nobody is going to want to see or smell this dead mare with all of her guts out when the sun comes up.'" Persisting, the veterinarian asked why the mare had been so sick in the first place. He was not a regular client; she had never met the man. The farmer said that the horse had been sick for three days, walking kind of funny, not eating well, acting strange. The veterinarian asked the million-dollar question. "No," the farmer replied, "she's not been vaccinated for rabies."

Veterinarian, while telling her story, is recreating her own dialogue.

At this point, she knew her dealings with the stubborn farmer were going to become considerably more difficult. "We need to take her head off and check for rabies," she said. "We argued for a while, but I insisted." Reluctantly agreeing, the farmer stepped back to watch. "So now I'm sawing the head off out in the middle of the rain. I finish, stick it in a bucket." The veterinarian's truck was parked on the other side of a fence dividing the field from the highway. Her plan was to hand the bucket over the fence to the farmer to put it on her truck, but now, suddenly, the farmer was nowhere to be found. So she balanced the bucket on top of the fence so that she could climb over and carry it to where her truck was parked. No sooner did she get on the fence, when the bucket fell over and the horse's head rolled into the middle of the highway. "I ran like hell, scooped the head up, threw it into my truck and jumped in. Whoever drove by during that whole fiasco probably thought The Godfather was happening all over again." The animal was not rabid, but the veterinarian had been obliged to order the necessary tests.

Inner point of view.

The veterinarian locates a spot in the barn directly beside an electric outlet and plugs in the disbudding iron. She walks outside, opens a pen in which two calves are waiting, selects a brown spotted calf ("The kind that makes chocolate milk," she jokes) and brings it inside. Working quickly, she shaves the hair from around the horns, then reaches into her bag for Lidocaine, a pain blocker, which she has already siphoned into a hypodermic needle. She injects the Lido-caine directly around the horn. Next comes the electric disbudding iron, which resembles a branding iron, round, like a large "O," not un-like a packaged donut with a hole in the middle. She grabs the calf's ear, wedges its head against her body, inserts the "O" of the iron through the calf's horn, and then, bringing the iron slowly downward, digs the hot iron into the calf's little head.

Intimate detail.

First there is a wisp of bluish-white smoke, and then the dank, stark stench of burning fur. Then comes the primeval aroma of roast-ing skin, followed by the sound of searing bone, as she applies increas-ing pressure. She twists the iron back and forth repeatedly until smoking copper-colored rings show through above the ears. It looks as if the smoke is emanating from the calf's head, as if the soul of this tiny helpless animal has suddenly been apprehended by the devil. "The horn is growing from cells within and below the hair, and so if you kill the skin around the horn, there will never be another horn returning. Animals sense the heat, but do not feel the pain," she adds. In the days of the wide-open range, horns were needed by livestock for protection. Today, horns serve no practical purpose and in fact may be used aggressively and cause harm to a farmer's valuable herd.

Information.

Veterinarians are asked to perform a number of such procedures, including the removal of wattles—appendages of skin that hang down from the necks of goats. For this procedure, she will snip off each wat-tle with a gigantic clipper, as if she were clipping fingernails. "The an-imal may not experience pain, although losing part of your anatomy can't be particularly pleasant." For cosmetic purposes, veterinarians may remove the third teat on the developing mammary gland of pygmy goats, a genetic flaw disqualifying the goat from competition or breeding. Using a local anesthetic to dull the pain and snipping the teat with a clipper resembling ordinary pliers, the procedure is com-pleted in three minutes flat.

Scene continues.

Disbudding of the second calf does not go as smoothly as in the first instance, perhaps because the first calf defecated on the floor dur-ing the procedure, and so now the second calf, an emaciated pale white baby of about four months, is slipping. As the calf struggles, its flying hooves pepper the veterinarian's khaki pants with feces and track it on her leather tennis shoes. "They love to stand on your feet," she says.

The veterinarian burns in the disbudding iron, twists it round and round, the calf jumping with each grinding twist. She blows a cloud of smoke away from her face. "It would be nice to have a little fan on your shoulder," she says. After the disbudding is finished, she rubs the hot circle of the iron on top of the tiny remaining buds, one at a time, to cauterize them. She sprays the burning circles with yellow anti-bacterial Furox and returns the calves to their pen. The horns will fall off in a couple of weeks. The calves will remember nothing, she says.

Note also specificity of detail.

Back in the truck, the veterinarian picks up our conversation, as if the disbudding never occurred or was much too common and ordinary to discuss. "There was a woman at a riding stable where I was working, a schoolteacher named Pat. Her horse was old and thin, and very lame; she could no longer ride him. But every day, she went to that barn and took him for a walk and gave him carrots; she'd always be hanging out and letting him graze. And I would go over to him and pet him and say, 'Oh, Shadow looks good.' I never left the stable without saying hello or goodbye to Shadow.

Scene 7.

"That year, I went away for the Christmas holidays, and while I was gone, Shadow had emergency surgery, and it turned out he was dying. But Pat wouldn't let anybody put him to sleep until I came back. She wanted me to drive to Limerick, a pet cemetery, and euthanize Shadow there so that we could bury him, but by the time I got back, it was too late. He needed to be euthanized immediately. I said, 'Pat, you need to say goodbye; he's suffered enough.'" When Pat walked into the stall and whispered his name, Shadow lifted his head, turned to look at her and started to nicker. "We all started to cry." Later, we loaded the horse on the trailer for her so that she could bury him.

"Not long afterward, the woman sent me a letter about how it meant so much to her that I would say 'hi' to Shadow. I remember reading the letter and thinking, 'Isn't that something? Just me stopping and saying hello to her horse made her feel like he was really important.' Those are the kinds of things that some clients want you to do; some clients want to feel that veterinarians really care about their animal.

"Four days before last Christmas, I had to put an old horse down for a little girl who had asthma. She would go to the barn with a mask on her face every day and take care of that horse. He got real sick the weekend before Christmas; I was on duty, and I was up all night with him for two nights, and he wasn't getting better. She had run out of funds, and we decided to euthanize him. Even now I can picture that little girl's face as she walked into the barn with the little mask on and . . . I was the only one who had to kill her horse. It was the worst Christmas of my life."

At the end of the day, back at her office, the veterinarian stoops on a patch of grass adjacent to the parking lot, examining a brown Nubian goat inflicted with a rare kidney disease far too expensive for its owner to afford to treat. The goat's owner is a woman with whom she has worked for a half dozen years who is suffering from an increasingly debilitating case of multiple sclerosis. The conversation is short and to the point; the woman's options are significantly limited. "Okay," she says to the veterinarian, holding her hand like a traffic policeman, palm straight forward, signaling STOP. "That's enough talk." Looking back, I realize that the euthanasia happened quite quickly, but at the time it occurred, the process seemed agonizingly long. I watched it as if it were being played back to me in slow motion.

The veterinarian takes out a catheter with a long tube filled with pink liquid (sodium phenobarbital) and injects it into the goat's neck. First blood splatters onto the veterinarian's hand from the catheter. For an instant, the little goat seems to simultaneously inflate itself— and momentarily freeze—mid-air. Then comes a silent single shudder that ripples like quiet thunder through every dip and graceful curve of her dramatic and biblical body. Finally, the goat caves in and collapses on the grass with a muffled thud.

Now the woman cries. She sits on the ground and pets her goat, stroking the goat's head and laying each ear, one at a time, on top of the forehead, tears streaming down her wrinkled cheeks. The veterinarian reaches down and attempts to close the goat's eyes with the palms of her hands. But the eyes open back up again, continuing to assert themselves. Those eyes are ice blue. They look like diamonds or stained glass glinting in the sun.

I don't know why the veterinarian selected such a public place to perform such a private act. Many people seemed to be going about their day as if nothing had changed, as if an animal hadn't lost a life and a woman, who herself is slowly dying, hadn't lost a friend. On the other side of the grass, a stable hand loading a horse on a trailer is talking loudly to a companion. Maintenance workers drive by, smiling and waving. The goat continues to shudder and groan, the woman stroking its ears.

Note the writer's voice and participation—but only a part of the story when he is involved.

"He's already dead," the woman says aloud. "Even though he's making these noises, I know they're involuntary. He's not coming back." Soon the woman struggles to her feet, hobbles back to the road and climbs shakily into her pickup truck. She starts the motor and drives away. I can see her watching us in her rearview mirror. Now the veterinarian and I are standing alone on the grass, staring quietly down at the goat. "It was a nice goat," the veterinarian says. "I wanted to tell the woman, 'Let's put her in the hospital and I'll pay the charges to fix her up.' It would have cost $300. But I do too much of that; I just didn't want to spend my own money this time." Soon the veterinarian disappears into her office. I sit down beside the brown goat; I stroke its ears and look into its ice-blue eyes.

FOLLOW-UP COMMENTARY

Highlighted block 1 is barely a scene. Not much happens—but enough. Because you can lose your reader so quickly, you want to start with action and momentum. Later you will see that this first semiscene is actually part of the "frame."

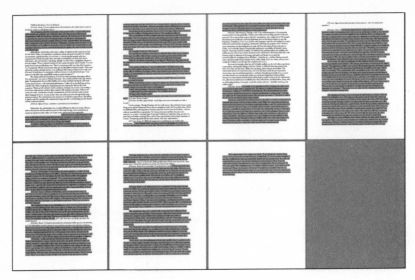

"Difficult Decisions" with scenes highlighted.

Highlight block 2 is a good scene from beginning to end. There's dialogue, description, detail. Information is embedded in the scene so the reader learns while the action plays out. This is a recreation of an event that happened to the writer and the veterinarian. In contrast, most of the other scenes in "Difficult Decisions" are stories from the veterinarian's past.

Highlight block 3 is a short scene or self-contained story. It's a quotation, while highlight blocks 4 and 5 are mostly stories the veterinarian tells, which I've paraphrased and dramatized. But they're all self-contained stories, with a beginning and an end. Something happens.

Highlight block 6 is another recreation, and a good deal of information is embedded in the story. There are two scenes here—two disbudding sequences. But the two events are simultaneous and occur in the same place, so it's one story. (It hardly matters if this is one or two blocks—they pass the yellow test.)

Highlight blocks 7 and 8 are stories the veterinarian told, that I paraphrased and dramatized. Highlight block 9 is a recreation of the title of the piece—difficult decision.

To summarize: There are nine blocks of highlight—nine scenes in this 3,700-word essay. Some are recreations of situations I experienced; others I recreated, based on stories the veterinarian and others told me. In each of the blocks of highlight something happens; they can stand alone. Sometimes there's information between each scene, and in other instances, one scene flows into another, with information embedded within it. Information teaches the reader about the person, place, or subject and helps clarify the story.

About three-quarters of the essay is highlighted. You don't need to have as much highlighting in your essay, but generally speaking, the more you have, the better the piece, as long as it is balanced out with information. Neither style nor substance should overwhelm the reader; when they are combined, however, the reader can be overwhelmed and informed at the same time. I feel this way about Lauren Slater's "Three Spheres," reprinted below. It is mostly story and scene, but it is powerful and compelling, as well as a learning experience for the reader, from start to finish.

"Three Spheres," by Lauren Slater

Linda Whitcomb: Initial Intake Notes

Ms. Whitcomb is a 37-year-old SWF who has had over 30 hospitalizations, all for suicide attempts or self-mutilation. She scratches her arms lightly when upset. Was extensively sexually abused as a child. Is now requesting outpatient therapy for bulimia. Ms. Whitcomb says she's vomiting multiple times during the day. Teeth are yellowed and rotting, probably due to stomach acids present during purges.

Client has been in out-patient therapy with over 70 (!) social workers, psychologists and psychiatrists. She has "fired" them all because she cannot tolerate their limit setting. She has threatened to sue "at least eight, maybe more," because "they never gave me what I needed. They were a menace to the profession." Please note: Client has never carried through with any of her threats to sue. She does, however, demand complete access to her health-care providers. Has a history of calling her therapists in the middle of the night, screaming that she needs to see them right away, and self-mutilating when her requests are refused.

During her intake and evaluation appointment, client presented as teary and soft spoken. She wore large hoop earrings and much makeup. She said she believes she has gout and asked to be pre-scribed medication for it. Became belligerent when refused. Possi-bly this client is delusional, although she was fully oriented to all three spheres—person, place and time—knowing who and where she was, and demonstrating capacity to locate historical figures in their appropriate periods. Proverb interpretation: somewhat con-crete. Serial sevens: intact. Recommendation: psychological testing; 1x weekly behavioral therapy to address eating disorder; possible admission as an inpatient if she cannot get bulimia under control.

"So who wants to take the case?" Dr. Siley, the director of the outpatient portion of the unit where I work, asks. He folds the initial intake evaluation from which he's been reading back into its green file.

None of the other clinicians offer. A woman as outrageously de-manding and consistently suicidal as this one is would add a lot of pressure to anyone's job. Ellen looks away. Veronica busies herself with the pleats on her skirt. The staff room stays quiet.

"What about you?" Dr. Siley says, looking in my direction. He knows my numbers are down. My job description states I'm respon-sible for seeing at least 20 outpatients, in addition to the chronic schizophrenics in the residential program.

"Well," I say, "she sounds like a lot of work."

"Who isn't?" Veronica says.

"Why don't you take her then?" I say.

"I'm full," Veronica says.

"And you aren't," Dr. Siley adds, pushing the file across the table toward me.

The phone rings six, maybe seven times, and then I hear a tiny voice on the other end—"Hello," it whispers, and I announce myself, the new therapist, let's make an appointment, look forward to meeting you, here's where the clinic is, in case you forgot—

"Can't," the voice weeps. "Can't can't." I hear the sound of choking, the rustle of plastic. "Ten times a day," the voice says. "Into 30 three-gallon bags. I've spent," and sobbing breaks out over the line, "I've spent every last penny on frozen pizzas. There's blood coming up now."

"You need to be in a hospital then," I say.

"Oh please," the voice cries. "Put me in a hospital before I kill myself. I'm afraid I'm going to kill myself."

I tell her to sit tight, hang on, and then I replace the receiver. I know the routine by heart. I call 911, give the ambulance company her name and address, tell them there's no need to commit her because she said she'd go willingly. Next they'll take her to an emergency room and after that she'll be placed on an inpatient unit somewhere in this state. She can't come into our own program's inpatient unit because she's neither schizophrenic nor male, the two criteria for admission. She'll stay wherever she is put anywhere from three days to four weeks, enough time, probably, for her to forget I ever called, to forget she ever wandered into the clinic where I work. At the hospital they'll likely set her up with an aftercare psychologist affiliated with their own institution, and he, or she, will have to deal with what sounds like her enormous neediness. And I, lucky I, will be off the case. Or so I think.

Two days later a call comes through to my office. "Ms. Linda Whitcomb tells us you're her outpatient therapist. Could you come in for a team meeting next Monday afternoon?"

"Well, I don't even know her, actually. I was assigned the case but before I could meet her she had to be hospitalized. Where is she?"

"Mount Vernon. I'm her attending psychologist here. Would you be willing to meet with us regarding her aftercare plans?"

Mount Vernon, Mount Vernon. And suddenly, even though it's been years, I see the place perfectly all over again, the brick buildings, the green ivy swarming the windows. The nurses who floated down the halls like flocks of seagulls, carrying needles in their beaks. My heart quickens; a screw tightens in my throat.

"Mount Vernon?" I say. Of all the hundreds of hospitals in Massachusetts, why did it have to be this one? And another part of me thinks I should have been prepared, for eventually past meets present; ghosts slither through all sealed spaces.

"Look, I don't know the woman at all," I repeat, and I hear something desperate in my voice. I try to tamp it down, assume a professional pose. "I mean," I say, "the patient, although technically assigned to me, has not begun a formal course of psychotherapy under my care."

A pause on the line. "But technically," the voice retorts, "she is under your care, yes? You have some sort of record on her? Your clinic agreed to take the case?"

"Yes," I say. "Well . . . yes."

"Next Monday then, one-o-clock, Wyman—"

"Two," I interrupt bitterly. "Wyman Two."

"Good," she says. "We'll see you then."

What else can I do? Technically, I have been assigned the case. But this isn't any longer about the case; my hesitations now don't have to do with Linda Whitcomb and her stained teeth, but with ivy on the brick, the shadow of a nurse, a needle, the way night looked as it fell beyond the bars and the stars were sliced into even segments. I remember looking out the windows on Wyman Two; I remember Rosemary swallowing her hidden pills, how she danced the Demerol onto her tongue and later sunk into a sleep so deep only the slamming cuffs of a cardiac machine could rouse her. Liquid crimson medicines were served in plastic cups. The rooms had no mirrors.

But the reflections came clear to me then, come still in quiet moments when past meets present so smoothly the seams disappear and time itself turns fluid. Sometimes I wish time stayed solid, in separable chunks as distinct as the sound of the ticking clock on my mantel right now. In truth, though, we break all boundaries, hurtling forward through hope and backwards on the trail made by memory.

But what else can we do except reach, except remember? What else can I do, having been assigned this case? I will go in, go down. Go back.

American culture abounds with marketplace confessions. I know this. And I know the criticisms levied against this trend, how such open testifying trivializes suffering and contributes to the narcissism polluting our country's character. I agree with some of what the critics of the confessional claim. I'm well aware of Wendy Kaminer's deep and in part justified scorn for the open admissions of Kitty Dukakis, who parades her alcoholism for all to observe, or for Oprah who extracts admissions from the soul like a dentist pulls teeth, gleefully waving the bloodied root and probing the hole in the abscessed gum while all look, without shame, into the mouth of pain made ridiculously public. Would it not be more prudent to say little, or nothing, to hold myself back like any good doctor, at most admitting some kind of empathic twinge? For what purpose will I show myself? Does it satisfy some narcissistic need in me— at last I can have some of the spotlight? Perhaps a bit, yes? But I think I set aspects of my own life down not so much to revel in their gothic qualities, but to tell you this: that with many of my patients I feel intimacy, I feel love. To say I believe time is finally fluid, and so are the boundaries between human beings, the border separating helper from the one who hurts always blurry. Wounds, I think, are never confined to a single skin but reach out to grasp us all. When you die, there's that much less breath to the world, and across continents someone supposedly separate gasps for air. When—Marie, Larry, George, Pepsi, Bobby, Harold—when I weep for you, don't forget I weep as well for me.

I have to drive out of the city to get there, down 40 miles of roads I've avoided for the past eight years. Where there was once farmland, horses spitting sand as they galloped, wide willow trees I sat under when the nurses let me out on passes, there are now squat square houses dotting the hills. But the building's bubbled dome rises unmistakably over a crest as I round the corner, floating there in the distance like a glittering spaceship, looking exactly the same as it did almost a decade ago. Walking back from passes I would see that domed bubble, that silver blister bursting against a spring sky, and I would count one, two, three, getting closer, my heart hammering half with fear, half with relief. Safe again. Trapped again. Safe again. Trapped aga—

And I have the same heart in the same socket of chest, and it hammers like it used to and I find myself thinking the same words safe again, trapped again. My palms sweat on the steering wheel. I remind myself: I am not that girl. I am not that girl. I've changed. I've grown. I am now a psychologist who over the years has learned to give up her Indian print sundresses and bulky smocks for tailored skirts, who carries a black Coach leather briefcase. How often, though, I've marveled at the discrepancy between this current image of me and the tangled past it sprang from. Sometimes I've imagined shouting out in staff meetings, in front of all my colleagues who know me as a spunky, confidant doctor, how often I've wanted to say Once I too . . .

And what I would tell them goes something like this. On five separate occasions, spanning the ages from 14 to 24, I spent considerable portions of my life inside the very hospital whose graveled drive I am now turning into. Until what could be called my "recovery" at 25 or so, I was admitted to this institution on the average of every other year for up to several months. And even today, at 31 years old, with all of that supposedly behind me, with chunks of time in which to construct and explain the problems that led me to lock-up, I find myself at a loss for words. Images come, and perhaps in the images I can illuminate some of my story. I am 5 years old, sitting under the piano, as my mother, her face a mask of manic pain, pummels the keys. Beneath the bench I press the golden pedals, hold them all down at the same time so our house swells with raw and echoing sounds, with crashing crescendos and wails that shiver up inside my skin, lodging there a fear of a world I know is impossible to negotiate, teetering on a cruel and warbling axis. And later, lying in my bed, she murmurs Hebrew while her fingers explore me and a darkness sprouts inside my stomach. A pain grows like a plant and when I'm 12, 13, I decide to find the plant, grasping for its roots with a razor blade. Stocked solid with the romance of the teen-age years, with the words of the wounded Hamlet and the drowned Virginia Woolf, whom I adored, I pranced on the lawn of my school, showing off the fresh gashes—Cordelia, a dwarf, a clown, Miss Haversham. I loved it all. I wept for the things inserted into me, the things plucked out of me. And I knew, with the conviction of adolescence, that pain confers a crown. I was removed to the hospital, then a foster home, then the hospital, again and again. Later on, in my late teens and early 20s, I starved myself, took pills to calm me down, wanted a way out. And finally I found one, or one, perhaps, found me.

I am not that girl any longer. I tell that to myself as I ride up the hospital's elevator. I found some sort of way into recovery. But I know, have always known, that I could go back. Mysterious neurons collide and break. The brain bruises. Memories you thought were buried rise up.

I rise up in the elevator and the doors part with a whisper. Stepping off, I find myself face to face with yet another door, this one bolted and on it a sign that says: "Enter With Caution. Split Risk."

And now I am standing on the other side of that door—the wrong, I mean the right, side of the door, and I ring the buzzer. I look through the thick glass window and see a nurse hustle down the hall, clipboard in hand. I recognize her. Oh my god, I recognize her! I hunch, dart back. Impossible, I tell myself. It's been over eight years. Staff turnover in these places is unbelievably high. But it could be her, couldn't it? And what happens if she recognizes me? My mouth dries and something shrivels in my throat.

"Dr. S?" she asks, opening the door. I nod, peer into her eyes. They're the blue of sadness, thickly fringed. Her lips are painted the palest sheen of pink. "Welcome," she says, and she steps back to let me pass. I was wrong, I've never seen this woman in my life. I don't know those eyes, their liquid color, nor the voice, in whose tone I hear, to my surprise, a ring of deference. Doctor, she actually calls me doctor. She bends a bit at the waist, in greeting, acknowledging the hierarchies that exist in these places—nurses below psychologists, psychologists below psychiatrists. Patients are at the bottom of the ladder.

With a sudden surge of confidence, I step through. The reversal is remarkable, and for a second makes me giddy. I'm aware of the incredible elasticity of life, how the buckled can become straight, the broken mended. Watch what is on the ground; watch what you step on, for it could contain hidden powers and, in a rage, fly up all emerald and scarlet to sting your face.

And here I am, for the briefest moment, all emerald, all scarlet. "Get me a glass of water," I imagine barking to her. "Take your pills or I'll put you in the quiet room."

Then the particular kind of dense quiet that sits over the ward comes to me. Emerald goes. Scarlet dies down. I am me again, here again. I grip my briefcase and look down the shadowy hall, and it's the same shadowy hall, loaded with the exact same scents, as it was so many years ago. The paint is that precise golden green. The odor is still undefinable, sweet and wretched. Another woman comes up, shakes my hand. "I'm Nancy," she says, "charge nurse on the unit."

"Good to meet you," I say. And then I think I see her squint at me. I've the urge to toss my hair in front of my face, to mention a childhood in California or Europe, how I've only been in this state for a year.

"We're meeting in the conference room," Nancy says. Clutching my briefcase, I follow her down the corridor. We pass open doors and I hold my breath as we come to the one numbered 6, because that was my bedroom for many of the months I stayed here. I slow down, try to peer in. Heavy curtains hang, just as they used to, over a large, thickly meshed window. There are the stars I want to say, for in my mind it's night again, and someone is rocking in a corner. Now, in the present time, a blond woman lies in what used to be my bed. On that mattress swim my cells, the ones we slough off, the pieces of ourselves we leave behind, forever setting our signatures into the skin of the world. As she sleeps, my name etches itself on her smooth flesh, and my old pain pours into her head.

And just as we are passing her by completely, the woman leaps out of bed and gallops to the door. "Oh Nancy," she keens. "I'm not safe, not safe. Get my doctor. I want my doctor."

"Dr. Ness will be up to see you at 4," Nancy says.

Suddenly the woman snarls. "Four," she says, "Dr. Ness is always late. Always keeps me waiting. I want a new doctor, someone who'll really care. A new doctor, a new . . . "

Her voice rises and she sucks on her fist. "Stop it, Kayla," Nancy says. "Take your fist out of your mouth. You're 29 years old. And if you want a new doctor, you'll have to bring it up in community meeting."

Kayla stamps her foot, tosses her head like a regal pony. "Screw you," she mutters now. "Screw this whole fucking place," and then she stomps back into her bed.

When we're a few feet beyond the scene, Nancy turns to me, smiles conspiratorially. I feel my mouth stretched into a similar smirk, and it relieves yet bothers me, this expression toward a patient. "Borderline," Nancy says matter of factly, giving a crisp nod of her head.

I sigh and nod back. "They're exhausting patients, the ones with borderline personalities." I pause. "But I prefer them to antisocials," I add, and as I say these words I feel safe again, hidden behind my professional mask. I am back on balance, tossing jargon with the confidence of a Brahmin in a village of untouchables. There is betrayal here, in what I do, but in betrayal I am finally camouflaged.

Of all the psychiatric illnesses, borderline personality disorder may be the one professionals most dislike to encounter. It's less serious than, say, schizophrenia, for the borderline isn't usually psychotic, but such patients are known for their flamboyant, attention-getting, overly demanding ways of relating to others. Linda, according to her intake description, is surely a borderline. Such patients are described with such adjectives as "manipulative" and "needy," and their behaviors are usually terribly destructive, and include anorexia, substance abuse, self-mutilation, suicide attempts. Borderlines are thought to be pretty hopeless, supposedly never maturing from their "lifelong" condition. I myself was diagnosed with, among other things, borderline personality disorder. In fact, when I left the hospital for what I somehow knew would be the very last time, at 24 years of age, I asked for a copy of my chart, which is every patient's right. The initial intake evaluation looked quite similar to Linda's, and the write-ups were full of all kinds of hopeless projections. "This young woman displays a long history marked by instability in her interpersonal and intrapsychic functioning," my record read. "She clearly has had a long career as a mental patient and we will likely encounter her as an admission again in the future."

I recall these words now, as we enter the conference room, where several other nurses and doctors sit around a table with a one-way mirror on the far wall. I scan their faces quickly, praying I look as unfamiliar to them as they do to me. I don't recognize any of the people in here, and I'm hoping against hope they don't recognize me. Still, even if we've never met, I feel I know them somehow, know them in a deep and private part of me. "Ta da," I have the angry urge to shout out, bowing to the bearded psychiatrist at the oval's head, standing arms akimbo, twirling so my skirt swells out. "Here I am," I'd like to yell, "yes sireee, encountered again. Guess who you're looking at; guess who this is. The Borderline! And sure enough folks, I did mature out, at least a little . . . "

But of course I won't say such a thing, wouldn't dare, for I would lose my credibility. But the funny thing is, I'm supposedly in a profession that values honesty and self-revelation. Freud himself claimed you couldn't do good analytic work until you'd "come clean" with yourself in the presence of another, until you'd spoken in the bright daylight your repressed secrets and memories. Freud told us not to be so ashamed, to set loose and let waltz our mothers and fathers, our wetness and skins. Training programs for psychologists like me, and the clinics we later work in, have as a credo the admission and discussion of countertransference, which by necessity claims elements of private conflict.

At the same time though, another more subtle yet powerful message gets transmitted to practitioners in the field. This message says Admit your pain, but only to a point. Admit it but keep it clean. Go into therapy, but don't call yourself one of us if you're anything more than nicely neurotic. The field transmits this message by perpetuating so strongly an us versus them mindset, by consistently placing a rift between practitioners and patients, a rift it intends to keep deep. This rift is reflected in the language only practitioners are privy to, in words like glossolalia and echolalia instead of just saying the music of madness, and then again in phrases like homicidal ideation and oriented to all three spheres instead of he's so mad he wants to kill her or he's thinking clearly today, knows who, what, and where he is. Along these same lines, practitioners are allowed to admit their countertransference but not the pain pain pain the patient brings me back to, memories of when I was 5, your arms my arms and the wound is one. No. To speak in such a way would make the rift disappear, and practitioners might sink into something overwhelming. We—I—hang onto the jargon that at once describes suffering and hoists us above it. Suddenly, however, here I am, back in an old home; lowered.

I recognize the conference room as the place where, when I was 14, I met with my mother and the social worker for the last time. My father had gone away to live in Egypt. My mother was wearing a kerchief around her head and a heavy bronze Star of David wedged between the hills of her breasts. Years later, seeing the mountains of Jerusalem, cupping the scathing sand of the desert, hearing the primitive wails of the Hasids who mourned the Temple's destruction, I would think of my mother's burning body, a pain I could never comprehend.

This is the conference room where she, unstable, prone to manic highs and depressive lows, shot through with a perpetual anxiety that made her hands shake, this is the same conference room where she told me she was giving me over to the care of the state, giving me up to become a foster child. "I can't handle you anymore," she'd said to me, spit at me. "I no longer want you with me."

I bow my head in deference to something I cannot name, and enter the room. Things are screaming inside me and my eyes feel hot. Nancy introduces me all around and I take a seat, pull out a notebook, try to act as calm and composed as possible. "The patient Ms. Whitcomb," the bearded psychiatrist begins, "is not able to make good use of the hospital. She's an extreme borderline, wreaking havoc on the unit. We suspect her of some factitious posturing as well." He pauses, looks at me, clears his throat. I smile back at him but my mouth feels uncoordinated, tightness at its corners. I won't cry, won't cry, even though in the one-way mirror, in the criss-crossing of the creamy branches beyond the ward's windows, I see my mother again, her face coming to me clearly, her eyes haunted with loneliness and rage. I feel her fingers at my breasts and flinch.

"We think," a social worker named Miss Norton continues, "that we'll be discharging her in a matter of days, as soon as we get her stabilized on some meds. We take it you'll be picking up her case on an out-patient basis. Any ideas of how you'll work with her?"

I nod, pretend to make some notes on the pad. As my voice rises through my throat, I'm surprised at how smooth it sounds, a sleek bolt of silk. "Lots of limits," I say. "We know borderlines do well with lots of limits. This is the only context in which a workable transference can begin."

The bearded doctor nods. In the tree, my mother tongues her teeth and wind lifts her lovely skirt, embroidered with fragile flowers. And then she is not my mother anymore, but a little girl whose legs are white, a single ruby scar on scrubbed knee. And while part of me sits in the conference room, part of me flies out to meet this girl, to touch the sore spot, fondling it with my fingers.

For I have learned how to soothe the hot spots, how to salve the soreness on my skin. I can do it so no one notices, can do it while I teach a class if I need to, or lead a seminar on psychodiagnosis. I can do it while I talk to you in the evenest of tones. "Shhhh," I whisper to the hurting part, hidden here. You can call her borderline—call me borderline—or multiple, or heaped with post traumatic stress— but strip away the language and you find something simple. You find me, part healthy as a horse and part still suffering, as are we all. What sets me apart from Kayla or Linda or my other patients like George, Marie, Pepsi—what sets me apart from these "sick" ones is simply a learned ability to manage the blades of deep pain with a little bit of dexterity. Mental health doesn't mean making the pains go away. I don't believe they ever go away. I do believe that nearly every person sitting at this oval table now has the same warped im- pulses, the same scarlet id, as the wobbliest of borderlines, the most florid of psychotics. Only the muscles to hold things in check—to channel and funnel—are stronger. I have not healed so much as learned to sit still and wait while pain does its dancing work, trying not to panic or twist in ways that make the blades tear deeper, finally infecting the wounds.

Still, I wonder. Why—how—have I managed to learn these things while others have not? Why have I managed somehow to leave behind at least for now what looks like wreckage, and shape something solid from my life? My prognosis, after all, was very poor. In idle moments, I still slide my fingers under the sleeves of my shirt and trace the raised white nubs of scars that track my arms from years and years of cutting. How did I learn to stop cutting and col- lapsing, and can I somehow transmit this ability to others? I don't know. It's a core question for me in my work. I believe my strength has something to do with memory, with that concept of fluid time. For while I recall with clarity the terror of abuse, I also recall the green and lovely dream of childhood, the moist membrane of a leaf against my nose, the toads that peed a golden pool in the palm of my hand. Pleasures, pleasures, the recollections of which have injected me with a firm and unshakable faith. I believe Dostoyevsky when he wrote, "If man has one good memory to go by, that may be enough to save him." I have gone by memory.

And other things too. Anthony Julio wrote in his landmark study, The Invulnerable Child, that some children manage to avoid or grow out of traumatic pasts when there is the presence in their lives of at least one stable adult—an aunt, a neighbor, a teacher. I had the extreme good fortune to be placed in a foster home where I stayed for four years, until I turned 18, where I was lovingly cared about and believed in. Even when my behavior was so bad I cut myself in their kitchen with the steak knife, or when, out of rage, I swallowed all the Excedrin in their medicine cabinet and had to go back to the unit, my foster parents continued to believe in my abilities to grow, and showed this belief by accepting me after each hospital discharge as their foster child still. That steady acceptance must have had an impact, teaching me slowly over the years how to see something salvageable in myself. Bless those people, for they are a part of my faith's firmness. Bless the stories my foster mother read to me, the stories of mine she later listened to, her thin blond hair hanging down in a single sheet. The house, old and shingled, with niches and culverts I loved to crawl in, where the rain pinged on a leaky roof and out in the puddled yard a beautiful German shepherd, who licked my face and offered me his paw, barked and played in the water. Bless the night there, the hallway light they left on for me, burning a soft yellow wedge that I turned into a wing, a woman, an entire army of angels who, I learned to imagine, knew just how to sing me to sleep.

At a break in the conference, a nurse offers me a cup of coffee. "Sure," I say, "but first the ladies' room." And then I'm off, striding down the hallway I know so well, its twists and turns etched in subterranean memory. I go left, then right, swing open the old wooden ladies' room door, and sit in a stall.

When I come back, the nurse is ready with a steaming Styrofoam cup. She looks at me, puzzled, as she hands me my hot coffee. "You've been here before?" she asks.

My face must show some surprise, for she adds, "I mean, the bathrooms. You know where they are."

Oh," I say quickly. "Right. I've visited some of my patients on this ward before, yes."

"You don't have to use the patient bathroom," she says, smiling oddly, looking at me with what I think may be suspicion. "We don't recommend it," she adds. "Please use the staff bathroom, through the nurses' station."

"OK," I say. I bend my face into the coffee's steam, hoping she'll think the redness is from the rising heat. Of course. How stupid of me. What's she thinking? Can she guess? But in a way I am one of the patients, and she could be too. I'm not ready to say it yet though, weak one. Wise one. This time, memory has led me astray.

The conference resumes. I pay little attention. I'm thinking about the faux pas with the bathroom, and then I'm watching the wind in the tree outside the window. I am thinking about how we all share a similar, if not single pain, and the rifts between stalls and selves is its own form of delusion. And then I hear, through a thin ceiling, wails twining down, a sharp scream, the clattering of footsteps. I sit up straight.

"Delivery rooms," the social worker says, pointing up. "We're one floor under the maternity ward."

I smile and recall. That's right. Wyman Two is just one floor of what is an old large public hospital. The psychiatric unit we're on has always been wedged between labor rooms upstairs and a nursery downstairs. When I was a patient I could often hear, during group therapy or as I drifted into a drugged sleep, the cries of pushing women as their muscles contracted and in great pain their pink skins ripped, a head coming to crown.

"Why don't you meet with Linda now?" the psychiatrist says, checking his watch and gathering his papers. Everyone stands, signaling the end of the conference. "You can take one of the interview rooms," Nancy, the charge nurse adds. "They're nice places for doing therapy, comfortable."

I nod. I've almost forgotten about Linda and how she is the reason for my return here today. Now I walk with the rest out of the conference room and Nancy points down the long hall. "There," she says, her finger aiming towards a door on the left. "The third room. We'll bring Linda to you." And then, to my surprise, Nancy fishes deep into her pocket and pulls out a large steel ring of keys, placing them in my hand. They're the same keys, I know, from all those years ago, keys I was not allowed to touch but which I watched avidly whenever I could, the cold green gleam and mysterious squared prongs opening doors to worlds I didn't know how to get to. Keys, keys, they are what every mental patient must dream of, the heart-shaped holes keys fit into, the smart click as they twist the secret tumblers and unlatch boxes, velvet lined and studded with sea-jewels. Keys are symbols of freedom and power and finally separateness. For in a mental hospital, only one side has the keys; the others go to meals with plastic forks in their fists.

Slowly, I make my way down the hall to the interview room, stand outside the locked door holding the key ring. It feels cool, and I press it to my cheek. A hand there once, feeling me for a fever, stroking away my fear. Bless those who have helped.

A woman who looks far older than her 37 years is now making her way down the hall. Stooped she is, with tired red ringlets of hair. As she gets closer I see the dark ditches under her eyes, where years of fatigue and fear have gathered. I would like to put my finger there, sweep away the microscopic detritus of suffering.

"Linda," I say, and as she comes close to me, I extend my hand. "Hello," I say, and I can hear a gentleness in my voice, a warm wind in me, for I am not only greeting her, but myself.

We stand in front of the locked interview room and I fumble for the correct key. I start to insert it in the lock, but then halfway done, I stop. "You," I say to my new patient, Linda. "You take the key. You turn the lock."

She arches one eyebrow, stares up at me. Her face seems to say Who are you, anyway? I want to cry. The hours here have been too long and hard. "You," I say again, and then I feel my eyes actually begin to tear. She steps forward, peers closely, her expression confused. Surely she's never seen one of her doctors cry. "It's OK," I say. "I know what I'm doing." And for a reason I cannot quite articulate at the moment, I make no effort to hide the wetness. I look straight at her. At the same time, for the first time today, my voice feels genuinely confident. "Take the keys, Linda," I say, "and open the door."

She reaches out a bony hand, takes the keys from me, and swings open the door. The interview room is shining with sun, one wall all windows. I've been in this room, too, probably hundreds of times over the years, meeting with the psychiatrists who tried to treat me. I shiver with the memory. Ultimately it was not their treatments or their theories that helped me get better, but the kindness lodged in a difficult world. And from the floor above comes the cry of a protesting baby, a woman ripped raw in birth. She is us. We are her. As my mother used to say, rocking over the Shabbat candles, chanting Jewish prayers late, late into the night, "Hear O Israel. The Lord is God, The Lord is one, and so are we as a people."

She would pause then, her hands held cupped over the candlesticks. "We are one," she would repeat to me after a few moments, her strained face peering at me through shadows. "As a people we are always one."

Sometimes I miss her.

My patient and I sit down, look at each other. I see myself in her. I trust she sees herself in me.

This is where we begin.

Highlighting "Three Spheres" and "Yellow Taxi"

As I said in the beginning, this is powerful and quite scenic, eliciting interest and emotion from the reader. Slater surprises and connects. Let's go through it together and see how she makes it work.

It begins with three recognizable scenes, one after another, which Slater separates using space breaks.

Scene 1 begins with dialogue: "So who wants to take the case?" (page 152).

Scene 2 begins: "The phone rings six, maybe seven times" (page 152).

Scene 3 begins: "Two days later, a call comes through to my office" (page 153).

There are also some less obvious scenes in these pages—I call them "sneaky scenes," or "scenes within scenes." Look at scene 2 and the paragraph beginning, "I tell her to sit tight." Slater is telling the reader what will happen to her patient—and she is recreating it for us as a story. It's a scene within a scene.

Then at the end of scene 3, Slater sits in her office after the Mount Vernon phone call and remembers a haunting event from her own life. Fiction writers call this use of a memory a *flashback*—and there's no reason creative nonfiction writers can't use flashbacks too, especially in memoir when, like Lauren Slater, we are reliving our lives.

So whether you conclude you have three scenes or five scenes at this point, the idea is that most of what the reader is reading is story.

Scene 4 begins: "I have to drive out of the city" (page 155).

Note that there are many mini memories, all stories, within this larger block—scenes within scenes. Driving to Mount Vernon is a place setting, an isolated instance, allowing the writer to go back in time.

Notice how Slater's stories inform as well as dramatize. The reader needn't be told about her cruel, crazy mother. We see her at the piano bench and hear the "crashing crescendos" of the keys, feel the fear and the "shivers" inside Slater's skin. Information is transformed into dramatic action. This is masterful showing and not telling—the reader learns and observes simultaneously.

Scene 5 brings Slater inside the hospital (page 157). Nancy, a nurse, escorts her through the hospital to the conference room. On the way, Slater sees Kayla, a patient, acting out—from a room Slater once occupied.

Scene 6 can be pinpointed at another space break: "I recognize the conference room" (page 161). The meeting begins and Slater attempts to concentrate and participate while her mind flashes back, repeatedly.

Scene 7 begins at another space break and Slater mistakenly goes to the patients' bathroom, out of habit, rather than the bathroom reserved for visitors and staff (page 164).

In scene 8 the conference resumes, and in scene 9, Dr. Slater meets her patient (page 166).

Though I've chosen to break this up into nine blocks of highlight—nine general scenes, there's a complex web of scene and stories and images throughout the essay that contribute to its power and impact.

To see more of this web, complete Exercise 12. Or, if you want to progress into the deconstruction phase more quickly, proceed to Exercise 13. And if you think you've had enough reading for the moment or you are going through "deconstruction overload," common among my students, then skip Exercise 13 and move forward. You can always return to any of this reading and review how writers do their work. Every time you read, you will likely see something different.

EXERCISE 13

Deconstruct "Yellow Taxi" (below)—a fitting highlighting assignment. Look for scenes, sneaky scenes (scenes within scenes), dialogue, specificity of detail. Want to see how I've deconstructed these pieces? Go to the teacher's manual on my website, www.leegutkind.com, and find out.

But first, let me give you some hints. There are at least fifteen short scenes or anecdotes in this essay, connected through an overall focus rather than narrative. I have highlighted the first three to help you out. In previous chapters, I have talked about Joseph's use of personal and public history, as well as fascinating ancillary information to help the reader feel more at one with the essay. Look also for areas where she combines reflection and information. She is helping us understand what she has been through, how she has been tested and taught. The sentence in the last paragraph pinpoints the essence of the essay: "We go on with the dead inside us."

"Yellow Taxi," by Eve Joseph

To work with the dying is to wade into mystery. In some situations professional training will be invaluable; in others, it will be of no use at all. On my first community visit as a hospice counselor, a

naked woman stood on the dresser beside her bed and flung a perfume bottle at my head; she thought she was in the war and her ar-
senal consisted of little colored bottles of eau de toilette. She had
captured the ridge and was there for the long haul. Two injections
of Haldol by the nurse eventually cleared the woman's delusions,
but what helped me to understand what the woman was seeing on
that ridge and to talk her down into the safety of her bed—the
bunker, we called it—were my mother's stories of the war.

It is a complicated thing to be employed to help people die. On
the one hand, each situation, each person, is unique, and each death
a profound experience; on the other, the job is like any other. You
set your alarm to wake up and grab a coffee on your way to work.
Traffic is bad, and you know the last parking spot is going to be gone.
You vow again to leave earlier, but that never happens. As with any
job, a certain set of skills is required; however, you never know exactly what it is you will need to be of some help.

A man dying of leukemia once asked me if I did anything useful.
In his last months he had built a farmer's market on his land so that
his wife and four sons would be able to support themselves after his
death. Without thinking I answered that I baked loaves of bread. It
was a lie, but it became a fortuitous lie. He told me to bring my
loaves to the market and said his family would keep half the profit;
the other half was mine. The first month after his death I decided
I'd do what I told the man, and I made five hundred dollars selling
banana, chocolate, blueberry, pumpkin, apple, and zucchini loaves.
I followed recipes; I made them up. A few years later, when my marriage ended, I supported myself and my children with money from
the loaves I sold at the man's market.

It's that way with the work of helping the dying; you start out
with good intentions and sometimes end up in a bunker reeking of
perfume.

The hospice where I worked in 1985 has been paved over and is
now a parking lot. The chestnut trees that lined the street outside

the patients' rooms are gone, along with the wild cherry trees that bloomed each February in a kind of mockery of winter. Bay Pavilion, as the old hospice was called, was a one-story horseshoe-shaped building built around a garden. These days they call hospice gardens "healing gardens." Back in 1985 the garden made no such claims; a gardener's garden, its raison d'être was to revel in its own beauty. For some patients it was the garden of their childhood; for others, it was the garden they wished they'd always had. This is not to say that Bay Pavilion was paradise but to muse over the idea it was only a step or two away from it.

In one of the rooms facing the courtyard, cherry blossoms blew in through an open window and fell onto a sleeping woman. I was in the room with her husband, whom I had met only moments before, when he had collapsed in my arms and said, "If there is a God and this is his plan, how can I ever believe in that God again; and if there is no God how can I live?" I was new to the work and had no answer for him. I hadn't even begun to formulate the questions. I remember looking at her pale skin and black hair and thinking she looked like Snow White in a Red Cross bed. Her window, like all the others on the unit, was kept slightly open in order for the spirit to leave.

Derived from the Latin *hospitium,* meaning both "host" and "guest," the word hospice represents an idea as well as a place. In Homeric times all strangers were regarded as guests; it was an obligation to be hospitable to strangers, an obligation imposed on civilized man by Zeus himself, one of whose many titles was xeinios, "protector of strangers." In the Odyssey, Alcinous, king of the Phaeacians, offers hospitality without knowing who Odysseus is: "Tell him, then, to rise and take a seat on a stool inlaid with silver and let the housekeeper give him some supper, of whatever there might be in the house."

The word hospice was used in the fourth century by monks who welcomed and provided sanctuary for pilgrims; it wasn't until the mid-1800s that it became exclusively associated with the care of the dying. The modern hospice, as we know it, did not come into being until 1967, when St. Christopher's Hospice was opened in London by Cicely Saunders, a young physician previously trained as a nurse and a social worker. The term "death with dignity" became a rallying cry for those working with the dying.

When I looked up the root of the word hospitality, I initially misread "friendliness to guests" as "friendliness to ghosts" and thought later that was not entirely inaccurate. It has been said by those who can see that the dead walk the corridors: mothers holding hands with daughters, grandfathers and grandmothers, husbands waiting for their wives, and others nobody knows, who are just there waiting.

One woman I worked with stared at the top left-hand corner of her room for days waiting for her late husband to come for her; others came, she told us, but she didn't know them and refused to go. On the morning of her death she said her husband had come. He'd tipped his hat in the slightly mocking way he'd always done in life, and she smiled. A wide, radiant smile.

A young man dying of AIDS asked me to be careful when I went to sit on a couch in his room; he didn't want me to sit on the old woman who had appeared three days ago with a bag of wool and needles. He asked me if I thought her arrival meant his death was near; I looked over my shoulder toward the empty couch and said my guess was that he had a bit of time, since she had brought her knitting.

I don't see spirits. But once, years ago, when I was eight months pregnant, I heard singing and drumming coming from the site of a Shaker church that had burned to the ground years before. My mother-in-law said spirits were singing to welcome the baby, but I was never sure what I'd heard or whether I had really heard anything at all.

Our first experiences with loss shape us in ways we don't understand at the time. When I was six, I roller-skated home like a bat out of hell from my friend's house with the still warm, limp body of a yellow budgie in my hand. I didn't know what death meant, but I knew it was big. My first funerals for animals were shaped not by belief in a send-off to the afterlife but out of love of ceremony—with the little graves, the procession, the tea parties on the lawn afterward.

When I was twelve, my older brother was killed in a car accident. It was 1965, the year Allen Ginsberg introduced the term "flower power," and Malcolm X was shot dead inside Harlem's Audubon Ballroom, the year T. S. Eliot died, and Bob Dylan's "Like a Rolling Stone" was on its way to becoming a new anthem. In North America, at that time, death was regarded as a taboo subject. Most people died in hospitals, away from view. Grief was not openly discussed, and not a lot was known about what to do with a kid whose brother had suddenly died on the other side of the country.

In the late Middle Ages, no funeral procession was complete without a delegation of children from orphanages or foundling homes. In the 1870s, children played with death kits complete with coffins and mourning clothes. Up until the late nineteenth century the preparation of the bodies of the dead occurred mostly in peoples' homes. It wasn't until the 1920s that death moved to hospitals and funeral homes, and people began believing children needed protection from the reality of death.

I spent the days between the phone call and the funeral playing with plastic horses in the basement. The smell of lilies drifted down the stairs, and when I surfaced, the funeral was over and everyone had gone home. I watched my mother gather armfuls of lilies and throw them in the trashcan. The lilies would have been *Lilium longiflorum*, trumpet-shaped flowers native to the Ryukyu Islands of Japan, the lilies mentioned in the Bible as the white-robed apostles of hope found growing in the Garden of Gethsemane after Christ's crucifixion, lilies that were said to have sprung up where drops of blood fell.

Thirty years later, I found a poem by a friend of my brother, in which I learned that his body had been shipped across Canada by train in a blue casket. Why that stays with me I can't fully explain. There is a story about a tribe of nomads crossing the Sahara Desert and pausing every few hours in order to let their spirits catch up with them. It seems right that it took my brother four days to arrive at the place he would be buried, right that he came across the country in a casket the color of the sky.

With death we see, as did C. S. Lewis, there are no lights on in the windows of the house, and we wonder if it was ever inhabited. I had no idea, when I studied social work and went to work for more than twenty years at a well-established hospice, that I was trying to sight grief through the scope of my past experience. I needed to find my way out of the basement.

The hospice that replaced the Bay Pavilion is located on the third and fourth floors of an old maternity hospital not far from downtown Victoria. In 1979, six years before I was hired as a counselor there, I gave birth to my first daughter in one of the rooms I later helped people die in.

There are seventeen beds on the unit, seven of them reserved for the imminently dying, nine allocated for patients with less than six months to live, and one for respite care that can be used by patients in the community for up to one week, a room I once heard a family member refer to as her "time-out" room. When you step out of the elevator onto the third floor you pass a vase filled with flowers to your left and a large hand-embroidered quilt on your right. The quilt contains the names of patients who have died; it is full, so new names are entered on a parchment scroll lying on the table beneath the quilt.

More than four hundred volunteers with various skills work at the hospice. Some sing, some play the piano in the family lounge, some know Reiki and therapeutic touch; many of them make tea and sit with the dying in their rooms. They come from all walks of life: they are doctors, teachers, filmmakers, waitresses, beauticians, dog trainers, painters and potters, CEOs, cops, and widows. Many, though not all, are retirees. There aren't many young volunteers; this is not their country yet.

On Sundays, Akako, a volunteer skilled in calligraphy, sits down at the table and carefully adds the names of patients who died that past week to the scroll. Some weeks there are three or four names; other weeks there are more. She remembers one week when it took her more than four hours to add twenty-three names to the list.

The nurses and doctors who do this work understand the language of pain. As the Bedouin must have for wind, the dying and those who care for them have many words for pain: sharp, dull, aching, crushing, searing, tingling, red, white, hot, cold, malevolent, familiar, catlike, ghostlike, jabbing, cutting, burning, flickering, flashing, ravenous, gnawing, coiling. (The Inuit, we are now told, have really only twelve words for snow.) For some it just hurts like hell; for others there are no words at all.

A language, says ethnobotanist Wade Davis, is not simply a set of grammatical rules or a vocabulary; it is a flash of the human spirit, a window of sorts into the cosmology of our individual lives. Many people, in their last days, speak of one thing in terms of another. Metaphor, the engine of poetry, is also the language of the dying. Those who work with the dying must learn to think like the poet who reaches for language the way a child reaches for the moon, believing it can be held in the hand like an orange at the same time it shines on in the night sky.

Without metaphor how could we comprehend the stars as small fires burning through the roof of the tent? Without metaphor how could we understand the man on his deathbed who tells you a yellow cab has pulled up outside his house, and even though the taxi has the wrong address, he says he'll go anyway? Or the woman who asks where she will live when they jackhammer her street? How could we understand the patient who repeatedly asks if her suitcase is packed and ready to go, the Buddhist who insists that the heads be chopped off all the flowers in her garden in case their beauty holds her back; how could we see what the woman crouched on her knees on her hospital bed sees when she smiles and tells the doctor she is peeking into heaven?

At birth, a newborn baby has approximately three hundred bones, while on average, an adult has two hundred and six. Our bones fuse as we grow; we are building our scaffolding without even knowing it. The twenty-four long, curved bones of our ribcage form a structure that shelters the heart, lungs, liver, and spleen. Like exotic birds we live within the safety of our bony cages.

One summer night a twenty-eight-year-old patient, with a rare form of bone cancer, asked to be wheeled outside in her hospital bed to sleep beneath the stars. In the days preceding her death, the bones of her ribcage were so brittle that one or two broke whenever she rolled over. I was horrified to learn that our bones could snap like dry twigs.

Pain speaks a number of languages. On one level it needs no translation; on another level it requires that we become translators and interpreters of another's pain if we are to be of any help. For her immediate physical pain, the young woman was on a morphine drip with breakthrough doses given subcutaneously through a butterfly in her upper arm. She was also seeing a counselor, Jo Dixon, who understood pain from a different perspective. Jo sat on the woman's bed every day and listened to her talk about what it was like to be trapped in her body. They talked about how each bone breaking was an opening, how the cage cracking was the only way she could fly free. The young *woman used* morphine to get on top of the pain and metaphor to try to understand it.

The metaphoric language of the dying is the language of the boatman. Metaphor, derived from the same word in Greek, in which it means "to transfer" or "to carry across," is the language of transition: a bit like the false work of the whole dying process, it holds us up until the crossing is strong enough to get us to the other side. In Athens, delivery trucks career around the streets with METAPHOR written on their sides. Pedestrians, I've heard, use their own metaphors when jumping out of the way. Aristotle believed the use of metaphor was a sign of genius: the dying as geniuses. On some level we know we will all be there one day, climbing into the yellow cab idling at the front door.

In my experience, very few people are aware of hospices until they need them. The actual work that goes on is invisible; we keep death as far away from us as we can. Hospices are part of a health system, and hospice workers part of an overriding bureaucracy. Traditionally, healers often lived on the outskirts of the village; shamans, prophets, tricksters, magicians, holy men, eccentrics, crazy men and women had a specific role to play as mediators between the living and the dead. There were times, over the years, when I thought that's what those of us working with the dying needed: huts on the edge of the city, places where people like Jo would be revered and feared, and, instead of biweekly pay checks, people would approach with stories, scraps of memory, a goat, a bag of potatoes, a basket of eggs, a chicken.

I was wrong about the trees. Today, driving past the parking lot the original Bay Pavilion has become, I see one oak still standing, the same tree Joseph Garcin's room overlooked. Metaphor didn't interest Joseph: "One leaf falling," he said, "can occupy me all day." But metaphor still concerns me—in his last week Joseph couldn't understand why it was taking him so long to die. Every night he knocked at death's door, asking to be let in.

Each of us brings our own beliefs to the work—beliefs based on our history with death, our culture, religion or lack of, beliefs based on mythology and psychology and on our motives and expectations. We come to our beliefs one death at a time. On New Year's Day, the Japanese believe, the dead arrive on the back of a horse, and, when the holiday is over, they return to their world in small wood and paper boats bearing a lighted candle. In Africa, a widow might run a zigzag course through the woods after her husband's burial so that his ghost will not follow and haunt her. Spain, says García Lorca, is a country open to death. Everywhere else, death is an end. "Death comes and they draw the curtains. In Spain they open them." Many Spaniards, he writes, live indoors until the day they die and are taken out into the sunlight.

What beliefs compel the living to carry the dead out into the sun? A mother whose premature baby spent her short life in a hospital asked only that her daughter be allowed to die outside. The doctor agreed to take her off life support and bag her, giving her oxygen by hand, until she was out of the hospital. A strange cortege of nurses, family, and friends walked single file behind the doctor through the corridors, out the back door, and across the parking lot to a nearby grassy hill. The baby's grandfather took up his drum and sang a farewell song to her. She breathed on her own for a good five minutes; when she took her last breath, a single clap of thunder reverberated across the sky. The grandfather believed the clap of thunder meant the Creator had opened the heavens, swooped down, picked the baby up in his arms, and booted it right on back to heaven.

A few years ago I read a story by the poet P. K. Page about an ornithologist who raised song birds in isolation in order to understand how they learned to sing. On their own, the birds cobbled together a kind of song, not species perfect, but a song nonetheless. When they were introduced to the songs of other birds, not of their own species, he discovered they chose the notes and cadences that completed their own species song.

In my work with the dying I was drawn instinctively to certain rituals and practices. I know very little of my Jewish ancestry, since my lineage is on my father's side, and Jewish identity is passed through matrilineal descent. From Baghdad and Russia to Calcutta and Shanghai and on to Israel, my ancestors studied Kabbalah and steeped themselves in Jewish and Arabic philosophy; they were Levys and Cohens and had names like Seemah, Mozelle, Solomon, and Dafna. Still, I do not qualify as a Jew. On the other hand, my marriage to a Coast Salish man made me legally an Indian under section 12 (1)(b) of the Indian Act. I am at home in the longhouse and a stranger in the synagogue.

I drew on native beliefs and rituals about death and dying in my work. It made sense to light a candle in order to hold the spirit in the last days and hours; it made sense that someone should sit with the body from the time of death until burial or cremation so that the spirit would not feel frightened or abandoned; it seemed right to pick up a handful of dirt and throw it onto the coffin before the plot was filled in, a last handshake, as the Coast Salish people call it.

What I didn't know and was stunned to find out one afternoon, reading Kaddish by Leon Wieseltier in the sun in my backyard, was that the native rituals that had resonated with me were also the rituals and beliefs of Jewish culture. From lighting candles and sitting with the body to covering mirrors and throwing dirt into the grave—I had unwittingly been learning my own species song, wading knee-deep, waist-deep, over-my-head-deep into mystery.

In addition to bringing our beliefs to the work, we also bring what we do not yet know about ourselves. We don't know our tolerance or our saturation point. We don't know what enough will look like. A nurse I knew, who burned out after eighteen years on the job, calculated she had helped over fifteen hundred people die. She left hospice and went to work in labor and delivery, where she vowed to deliver fifteen hundred babies before retiring.

My memories of life are stronger than those of death in the room I gave birth in. I remember lying beside a long window through which the sun was streaming in and looking over at my brand new baby daughter lying in her bassinet. I remember the sensation of falling in love: the quick jerk of it, the way one sometimes finds oneself falling backward into sleep and flailing to keep from disappearing into the void.

I believe it would be a fine thing to leave the world in a small wood and paper boat holding a lighted candle.

In my mother's last year she so weak she was unable to leave her house; in her last months she was confined to her bedroom. Later when I saw her in the hospital morgue, she was lying on a steel gurney in a half-zipped body bag. Her face was uncovered, and her hands, with their magenta nails, were resting on her chest. I asked the undertaker, when he arrived, to leave her face uncovered—which he did, although reluctantly, as it was against protocol. When we took her outside to the waiting van to take her body to the funeral home, rain fell on her cold face. The rain fell on her without knowing she was dead; it fell on her as it fell on earth. It fell on her the way it fell on Holly Golightly and Cat in Breakfast at Tiffany's, and it fell on her the way it had fallen on the attic roof when I was a girl and everywhere water was running, and my mother and I were dry in our adjoining beds and full of sleep.

We labor to be born and we labor to die. The obvious analogy is the clichéd one: we come from the unknown and depart for the unknown; however, the similarities are striking in other ways. Breath is crucial to both kinds of labor. Prenatal classes focus on breath and pain; the progression in Lamaze classes is from deep to shallow breathing. The dying, too, move from regular deep breaths to rapid mouth breathing. At the end, the dying often look like fish out of water, their mouths opening and closing in a kind of reflex. One could almost mistake these last breaths for silent kisses.

Babies arrive on their own time; there is an estimated due date, but it is the baby who releases a signal and triggers labor. Much like the white rabbit in Alice in Wonderland, the dying, too, are often preoccupied with time. I'm late, I'm late for a very important date; no time to say hello, good-bye. I'm late, I'm late, I'm late. Sometimes they wait for someone to arrive from out of town; sometimes they die when people have stepped out of the room to have a smoke.

You can't help but wonder. When I worked on the crisis team in the community, I went with a nurse to the home of a woman who seemed unable to die, a bee buzzed insistently against the inside of a sliding glass door until someone finally slid it open and let the bee out. The dying woman took her last breath when the door was opened and was gone before it closed again. To find a honey tree, says Annie Dillard, paraphrasing Thoreau, you must first catch a bee when its legs are heavy with pollen and it is ready for home. Release it and watch where it goes and follow it for as long as you can see it; wait until another bee comes, catch it, release it and watch. Keep doing that, and sure enough it will lead you home. Bee to bee leading us home. How does the spirit leave? We don't know, but every window on the hospice unit is open, just a crack, just in case.

In 1969, with her book *On Death and Dying*, Elisabeth Kübler-Ross brought the subject of death out of the privacy of medical schools and delivered it to the streets. She gave the layperson a language and a framework to understand the process of grief. Her five stages of grief provided new ways to think and speak about loss and helped give a sense of movement to the dying process. Her model is largely responsible for the ubiquitous idea of the "good death," the idea that there is a best way to approach the end of life, that we will reach acceptance before our last breath. A central concept of a good death is one that allows a person to die on his or her own terms, relatively pain free, with dignity. As if we have control. I was regularly asked, by family members, to describe the dying process. I would tell them about how people often lapse into a coma in the days preceding death and how breath moves from the deep and regular to the shallow and intermittent. I would explain apnea and how many people hold their breath for long periods of time, up to three minutes sometimes, and how all others in the room also hold their breath until the gasping breath breaks the silence in the room. I would explain that people rarely die in the space between breaths, that they return to the body as if they have been on a practice run. I would go over the possibility that phlegm would build up, resulting in what is known as a "death rattle," a term that invokes a kind of dread, a term that conjures up scenes like the one Dostoevsky described in *Crime and Punishment*: "She sank more and more into uneasy delirium. At times she shuddered, turned her eyes from side to side, recognized everyone for a minute, but at once sank into delirium again. Her breathing was hoarse and difficult; there was a sort of rattle in her throat." I would talk about how the hands and feet get cold as blood leaves the extremities and pools around the heart and lungs in a last attempt to protect the vital organs and how those hands and feet turn blue shortly before death. And I would talk about how breath leaves the body, how it moves from the chest to the throat to little fish breaths at the end.

For a long time this work was for me a calling: not religious, not selfless. I left hospice three years ago after nearly twenty years. I can't say that I've ever come up with an adequate answer for the questions about God and fairness from the man whose wife lay dying as the cherry blossoms drifted in through the open window. The closest I've come is my own realization of what hospice work asks of us: that we enter the darkness without a map of the way home, that we accompany people as far as we can. "Closure," says a friend of mine, "is a pile of crap." We go on with the dead inside us. My brother, the woman whose bones broke like twigs, the boy dying of AIDS. My mother. The innumerable others.

Reflection

Eve Joseph's essay is moving, vivid, scenic from start to finish—and especially profound. Off and on through the essay she steps aside in order to speak directly to the reader, clarifying her viewpoint and perhaps seeking to be more clearly understood. We do this in conversation with friends when we say, "Do you realize how important this is to me? Do you understand where I'm coming from? What this means?" She is reflecting on the information, ideas, and events she is communicating so vividly and emotionally to her reader. Reflection is a challenging but essential part of creative nonfiction, especially in personal essay and memoir.

In "Three Spheres," Lauren Slater tries repeatedly to make sense of what's happened to her and reflects about why she's writing about it now. At the end of scene 3 (page 154), at the text break, she begins to add context to her story by discussing what she calls "marketplace confessions" and the "narcissistic need in me" to share and thereby purge herself of her story. Later she ponders "the incredible elasticity of life, how the buckled can become straight, the broken mended." These are all judgments, assessments, reflections of what she's written and what it might mean to her and in context to the reader.

Owing to the nature of her topic, Joseph is especially reflective in her essay. Nearly every scene she writes is bolstered by the wisdom she gained through her experience not only as a hospice coordinator but also as a mother, daughter, and poet. Her first three paragraphs are short but vivid scenes, each with subtle reflective commentary.

Note that Slater and Joseph often couple reflection with history, as in this passage from Joseph:

> The word hospice was used in the fourth century by monks who welcomed and provided sanctuary for pilgrims; it wasn't until the mid-1800s that it became exclusively associated with the care of the dying. The modern hospice, as we know it, did not come into being until 1967, when St. Christopher's Hospice was opened in London by Cicely Saunders, a young physician previously trained as a nurse and a social worker. The term death with dignity became a rallying cry for those working with the dying.
>
> When I looked up the root of the word hospitality, I initially misread "friendliness to guests" as "friendliness to ghosts" and thought later that was not entirely inaccurate. It has been said by those who can see that the dead walk the corridors: mothers holding hands with daughters, grandfathers and grandmothers, husbands waiting for their wives, and others nobody knows, who are just there waiting.

EXERCISE 14

Go back and examine Joseph's piece. Focus on the reflective elements and note that her reflections come directly from the text. You can see the connection. She's not pontificating; there's a difference. Now go to the writing you have been doing. Are there reflective elements? Perhaps not—or at least not yet. Sometimes it takes a while to understand why you are telling a story and what it means to you—or the world.

DEALING WITH THE DEAD

Question: I'd like to write about my grandmother—or someone else from my family. I want to write in scenes, as you recommend. But most of the people I want to write about are dead. So how can I do that? Isn't that making stuff up?

Answer: I hope you aren't making anything up—and you don't have to make stuff up. You are *recreating*—not creating—so the reader will understand and allow you to take certain liberties.

Recreation or "Reconstruction"?

It's a given that a writer of creative nonfiction takes some license in recreating a circumstance, event, or memory—as a friend might do when telling a story to another friend. This is vital to creating compelling narratives; the only caveat is that the writer must remain as true to the spirit and facts of the circumstances as possible.

Angela's Ashes is a powerful and cinematic narrative. When Frank McCourt captured his tormented young life growing up in Ireland, he was recreating from memory the lives of his family. He didn't have transcriptions of their conversations and film footage of their activities so many decades ago. Readers granted him the latitude to paint his word pictures as he remembered them because his voice was authentic and the details he provided—those that could be fact-checked—were accurate. And McCourt was writing memoir. It is much easier to recreate and to make assumptions about your own life as opposed to recreating the lives of others. You can sound more believable, especially difficult when there are no living witnesses. Narrative historians who are recreating someone else's life, like David McCullough, however, turning history into documentary nonfiction drama, must be careful and persistent and prove themselves through research.

Here's a description of how E. F. Farrington, the sixty-year-old master mechanic of the Brooklyn Bridge, tested the first span of wire cables more than 150 years ago from McCullough's book *The Epic Story of the Building of the Brooklyn Bridge* (2001):

> There was great shouting from down below, and up ahead, on top of the tower, people were waving hats and handkerchiefs. Then all at once, as he went swinging out over the housetops between the anchorage and the tower, Farrington freed himself from the rope about his chest and stood up on the seat. Holding on first with one hand, then the other, he lifted his hat in response to the continuing ovation. Then he sat down again. People were running through the streets beneath him now, shouting and cheering as they ran. He waved, he blew them kisses. Sailing steadily along all the while, his course was nearly horizontal at first, like that of a heavy bird taking flight, because of the sag in the rope. His light coat blew open and began fluttering in the wind. And then he was beyond the sag and climbing sharply, almost straight up, a coat—flapping, gently twirling form that looked very small, fragile, and very birdlike now against the granite face of the tower.
>
> A tremendous cheer went up from the streets and rooftops, followed quickly by a salute from the little cannon across the river. His time from anchorage to tower was three and three-quarter minutes.

McCullough had to use existing documents to create his narrative drama, but Rebecca Skloot was able to combine existing documentary material with personal interviews of relatives and friends in her reconstruction of the life and story of Henrietta Lacks for her book, *The Immortal Life of Henrietta Lacks* (2010). Lacks died of cancer in 1951, but her cells, the first human cells ever to do so, reproduced rapidly—and survived—in a lab at Johns Hopkins. (Other lab-grown cells died quickly.)

HeLa—what the cells were called (for the first two letters of Lacks's first and last names)—were subsequently used in research labs all over the world. Lacks, a thirty-one-year-old African American, tended her five children and endured scarring radiation treatments in the hospital's "colored" ward, oblivious to the fact that her cells were being cultivated for a research project.

Skloot's creativity in combining existing research with new interviews is a perfect example of a writer's ingenuity in recreating stories and characters when there are only a few living witnesses and sparse documentation. No one knew in 1950 that Henrietta would literally become immortal, so no one was watching. Here's an excerpt from *The Immortal Life of Henrietta Lacks* first published in *O* magazine, which also provided this introduction to its readers:

> When Henrietta Lacks was diagnosed with cancer in 1951, doctors took her cells and grew them in test tubes. Those cells led to breakthroughs in everything from Parkinson's to polio. But today, Henrietta is all but forgotten. In an excerpt from her book, *The Immortal Life of Henrietta Lacks,* Rebecca Skloot tells her story.
>
> In 1951, at the age of 30, Henrietta Lacks, the descendant of freed slaves, was diagnosed with cervical cancer—a strangely aggressive type, unlike any her doctor had ever seen. He took a small tissue sample without her knowledge or consent. A scientist put that sample into a test tube, and, though Henrietta died eight months later, her cells—known worldwide as HeLa—are still alive today. They became the first immortal human cell line ever grown in culture and one of the most important tools in medicine: Research on HeLa was vital to the development of the polio vaccine, as well as drugs for treating herpes, leukemia, influenza, hemophilia, and Parkinson's disease; it helped uncover the secrets of cancer and the effects of the atom bomb, and led to important advances like cloning, in vitro fertilization, and gene mapping. Since 2001 alone, five Nobel Prizes have been awarded for research involving HeLa cells.
>
> There's no way of knowing exactly how many of Henrietta's cells are alive today. One scientist estimates that if you could pile all the HeLa cells ever grown onto a scale, they'd weigh more than 50 million metric tons—the equivalent of at least 100 Empire State Buildings.

Today, nearly 60 years after Henrietta's death, her body lies in an unmarked grave in Clover, Virginia. But her cells are still among the most widely used in labs worldwide—bought and sold by the billions. Though those cells have done wonders for science, Henrietta—whose legacy involves the birth of bioethics and the grim history of experimentation on African-Americans—is all but forgotten.

The following is an excerpt from *The Immortal Life of Henrietta Lacks.*

On January 29, 1951, David Lacks sat behind the wheel of his old Buick, watching the rain fall. He was parked under a towering oak tree outside Johns Hopkins Hospital with three of his children—two still in diapers—waiting for their mother, Henrietta. A few minutes earlier she'd jumped out of the car, pulled her jacket over her head, and scurried into the hospital, past the "colored" bathroom, the only one she was allowed to use. In the next building, under an elegant domed copper roof, a ten-and-a-half-foot marble statue of Jesus stood, arms spread wide, holding court over what was once the main entrance of Hopkins. No one in Henrietta's family ever saw a Hopkins doctor without visiting the Jesus statue, laying flowers at his feet, saying a prayer, and rubbing his big toe for good luck. But that day Henrietta didn't stop.

She went straight to the waiting room of the gynecology clinic, a wide-open space, empty but for rows of long, straight-backed benches that looked like church pews.

"I got a knot on my womb," she told the receptionist. "The doctor need to have a look."

For more than a year Henrietta had been telling her closest girlfriends that something didn't feel right. One night after dinner, she sat on her bed with her cousins Margaret and Sadie and told them, "I got a knot inside me."

"A what?" Sadie asked.

"A knot," she said. "It hurt somethin' awful—when that man want to get with me, Sweet Jesus aren't them but some pains."

When sex first started hurting, she thought it had something to do with baby Deborah, who she'd just given birth to a few weeks earlier, or the bad blood David sometimes brought home after nights with other women—the kind doctors treated with shots of penicillin and heavy metals.

About a week after telling her cousins she thought something was wrong, at the age of 29, Henrietta turned up pregnant with Joe, her fifth child. Sadie and Margaret told Henrietta that the pain probably had something to do with a baby after all. But Henrietta still said no.

"It was there before the baby," she told them. "It's somethin' else."

They all stopped talking about the knot, and no one told Henrietta's husband anything about it. Then, four and a half months after baby Joseph was born, Henrietta went to the bathroom and found blood spotting her underwear when it wasn't her time of the month.

She filled her bathtub, lowered herself into the warm water, and slowly spread her legs. With the door closed to her children, husband, and cousins, Henrietta slid a finger inside herself and rubbed it across her cervix until she found what she somehow knew she'd find: a hard lump, deep inside, as though someone had lodged a marble the size of her pinkie tip just to the left of the opening to her womb.

Henrietta climbed out of the bathtub, dried herself off, and dressed. Then she told her husband, "You better take me to the doctor. I'm bleeding and it ain't my time."

Her local doctor took one look inside her, saw the lump, and figured it was a sore from syphilis. But the lump tested negative for syphilis, so he told Henrietta she'd better go to the Johns Hopkins gynecology clinic.

The public wards at Hopkins were filled with patients, most of them black and unable to pay their medical bills. David drove Henrietta nearly 20 miles to get there, not because they preferred it, but because it was the only major hospital for miles that treated black patients. This was the era of Jim Crow—when black people showed up at white-only hospitals, the staff was likely to send them away, even if it meant they might die in the parking lot.

When the nurse called Henrietta from the waiting room, she led her through a single door to a colored-only exam room—one in a long row of rooms divided by clear glass walls that let nurses see from one to the next. Henrietta undressed, wrapped herself in a starched white hospital gown, and lay down on a wooden exam table, waiting for Howard Jones, the gynecologist on duty. When Jones walked into the room, Henrietta told him about the lump. Before examining her, he flipped through her chart:

Breathing difficult since childhood due to recurrent throat infections and deviated septum in patient's nose. Physician recommended surgical repair. Patient declined. Patient had one toothache for nearly five years. Only anxiety is oldest daughter who is epileptic and can't talk. Happy household. Well nourished, cooperative. Unexplained vaginal bleeding and blood in urine during last two pregnancies; physician recommended sickle cell test. Patient declined. Been with husband since age 14 and has no liking for sexual intercourse. Patient has asymptomatic neurosyphilis but canceled syphilis treatments, said she felt fine. Two months prior to current visit, after delivery of fifth child, patient had significant blood in urine. Tests showed areas of increased cellular activity in the cervix. Physician recommended diagnostics and referred to specialist for ruling out infection or cancer. Patient canceled appointment.

It was no surprise that she hadn't come back all those times for follow-up. For Henrietta, walking into Hopkins was like entering a foreign country where she didn't speak the language. She knew about harvesting tobacco and butchering a pig, but she'd never heard the words cervix or biopsy. She didn't read or write much, and she hadn't studied science in school. She, like most black patients, only went to Hopkins when she thought she had no choice.

Henrietta lay back on the table, feet pressed hard in stirrups as she stared at the ceiling. And sure enough, Jones found a lump exactly where she'd said he would. If her cervix was a clock's face, the lump was at 4 o'clock. He'd seen easily a thousand cervical cancer lesions, but never anything like this: shiny and purple (like "grape Jello," he wrote later), and so delicate it bled at the slightest touch. Jones cut a small sample and sent it to the pathology lab down the hall for a diagnosis. Then he told Henrietta to go home.

Soon after, Howard Jones dictated notes about Henrietta and her diagnosis: "Her history is interesting in that she had a term delivery here at this hospital, September 19, 1950," he said. "No note is made in the history at that time or at the six weeks' return visit that there is any abnormality of the cervix."

Yet here she was, three months later, with a full-fledged tumor. Either her doctors had missed it during her last exams—which seemed impossible—or it had grown at a terrifying rate.

Henrietta Lacks was born Loretta Pleasant in Roanoke, Virginia, on August 1, 1920. No one knows how she became Henrietta. A midwife named Fannie delivered her in a small shack on a dead-end road overlooking a train depot, where hundreds of freight cars came and went each day. Henrietta shared that house with her parents and eight older siblings until 1924, when her mother, Eliza Lacks Pleasant, died giving birth to her tenth child.

Henrietta's father, Johnny Pleasant, was a squat man who hobbled around on a cane he often hit people with. Johnny didn't have the patience for raising children, so when Eliza died, he took them all back to Clover, Virginia, where his family still farmed the tobacco fields their ancestors had worked as slaves. No one in Clover could take all ten children, so relatives divided them up—one with this cousin, one with that aunt. Henrietta ended up with her grandfather, Tommy Lacks.

Tommy lived in what everyone called the home-house, a four-room wooden cabin that once served as slave quarters, with plank floors, gas lanterns, and water Henrietta hauled up a long hill from the creek. The home-house stood on a hillside where wind whipped through cracks in the walls. The air inside stayed so cool that when relatives died, the family kept their corpses in the front hallway for days so people could visit and pay respects. Then they buried them in the cemetery out back.

Henrietta's grandfather was already raising another grandchild that one of his daughters left behind after delivering him on the home-house floor. That child's name was David Lacks, but everyone called him Day, because in the Lacks country drawl, house sounds like hyse, and David sounds like Day. No one could have guessed Henrietta would spend the rest of her life with Day—first as a cousin growing up in their grandfather's home, then as his wife.

Like most young Lackses, Day didn't finish school: He stopped in the fourth grade because the family needed him to work the to-bacco fields. But Henrietta stayed until the sixth grade. During the school year, after taking care of the garden and livestock each morn-ing, she'd walk two miles—past the white school where children threw rocks and taunted her—to the colored school, a three-room wooden farmhouse hidden under tall shade trees.

At nightfall the Lacks cousins built fires with pieces of old shoes to keep the mosquitoes away, and watched the stars from beneath the big oak tree where they'd hung a rope to swing from. They played tag, ring-around-the-rosy, and hopscotch, and danced around the field singing until Grandpa Tommy yelled for everyone to go to bed.

Henrietta and Day had been sharing a bedroom since she was 4 and he was 9, so what happened next didn't surprise anyone: They started having children together. Their son Lawrence was born just months after Henrietta's 14th birthday; his sister, Lucile Elsie Pleas-ant, came along four years later. They were both born on the floor of the home-house like their father, grandmother, and grandfather before them. People wouldn't use words like epilepsy, mental retar-dation, or neurosyphilis to describe Elsie's condition until years later. To the folks in Clover, she was just simple. Touched.

Henrietta and Day married alone at their preacher's house on April 10, 1941. She was 20; he was 25. They didn't go on a honeymoon because there was too much work to do, and no money for travel. Henrietta and Day were lucky if they sold enough tobacco each season to feed the family and plant the next crop. So after their wedding, Day went back to gripping the splintered ends of his old wooden plow as Henrietta followed close behind, pushing a homemade wheelbarrow and dropping tobacco seedlings into holes in the freshly turned red dirt.

A few months later, Day moved north to Turner Station, a small black community outside Baltimore where he'd gotten a job working in a shipyard. Henrietta stayed behind to care for the children and the tobacco until Day made enough money for a house and three tickets north. Soon, with a child on each side, Henrietta boarded a coal-fueled train from the small wooden depot at the end of Clover's Main Street. She left the tobacco fields of her youth and the hundred-year-old oak tree that shaded her from the sun on so many hot afternoons. At the age of 21, she stared through the train window at rolling hills and wide-open bodies of water for the first time, heading toward a new life.

After her visit to Hopkins, Henrietta went back to her usual routine, cleaning and cooking for her husband, their children, and the many cousins she fed each day. Less than a week later, Jones got her biopsy results from the pathology lab: "epidermoid carcinoma of the cervix, Stage I." Translation: cervical cancer.

Cervical carcinomas are divided into two types: invasive carcinomas, which have penetrated the surface of the cervix, and noninvasive carcinomas, which haven't. The noninvasive type is sometimes called "sugar-icing carcinoma," because it grows in a smooth layered sheet across the surface of the cervix, but its official name is carcinoma in situ, which derives from the Latin for "cancer in its original place."

In 1951 most doctors in the field believed that invasive carcinoma was deadly, and carcinoma in situ wasn't. So they hardly treated it. But Richard Wesley TeLinde, head of gynecology at Hopkins and one of the top cervical cancer experts in the country, disagreed—he believed carcinoma in situ was simply an early stage of invasive carcinoma that, left untreated, eventually became deadly. So he treated it aggressively, often removing the cervix, uterus, and most of the vagina. He argued that this would drastically reduce cervical cancer deaths, but his critics called it extreme and unnecessary.

TeLinde thought that if he could find a way to grow living samples from normal cervical tissue and both types of cancerous tissue—something never done before—he could compare all three. If he could prove that carcinoma in situ and invasive carcinoma looked and behaved similarly in the laboratory, he could end the debate, showing that he'd been right all along, and doctors who ignored him were killing their patients. So he called George Gey (pronounced "guy"), head of tissue culture research at Hopkins.

Gey and his wife, Margaret, had spent the last three decades working to grow malignant cells outside the body, hoping to use them to find cancer's cause and cure. But most of the cells died quickly, and the few that survived hardly grew at all. The Geys were determined to grow the first immortal human cells: a continuously dividing line of cells all descended from one original sample, cells that would constantly replenish themselves and never die. They didn't care what kind of tissue they used, as long as it came from a person.

So when TeLinde offered Gey a supply of cervical cancer tissue in exchange for trying to grow some cells, Gey didn't hesitate. And TeLinde began collecting samples from any woman who happened to walk into Hopkins with cervical cancer. Including Henrietta.

Jones called Henrietta on February 5, 1951, after getting her biopsy report back from the lab, and told her the tumor was malignant. Henrietta didn't tell anyone what Jones said, and no one asked. She simply went on with her day as if nothing had happened, which was just like her—no sense upsetting anyone over something she could just deal with herself.

The next morning Henrietta climbed from the Buick outside Hopkins again, telling Day and the children not to worry.

"Ain't nothin' serious wrong," she said. "Doctor's gonna fix me right up."

Henrietta went straight to the admissions desk and told the receptionist she was there for her treatment. Then she signed a form with the words operation permit at the top of the page. It said:

I hereby give consent to the staff of The Johns Hopkins Hospital to perform any operative procedures and under any anaesthetic either local or general that they may deem necessary in the proper surgical care and treatment of:

_____.

Henrietta printed her name in the blank space. A witness with illegible handwriting signed a line at the bottom of the form, and Henrietta signed another.

Then she followed a nurse down a long hallway into the ward for colored women, where Howard Jones and several other white physicians ran more tests than she'd had in her entire life. They checked her urine, her blood, her lungs. They stuck tubes in her bladder and nose.

Henrietta's tumor was the invasive type, and like hospitals nationwide, Hopkins treated all invasive cervical carcinomas with radium, a white radioactive metal that glows an eerie blue. So the morning of Henrietta's first treatment, a taxi driver picked up a doctor's bag filled with thin glass tubes of radium from a clinic across town. The tubes were tucked into individual slots inside small canvas pouches hand-sewn by a local Baltimore woman. One nurse placed the pouches on a stainless steel tray. Another wheeled Henrietta into the small colored-only operating room, with stainless steel tables, huge glaring lights, and an all-white medical staff dressed in white gowns, hats, masks, and gloves.

With Henrietta unconscious on the operating table in the center of the room, her feet in stirrups, the surgeon on duty, Lawrence Wharton Jr., sat on a stool between her legs. He peered inside Henrietta, dilated her cervix, and prepared to treat her tumor. But first—though no one had told Henrietta that TeLinde was collecting samples or asked if she wanted to be a donor—Wharton picked up a sharp knife and shaved two dime-size pieces of tissue from Henrietta's cervix: one from her tumor, and one from the healthy cervical tissue nearby. Then he placed the samples in a glass dish.

Wharton slipped a tube filled with radium inside Henrietta's cervix, and sewed it in place. He then sewed a pouch filled with radium to the outer surface of her cervix and packed another against it. He slid several rolls of gauze inside her vagina to help keep the radium in place, then threaded a catheter into her bladder so she could urinate without disturbing the treatment.

When Wharton finished, a nurse wheeled Henrietta back into the ward, and a resident took the dish with the samples to Gey's lab, as he'd done many times before. Gey still got excited at moments like this, but everyone else in his lab saw Henrietta's sample as something tedious—the latest of what felt like countless samples that scientists and lab technicians had been trying and failing to grow for years.

Gey's 21-year-old assistant, Mary Kubicek, sat eating a tuna salad sandwich at a long stone culture bench that doubled as a break table. She and Margaret and the other women in the Gey lab spent many hours there, all in nearly identical cat's-eye glasses with fat dark frames and thick lenses, their hair pulled back in tight buns.

"I'm putting a new sample in your cubicle," Gey told Mary.

She pretended not to notice. "Not again," she thought, and kept eating her sandwich. Mary knew she shouldn't wait—every moment those cells sat in the dish made it more likely they'd die. But they always died anyway. "Why bother?" she thought.

At that point, there were many obstacles to growing cells successfully. For starters, no one knew exactly what nutrients they needed to survive or how best to supply them. But the biggest problem facing cell culture was contamination. Bacteria and a host of other microorganisms could find their way into cultures—from people's unwashed hands, their breath, and dust particles floating through the air—and destroy them. Margaret Gey had been trained as a surgical nurse, which meant sterility was her specialty—it was key to preventing deadly infections in patients in the operating room.

Margaret patrolled the lab, arms crossed, leaning over technicians' shoulders as they worked, inspecting glassware for spots or smudges. Mary followed Margaret's sterilizing rules meticulously to avoid her wrath. Only then did she pick up the pieces of Henrietta's cervix—forceps in one hand, scalpel in the other—and carefully slice them into one-millimeter squares. She sucked each square into a pipette, and dropped them one at a time onto chicken-blood clots she'd placed at the bottom of dozens of test tubes. She covered each clot with several drops of culture medium, plugged the tubes with rubber stoppers, and wrote "HeLa," for Henrietta and Lacks, in big black letters on the side of each tube. Then she put them in an incubator.

For the next few days, Mary started each morning with her usual sterilization drill. She'd peer into all the incubating tubes, laughing to herself and thinking, "Nothing's happening." "Big surprise." Then she saw what looked like little rings of fried egg white around the clots at the bottom of each tube. The cells were growing, but Mary didn't think much of it—other cells had survived for a while in the lab.

But Henrietta's cells weren't merely surviving—they were growing with mythological intensity. By the next morning, they'd doubled. Mary divided the contents of each tube in two, giving them room to grow, and soon she was dividing them into four tubes, then six. Henrietta's cells grew to fill as much space as Mary gave them.

Still, Gey wasn't ready to celebrate. "The cells could die any minute," he told Mary. But they didn't. The cells kept growing like nothing anyone had seen, doubling their numbers every 24 hours, accumulating by the millions. "Spreading like crabgrass!" Margaret said. As long as they had food and warmth, Henrietta's cancer cells seemed unstoppable.

Soon, George told a few of his closest colleagues that he thought his lab might have grown the first immortal human cells.

To which they replied, Can I have some? And George said yes.

George Gey sent Henrietta's cells to any scientist who wanted them for cancer research. HeLa cells rode into the mountains of Chile in the saddlebags of pack mules and flew around the country in the breast pockets of researchers until they were growing in laboratories in Texas, Amsterdam, India, and many places in between. The Tuskegee Institute set up facilities to mass-produce Henrietta's cells, and began shipping 20,000 tubes of HeLa—about six trillion cells—every week. And soon, a multibillion-dollar industry selling human biological materials was born.

HeLa cells allowed researchers to perform experiments that would have been impossible with a living human. Scientists exposed them to toxins, radiation, and infections. They bombarded them with drugs, hoping to find one that would kill malignant cells without destroying normal ones. They studied immune suppression and cancer growth by injecting HeLa into rats with weak immune systems, who developed malignant tumors much like Henrietta's. And if the cells died in the process, it didn't matter—scientists could just go back to their eternally growing HeLa stock and start over again.

But those cells grew as powerfully in Henrietta's body as they did in the lab: Within months of her diagnosis, tumors had taken over almost every organ in her body. Henrietta died on October 4, 1951, leaving five children behind, knowing nothing about her cells growing in laboratories around the world.

Henrietta's husband and children wouldn't find out about those cells until 25 years later, when researchers from Johns Hopkins decided to track down Henrietta's family to do research on them to learn more about HeLa.

When Henrietta's children learned of HeLa, they were consumed with questions: Had scientists killed their mother to harvest her cells? Were clones of their mother walking the streets of cities around the world? And if Henrietta was so vital to medicine, why couldn't they afford health insurance? Today, in Baltimore, her family still wrestles with feelings of betrayal and fear, but also pride. As her daughter Deborah once whispered to a vial of her mother's cells: "You're famous, just nobody knows it."

How Did It Happen?

Rebecca Skloot pulled together the story Henrietta shared with Margaret and Sadie, based on interviews with surviving family members who knew Henrietta and David Lacks. But it's the details in the first paragraph, the first scene, that make the story come to life. Using Henrietta's medical records, Skloot established the date of Henrietta Lacks's visit to Johns Hopkins after the birth of her fifth child and verified the story that Sadie and Margaret told her about Henrietta finding the tumor herself in the bathtub. She laid the groundwork for essential scenic details through interviews with Henrietta's husband (who remembered that it was raining, that he parked under an old tree) and Henrietta's doctors and nurses (who remembered the waiting room and the admissions process Henrietta went through). Skloot then verified and fleshed out those stories through document research. She verified that it was raining that day through the weather bureau. Using archival photos, she was able to verify and enhance the descriptions sources gave her of rooms. She found a photo which confirmed that there was a tree outside where David said he parked. She shared that photo with a botanist to be sure it was an oak tree.

Skloot was an obsessed researcher. Like Truman Capote, she tracked down and interviewed anyone who might have anything to say about the Lacks family then and now. She raided the bowels of the hospital for old medical records and pieced together conversations between the Lackses and the Hopkins medical staff, as accurately and vividly as possible. She also recreated the tenor of the Jim Crow era in which Henrietta lived.

Skloot made her scenes real by being persistent, not trying to rush to publish, by carefully constructing and sculpting every scene from start to finish. *The Immortal Life of Henrietta Lacks* has been on the best-seller list in this country and many others for more than two years, as of this writing. Far from achieving instant fame, Skloot spent thirteen years, start to finish, writing the book.

THE SHOCKING TRUTH ABOUT THE *NEW YORK TIMES*

I have been discussing the opening scene of "Shared Prayers, Mixed Blessings" from the *New York Times* in my workshops and classes ever since it was published on the front page of the *New York Times* in 2000. It is a great example of how a nonfiction writer can use all the literary techniques available to the fiction writer. The scene allows Sack to combine dialogue and brief and evocative description to involve the reader in a story that has plot, suspense, and strong characters. The scene also introduces the main character, the person whom Sack was profiling—and at the same time capture the essence or focus of the story.

Recently I contacted Sack, told him how much I admired the story, especially that scene, and arranged to interview him about how it came together. For years I had been assuring my students that Sack had immersed himself in that church for long periods of time, that he knew the people in the story very well, and that he was present the day Howard Pugh and Roy Denson had their confrontation, ready to write down exactly what happened, just as Gay Talese was watching while Sinatra went *mano a mano* with Harlan Ellison.

"That's why you do immersions," I tell my students. "You hang out and wait for something to happen—and sooner or later something will happen—and you'll be there ready to write it all down."

My conversation with Kevin Sack didn't change my mind about immersion and the essential importance of being present and spending time with your subjects. But Sack surprised me by revealing a detail even his editor didn't know—until I told him.

But first: I was right about Sack's dedication to immersion: writing the story took about a year between conception and publication, Sack told me. He was working on other stories too, but this was his main focus. "I lived there—for services every Wednesday night and every Sunday, Sunday morning, Sunday night, Sunday school before church—and then I filled the rest of the week with lots of interviews, at the church and at people's homes; I went to choir rehearsals, I went to social events, I went to dinners at people's homes after church on Sunday, and retreats, barbeques."

So when did Sack see the Roy Denson/Howard Pugh church episode take place?

He didn't.

Sack met Howard Pugh at the church early on in his research. "He was an usher, and he was a lot more interested in ushering than sitting in a service, so we'd sit out in the lobby and talk and he ended up walking me around the church, showing me around, and I think he may have told me the Roy Denson story right then and there, which was encouraging. If I was getting that kind of stuff on the first day I was hopeful about what I'd get on the sixth month."

"So it wasn't anything you personally witnessed?" I asked. Frankly, I was surprised. I've recreated scenes hundreds of times for my own books and essays, and I'm certain many writers have similarly recreated stories for their own books and for magazines like *Esquire* or *The New Yorker*. But the *New York Times*? Somehow that was hard to believe.

"I did not witness it," Sack said. "I reconstructed it." Sack reinterviewed the people in the story, who confirmed the inner point of view—the information and feelings the reader received, as if Denson and the others perceived the situation. Denson "has not disagreed with my characterization," said Sack.

Sack was surprised that I was surprised.

"I just didn't think that the *New York Times* would recreate," I said. I should note that Sack used the term "reconstruct."

"I'm curious about how your editors felt about that," I asked.

"We do this all the time," Sack interrupted. "We're certainly never limited to writing about things we see with our own eyes. Seventy-five percent of reporting is reconstructing things we don't see."

"It wasn't a problem with the editors at all?"

"No."

I understand that much of journalism and all nonfiction writing is re-construction/recreation, but the scene was written so vividly I always assumed that Sack was there.

Sack said that many editors worked on the Race in America series that this article was a part of, but the line editor, Paul Fishleder, was the one he worked with more than anyone else. (There were five articles in the series.)

I was able to reach Fishleder and we had a good, open conversation. Fishleder allowed that the *Times* didn't do a lot of long-form narrative and so maybe didn't do it as well as magazines that had more experience with the genre. One thing I noticed about the *Times'* long-form narrative both in the newspaper and the magazine, in the race series and generally, is that the *Times* has a tendency to start strong with scene and story, as in the Sack piece, but soon loses the narrative, as in "Shared Prayers, Mixed Blessings." That first scene with Pugh and Denson may be the only full scene in the piece. There are a few partial scenes after that—but no full-blown scenes.

I asked Fishleder if he remembered the story, and he said that he'd read it right before I called him to prepare for our talk. I asked him how he felt about the fact that the first scene with Roy Denson and Howard Pugh was recreated.

At first he was speechless. He was taken by surprise, and he didn't answer the question for at least five minutes. He literally sputtered.

After a while he said he didn't remember all the details of the story as it came together. It was a long time ago. Which is true.

The fact that Sack recreated the story—or "reconstructed" it—doesn't take away from its power and effectiveness. It vividly demonstrates the difference between showing and telling.

The Narrative Line and the Hook

The stronger the scene and the faster you involve the reader in the scene, the more successful you'll be. So when writing a scene, think about thrusting your reader into the heat of the action as quickly as possible. Action comes before place and characters.

Lauren Slater does this in most scenes in "Three Spheres," as does Rebecca Skloot in "Henrietta Lacks." Little information is provided to the reader at the beginning of each scene—only what's necessary to the scene. The background is embedded later.

The background is, as they say in the movie business, the back story—not the front story.

> **Question:** But don't I have to tell my readers who I'm talking about, where we are, how we got there before I start the scene?
>
> **Answer:** Absolutely. No question. As I've said, the story is the reason personality and place exist. The story introduces all the relevant details and provides the background. So tell your story. You don't need to point out everything right away; tell the reader just enough to understand the scene.

Here's an example of a scene that hooks the reader with story and includes place and personality almost simultaneously, with just enough detail, from Jeannette Walls's 2005 best-selling memoir *The Glass Castle*:

I was sitting in a taxi, wondering if I had overdressed for the evening, when I looked out the window and saw Mom rooting through a dumpster. It was just after dark. A blustery March wind whipped the steam coming out of the manholes, and people hurried along the sidewalks with their collars turned up. I was stuck in traffic two blocks from the party where I was heading.

Mom stood fifteen feet away. She had tied rags around her shoulders to keep out the spring chill and was picking through the trash while her dog, a black-and-white terrier mix, played at her feet. Mom's gestures were all familiar—the way she tilted her head and thrust out her lower lip when studying items of potential value that she'd hoisted out of the Dumpster, the way her eyes widened with childish glee when she found something she liked. Her long hair was streaked with gray, tangled and matted, and her eyes had sunk deep into their sockets, but still she reminded me of the mom she'd been when I was a kid, swan-diving off cliffs and painting in the desert and reading Shakespeare aloud. Her cheekbones were still high and strong, but the skin was parched and ruddy from all those winters and summers exposed to the elements. To the people walking by, she probably looked like any of the thousands of homeless people in New York City.

It had been months since I laid eyes on Mom, and when she looked up, I was overcome with panic that she'd see me and call out my name, and that someone on the way to the same party would spot us together and Mom would introduce herself and my secret would be out.

This is powerful and intriguing. It leads with story, yet tells you enough about the characters to allow you to get into the narrative and makes you want to know more of the background. And she's provided some background in these three paragraphs. We know how Mom and the narrator were years ago, when "I was a kid." We have a quick but graphic description of Mom then, precipitated by the description of her now. There's just enough—all we need at the moment and no more.

Here's another example of a story line scene, this one from Chester A. Phillips's "Charging Lions," a segment of his MFA thesis that combines memoir, ethics, and scientific knowledge. This essay won the 2011 *Creative Nonfiction* Editors Prize for Best Creative Nonfiction Essay about Animals:

> "Wake up," Debbie shouted. "I think the lion's got Duchess' calf."
>
> I bolted away, sitting up in bed, disoriented. On warm nights we slept with the windows open and I heard the shrill bellowing that was Duchess' most distinctive characteristic, just as it was her mother's. When you spend every day for years getting to know any creatures, human or otherwise, you come to know such things; the differences of vocal inflection; calm or skittish or aggressive temperaments; degrees of adventurousness verses maternal instinct; intelligence and guile; the willingness to walk a long way . . . From the corral, the calls sounded again and again—loud, arranged by worry, a desperate mother's cries of distress.

The two examples from Walls and Phillips are memoir. Look at the first scene in Rebecca Skloot's immersion piece "Fixing Nemo," reprinted in its entirety (and highlighted) below. Note also that in this piece the scenes and the information are in longer blocks then some of the other examples. Do they still work?

"Fixing Nemo"

Dr. Helen Roberts was about to make the first incision in what should have been a standard surgery—a quick in-and-out procedure—when she froze. "Bonnie," she said, turning to her anesthesiologist, "is she breathing? I don't see her breathing." Roberts's eyes darted around the room. "Grab the Doppler," she told her other assistant. "I want to hear her heart. Bonnie, how's she doing?" Bonnie pushed up her purple glasses, leaned over the surgery table and lowered her face inches from the patient to watch for any signs of breath: nothing. "She's too deep," Roberts said, "go ahead and give her 30 c.c.'s of fresh water." Bonnie picked up an old plastic jug filled with pond water and poured two glugs into the anesthesia machine. Seconds later, a whisper of a heart rate came through the Doppler. Bonnie wasn't happy: "We have gill movement—but not much." Then the Doppler went silent and she reached for the jug. "Wait," Roberts said. "We have fin movement . . . damn, she's waking up—30 c.c.'s of anesthetic." Roberts sighed. "She was holding her breath," she said, shaking her head. "Fish are a lot smarter than people give them credit for."

Yes, Roberts and Bonita (Bonnie) Wulf were doing surgery on a goldfish. Not the fancy kind that people buy for thousands of dollars and keep in decorative ponds (though they do surgery on those too), but on a county-fair goldfish named the Golden One, which Roberts adopted when its previous owners brought it into her clinic outside Buffalo, saying they didn't have time to take care of it. Which is to say, it's a regular fish that could belong to anybody. Just like Lucky, the one-and-a-half-pound koi with a two-and-a-half-pound tumor; Sunshine, who was impaled on a branch during rough sex; Betta, with a fluid-filled abdomen; and countless goldfish with so-called buoyancy disorders, like the perpetually upside-down Belly Bob, or Raven, who was stuck floating nose down and tail to the sky. All those fish went under the knife.

Ten years ago, the chances of finding a fish vet were slim. But true to its history, veterinary medicine is steadily evolving to meet the demands of pet owners. Through the early 1900's, vets treated livestock mostly. You didn't treat cats and dogs—you usually shot those. But by the mid-50's, the world was in love with Rin Tin Tin and Lassie, and people started thinking, I shouldn't have to shoot my dog. By the 70's, dogs and cats could get human-quality medical care—but treating birds? That was insane. Instead, bird advice came from pet stores (and birds died of a "draft," a diagnosis akin to the vapors). Yet by the 80's, avian medicine had its own academic programs, a professional society, at least one monthly magazine and a large clientele. Today we have surgery for parakeets, organ transplantation for dogs and cats, chemotherapy for gerbils. But people who want to take fish to the vet—those people are still crazy. At least for the time being.

"I have no doubt fish medicine will become mainstream much like bird medicine did in the 80's," said Dr. David Scarfe, assistant director of scientific activities at the American Veterinary Medical Association. "It's actually happening far more rapidly than I'd imagined." According to the A.V.M.A., almost 2,000 vets currently practice fish medicine. That number is steadily growing, and the market seems solid: 13.9 million households have fish and spend several billions of dollars annually on fish supplies alone—tanks, water conditioners, food—not including veterinary care or the fish themselves, which can cost as much as $100,000, sometimes more.

Fish diagnostics range from a basic exam ($40), blood work ($60) and X-rays ($55) to the advanced: ultrasound ($175), CAT scans ($250). Veterinarians tube-feed fish. They give fish enemas, fix broken bones with plates and screws, remove impacted eggs, treat scoliosis and even do fish plastic surgery—anything from glass-eye implantation to "surgical pattern improvement," with scale transplantation, scale tattooing or unsightly-scale removal.

But some of the most common and vexing fish ailments are buoyancy disorders. They involve the swim bladder, an organ in the digestive tract prone to infections, obstructions and defects that destroy a fish's ability to regulate air, leaving it "improperly buoyant," to the point of floating or sinking in odd positions—usually upside down. Surgically inserting a tiny stone in the fish's abdomen to weigh it down is the best option, but since that costs anywhere from $150 to $1,500, depending on where and how it's done, many vets first recommend green-pea treatment: "Feeding affected goldfish a single green pea (canned or cooked and lightly crushed) once daily might cure the problem," Dr. Greg Lewbart wrote in a paper titled "Green Peas for Buoyancy Disorders." Lewbart is a top fish veterinarian, but even he isn't sure how pea treatment works.

When I tell people I'm writing about fish medicine, their reaction is almost always the same: why not flush the sick fish and get a new one? Actually, for several reasons. First, there are the money fish. "I've worked on several fish worth $30,000 to $50,000," Lewbart once told me. These are the fancy koi that work fish shows for big prizes, then retire to a life of reproduction. "I examined one in Japan an owner turned down $200,000 for," Lewbart says. That's what he calls a big fish. "People will spend thousands to fix them." But not all koi are show koi; many are what Lewbart calls U.P.F.'s: ugly pond fish.

Which brings us to the human-fish bond, and people who gasp if you mention flushing because they swear their fish have personalities so big they win hearts. I heard stories of Zeus, who weighed two pounds but dominated the house cat by biting onto the cat's paw and yanking it headfirst into the tank when it swatted the water. There was Sushi, the "gregariously affectionate" koi with recurring bacterial infections. And Zoomer, the "koi with a vendetta," who shot out of the water at her owner, David Smothers, and broke his nose—something his pet Ladyfish never would have done. She'd just cuddle with him in the pond and wiggle when he kissed her. David spent thousands trying to save Ladyfish when lightning struck near his pond, creating a shock wave that broke her back. He got X-rays, CAT scans, chiropractic adjustments and spinal surgery, then spent weeks in the pond, gently holding Ladyfish's tail during physical therapy. Nothing worked, and he still tears up when he talks about it.

The human-fish-bond people don't understand the money-fish people. "They don't even name their fish," Bonita Wulf says, sounding shocked. The organizers of the Singapore International Fish Show just announced a fish-adoption initiative, declaring that "fish have their lives, and they have feelings, too," so if fish don't win shows, it's "more humane to bring the fish up for adoption," rather than flushing them down the toilet. Others train fish to fetch and dunk basketballs. "Some of fish personality might be a feeding response," says Dr. Julius Tepper of the Long Island Fish Hospital, "but so is a lot of what we interpret as affection from cats." Sushi's owner doesn't buy that. "You have to meet Sushi to understand," she told me. So I went with Dr. Roberts to Marsha Chapman's house thinking, O.K., Sushi, show me this personality of yours.

"Sushi's in here," Marsha said, leading me to the 6-foot-long, 150-gallon tank in her family room. Marsha is a warm and motherly special-education teacher in her 50's who looks you in the eye and sounds as if she's talking to a room of second graders. "Hi, baby," she cooed. "How's Mama's girl?" Sushi darted to the surface of the tank and started splashing frantically. "That's right, show us how you wag your tail." And Sushi did (though a wagging fish tail looks just like a swimming fish tail to me). "She's just like a dog that way," Marsha said. "If I could hug her, I would."

Aside from Sushi's size (two feet long), her looks are unimpressive. Mostly white, a few orange spots, short nonflowing fins, trademark carp whiskers. Lewbart would call her a U.P.F., though not around Marsha, who reached in the tank and patted Sushi's head. "Look who's here, Sweetie," she said, "Say hi to Rebecca."

Sushi ignored me. But she did the "basketball dance" for Marsha, swimming in place, face against the glass, jerking back and forth and up and down. And Marsha did it right back. She put her red-lipstick-covered lips an inch from the tank opposite Sushi's. She clenched her fists, bent her elbows and knees, stuck out her butt and wiggled her body violently while making loud kissing noises. The more Marsha danced, the more Sushi danced. Then Roberts walked in the room saying, "Isn't he cute?" and Sushi hid. "Dr. Roberts thinks she might be a boy, but Sushi is a girl's name." Marsha tapped the tank. "Don't be afraid, Dr. Roberts makes you better."

Roberts is a petite "warm fuzzy fish vet" whose no-nonsense appearance—no makeup, a thick black plastic sports watch—almost clashes with the turquoise contacts that make her eyes beautifully inhuman. She surrounds herself with pewter fish and glass fish; papier-mâché, metal, wood and stone fish; and of course, her pet fish: Splotch, Carrot, Harrison, Ford and about 32 others, including B.O. (Big Orange), her favorite. He's "the dog of the pond" in the many fish pictures in her living room and office, or on her computer desktop. "Come on, Sush," Roberts said. "I'm your friend."

I stared into Sushi's tank for hours. Marsha put the "Twin Peaks" theme song on repeat, and I thought, Fun fish. She was active and sparkly, she swam back and forth, her muscles moving with the music in slow melodic waves. It was mesmerizing. But to me she was more like a Lava lamp than a pet. Then again, to her I was more like a piece of furniture than a human. I didn't feel Sushi's personality—I felt Dr. Roberts's and Marsha's. When Sushi swam by, their eyes widened, they smiled, touched the glass, said hello. When she turned, they said things like "Isn't she amazing?" and "She's so funny."

They know people might say they're crazy. "I don't care what people think," Marsha said. "I use my relationship with Sushi as a springboard for teaching special-education students about affection for unconventional people, like themselves." She stared into the tank, her voice suddenly serious. "It enlarges the world when you see how much possibility there is for loving people and animals who aren't usually given a chance."

The golden one finally stopped holding her breath, which meant Dr. Roberts could actually spay her. Well, at least that was the plan. "I'm pretty sure she's a female," Roberts said, "but it's always hard to tell with fish. If she turns out to be a boy, it's no big deal. We'll just neuter her." Roberts was born in England, raised in Italy and Georgia; her accent is soft, slightly rural and completely unidentifiable. "Goldfish are the rabbits of the fish world," she said when I asked why she was spaying her fish. "I don't want to face the ethical decision of what to do with all those babies."

Aside from the human-quality surgical instruments and monitors, the setup was 100 percent garden-supply store: one Rubbermaid tub full of pond water and anesthetic, clear plastic tubing attached to a submersible pump with duct tape. The Golden One lay on a plastic grate above the tub, yellow foam pad keeping her upright, tube in her mouth pumping anesthetic water from the tub, through her gills, then back again. Like a recirculating fountain.

It's the same setup used in the first account of pet fish surgery I could find, which was performed in 1993 and written about two years later by Dr. Greg Lewbart at the College of Veterinary Medicine at North Carolina State University. Lewbart, a professor of aquatic medicine, has short brown hair, graying sideburns and a soft blanket of freckles—like someone misted him with tan paint. "I don't tell my clients," he told me, hesitantly, "but I got into fish as a fisherman." He couldn't help laughing when he said this. "It's undeniably weird: I sometimes spend my weekends at the coast fishing." Then he paused. "I do mostly catch and release, but not always, and either way, it's unpleasant for the animal: I take the hook out, traumatize the fish, then throw it back in the water with a huge wound on its face or toss it into a cooler where it flops around for a few minutes. Then I go into work Monday, somebody brings in a goldfish, I console them, take their fish to surgery, then put it on postoperative pain medication."

Lewbart loves fish medicine—he flies around the world teaching and practicing it; he publishes scholarly articles and books on it. But he's not all fish. "My real love is marine invertebrates," he told me, like snails, worms, horseshoe crabs. "It's still a little down the road when people are going to start bringing those guys to the vet. But I think it'll happen in the same way fish medicine happened."

Fish medicine actually dates to the 1800's, but it didn't start to catch on until the 1970's and 80's, when scientists started publishing research articles on everything from fish hormones and nutrition to pondside operating tables. But that had nothing to do with pets. Until Lewbart published his surgery paper, references to fish medicine came from fisheries, marine biology and wildlife.

In the late 70's, a few obscure papers mentioned the burgeoning field of pet fish; some even said vets should make the transition from aquaculture to pets. But that didn't happen for more than a decade, until koi exploded into a multimillion-dollar industry, the Internet appeared and owners started typing "fish veterinarian" into search engines. When they found research papers by vets like Lewbart, owners started calling and e-mailing. "I never thought of being a fish vet," said Dr. Tepper of the Long Island Fish Hospital. "Then I got a call from a guy wondering if I treated fish or knew someone who did. I said, 'No, actually, I don't.' Then I was like, Why didn't I think of this earlier?"

Pet-fish medicine isn't exactly mainstream: many owners don't know fish vets exist; others look but can't find them. The A.V.M.A. and several vets are working on databases for referring clients, but they're not available yet. Until then, Lewbart will keep fielding 400 to 500 calls and e-mail messages a year from people with fish questions, and many owners will take matters into their own hands. Just like Bonita Wulf, who isn't an actual fish anesthesiologist; she's a fish hobbyist with a gravelly smoker's voice and a very large gun collection. (As Dr. Roberts says, you don't joke about flushing fish with a woman like Bonnie.) Wulf talks to her fish and carries pictures of them in her purse. "I've got grandkids too," she says with a grin, "but I only carry fish pictures." She has taken more courses in fish health and medicine than most veterinarians, and she started by Googling the word "koi." Inevitably, that leads to KoiVet.com, an all-you-need-to-know-about-fish site, and Aquamaniacs.net. Between the two, thousands of fish hobbyists join message boards for moral support and immediate do-it-yourself help during fish crises. They're starting to refer one another to fish vets, though traditionally fish medicine is one of the few areas where pet owners, as a rule, know more than veterinarians. But things have changed: veterinary schools are starting to teach fish medicine.

I recently went to North Carolina to visit a seminar at one of the only aquatic-medicine departments in the world, which Lewbart oversees. He and his colleagues also run a one-week intensive fish-medicine course, as well as the world's only aquatic-medicine residency. Their courses are always full. On the first day of the seminar, eight vet students from around the country learned to catch, anesthetize and transport fish. They drew blood, took fin and scale samples, looked under microscopes for parasites. They saw an underwater frog with a fluid-retention problem, a turtle filled with rocks it wasn't supposed to eat. The seminar is about 25 percent aquatic reptiles and 75 percent fish, but the first day, there were no sick fish. And it was sunny out, so Lewbart took everyone to Ben & Jerry's for a fish-medicine lecture. As he sat in the sun wearing black plastic sunglasses—ice cream in one hand, fish book in the other—Lewbart talked about fish cancer and carp herpes. "Are there any questions?" he asked eventually. A student from Pennsylvania raised his hand: "Can a person make a living as a fish vet?"

The answer is yes and no: despite hourly rates up to $100 for "tank calls," business would be tight for a full-time pet-fish vet right now. Some successful pet-fish vets work in fisheries, public aquariums, zoos or the tropical-fish industry; others supplement their practices with teaching and research. But most pet-fish vets must treat other animals too. "Dogs and cats are the meat and potatoes," Roberts says. "Fish are the spice." That's likely to be true for a while. "Fish medicine is still a hobby," Tepper says. "It costs me thousands of dollars a year." He blames this in part on seasonality—koi are dormant in winter—so he and others are encouraging preventive fish medicine. That's what's unusual about the Golden One's surgery: she's perfectly healthy. Spaying means Roberts won't have to face the ethical baby-placement issue, but it's also a business move. "If I can master this," says Roberts, "I can offer it to owners who say, 'I really love this goldfish, I just don't want a thousand more.' "

Fifteen minutes before the Golden One would be up and darting around her pond looking for food, Dr. Roberts poked around in the fish's abdomen. She told Wulf about her new video game, then stopped suddenly. "Look at that, Bonnie." Roberts pulled a long yellow gelatinous strand from the Golden One's belly. "That looks male, doesn't it?" Bonnie nodded. "Yep, Helen, that's male." Roberts laughed. "How could you be male? You look so female!"

"Don't spay that one," Bonnie said.

"O.K.," Roberts shot back, chipper as always. "We'll neuter him."
Then she turned to me and whispered: "Fish medicine isn't an exact
science yet. But we're working on it."

Plunging the Reader into the Story

Skloot's first scene leaves the reader intrigued by the situation and wanting
more. Readers wonder, Surgery on a goldfish? What's that all about? And
then they plunge in. This is what you want readers to do—commit quickly
so that there's no turning back.

In Phillips's "Charging Lions" readers wonder, Will Duchess live or die?
and then plunge in to find the answer. In *The Glass Castle* the reader wants
to know how mom and her daughter ended up in such a quandary. It takes
the entire book for readers to learn the answers, but since millions of copies
of the book have been sold, Walls is clearly doing something—many
things—right.

Background Means What It Says: In the Back

The faster you get readers involved in the story of your essay, the longer
they'll stay with you. No need to provide information that readers don't need
and cannot use at the moment, even if they will need to know it eventually.

Look carefully at the three "plunging in" examples above. Is there any
missing information that causes you to be confused or turned off or left in
the dark? Probably not. Of course, you want to know more about the Walls
family, Nemo, and Duchess, but so far in these beginnings, the reader is in
sync with the writer. There's nothing missing—just yet. So this leads to
some good advice: follow the story.

The Story Determines the
Research Information—the
Facts—You Gather and Provide

I remember once traveling with a respected radio journalist, observing the way he worked on assignment. I followed him for a day as he interviewed people, gathered facts, and asked questions. By the end of the day, he was ready to return to his home base a few hundred miles away. He said, "Now that I have the facts, I have to figure out how to tell the story."

This is the way traditional reporters work. The facts come first, even for writers and reporters like the one I'd followed that day, who knew he had to have a narrative. But in creative nonfiction, the facts and the story that communicate the facts are given equal emphasis and the story takes precedence in the writing. If you're starting with story, and if the vehicle to capture the reader is story, then the story determines the facts you provide to the reader—or at least the order and emphasis of the facts.

At this point, you might hear a "truth-o-meter" alarm go off, as journalists around the country proclaim, "Those creative nonfictionists are making stuff up."

Not so. Rebecca Skloot chose to tell the "human-fish bond" story through the surgery on Nemo, so the surgery and the way the surgery progresses determine what information the writer will communicate first to the reader. This is usually the most important information. Which is not

EXERCISE 15

Once again, return to the essays you have been writing—and reading in this book. Are the beginnings structured so that the reader is drawn in quickly? If not, start to think about the ways you can make your first few paragraphs—or pages—more compelling. Go through some of the magazines and essay collections you have at home or you see on the newsstand. Do they pass the "plunge-in" test? Try your hand at writing beginnings that immediately compel a reader to commit. Do five of them—even if you don't have a story to follow up with. Try the plunge-in test in conversation, as well. Say something intriguing to a friend that may only be tangentially related to what you actually want to talk about. Then see how much more interested she gets!

to say that some facts aren't omitted, particularly if they have nothing to do with the story's focus. To repeat: the story determines what information/facts the writer provides to the reader. The process is a package.

I once talked with a "book doctor" in Massachusetts who worked for many Ivy League academics attempting to write for a general audience. "They give me their book manuscript. It is all filled with jargon and technical information, and they say to me, 'Put in some color.' They think that's how it works—just scatter about some interesting anecdotes—and their book will be on the best-seller lists," she said. But that's not the way it works.

Whether it's immersion or memoir, the book is a package—style and substance, fact and story, with story determining the order and importance of the facts. This hierarchy, however, does not mean that you can make facts up.

Framing: The Second Part
of Structure (After Scenes)

_____

You've heard this before—and I say it one more time because it is a constant challenge: (1) The building blocks of creative nonfiction are scenes—little stories; (2) information is communicated through action as part of the scene or in between scenes; (3) story is the creative vehicle to present the nonfiction. It is a style and substance dance.

But you can't just write scenes, throw them in a pile, pick out the best of the bunch, and have a completed essay. That's a good start, but there's more to it. Scenes require some sort of order. One scene must follow another in a logical progression or pattern. That pattern, a story in itself, is called a frame.

A frame gives shape to a story and keeps readers turning pages (or scrolling on screens) to find out what happens from scene to scene. It's the plot of a story—the change in people, places, or objects—from beginning to end. Frame is the overarching narrative, the reader's journey, scene to scene from start to finish. The frame or overall narrative is almost always a story. It is a bigger and more general story, whereas scenes are smaller and more specific stories. So a frame can also be referred to as an overall narrative or "story structure."

Whatever term you use, almost every essay, every chapter, every book, is framed, loosely or tightly, in some kind of story. Let's take a look at how

"Difficult Decisions" is framed. What keeps the nine blocks of yellow—its scenes—together?

This essay is framed chronologically—a day in the life of a veterinarian. It starts in the morning at the veterinarian's office when the writer and the veterinarian meet and ends six hours later, back at the location where they started. "Three Spheres" is similarly chronological. It begins with Lauren Slater's resistance to accepting the "borderline" as a patient and ends two or three days later, with Dr. Slater meeting her patient. Many things go on within those few days, but the frame is a consistent progression of time.

Books are often ordered chronologically. One of my favorite examples is Tracy Kidder's *House*, which begins with a family buying land to build a house on it and ends eight months later when they move in.

Frames are necessary devices—not just in creative nonfiction but also in novels, movies, and TV shows. Consider an episode of *Law and Order* (not *Law and Order SVU*; I'm a *Law and Order* groupie—another of my vices).

Law and Order usually begins when a body is accidentally discovered: scene 1. The detectives arrive and scope out the crime scene, then sum up the circumstances of the murder. Lenny, the veteran detective, usually ends this—scene 2—with a funny or ironic comment. The scenes go on, one after another, in a logical progression. Suspects are interviewed, released, and finally arrested. The district attorney's office takes over and a trial ensues. More scenes. Tension. The frame—the overall plot—generally advances until, at the end, the viewer learns whether the subject who's arrested and tried is convicted. All the scenes are, in other words, framed in a larger story.

Many frames are not only chronological but compressed. "Fixing Nemo" has a logical chronology. But the suspense is heightened because the story begins in the middle of surgery, takes the reader on a roundabout journey through fish surgery, and ends when the surgery is completed— and the patient survives. So Skloot establishes a measure of suspense. There's something at stake for Nemo and for the reader. Will Nemo live or die?

As Part of the Frame, There's Something at Stake

We've already looked at the necessity of plunging readers into the action and making them commit. Almost always this has something to do with what is at stake—what might happen to them—for the characters, the writer, or both parties.

Here's another example, one of my favorite frames, for it always makes me smile. In her essay "Last Tango in Westwood," published in *Harper's* in 2003, Phyllis Raphael begins by describing a dinner she attended in the 1960s with Marlon Brando, then a young stud actor. He and Raphael are having a casual conversation in a restaurant full of people, including Raphael's husband, while Brando is secretly caressing her back and arm. They've never met before, but it's clear Brando is giving her a "signal," says Raphael, who writes, "his touch is heating up my skin like a sun reflector in the California desert. Heat is traveling up my arm, through my body, and into my head. I am being careful not to move, even when I breathe. Neither Brando nor I make any visible sign of what is transpiring between us. Since I became aware of his touch, I haven't altered my expression, and Brando, even when looking directly at me, appears oblivious."

"Last Tango in Westwood" is about 4,000 words long and is mostly about Brando and the actress Rita Hayworth, who's also at the table in the restaurant, as well as other show business folks, including Raphael's own aborted acting career. But the story is framed by Brando's secret interactions with Raphael—whether he'll seduce her (he tries, right in front of her husband, by inviting her home with him) and whether she's enticed. Clearly there's something at stake that will keep the reader engaged.

So consider this when you are deciding on a frame—a way of presenting your scenes: "What's at stake for my character?"

Altering Chronology

Frames need not advance in a beginning-to-end chronology. Writers can start a frame in the middle, as John McPhee does in his classic essay, "Travels in Georgia," published in *The New Yorker* in 1973, which begins with a scene when he and two traveling companions, Sam and Carol—naturalists with the Georgia Natural Areas Council—discover a snapping turtle DOR (dead on the road) and scrape it off the highway, intending to eat it for dinner.

Shortly thereafter, they arrive at the bank of a river, where a dragline crane operator named Chap Causey is widening the riverbed. McPhee and his companions are on a 1,300-mile ride through the state, examining wetlands; they are environmentalists, and they want to conserve the wetlands as habitat for wildlife. This scene with the crane gobbling up the riverbank is a stark illustration of what's at stake, and provides a vivid and engaging beginning for the essay.

McPhee then loops back to the beginning of his journey—long before the snapping turtle or Chap Causey. In the next twenty-five pages—nearly two-thirds of the story—he explains how he came to travel with Sam and Carol and develops them more fully as characters. They stop for more DORs and spend time at Carol's house with her menagerie of rescued animals and collection of animal bones. They camp out, eat DOR muskrat, and paddle down a river in the moonlight.

Each of these scenes advances the story—they are all connected to its focus. We learn many things about Carol, for example, all related to her passion for preserving Georgia's wetlands. An essay is more than a collection of terrific scenes and information, no matter how cleverly organized. Each part of the frame must have a specific emphasis or theme that relates to the larger story.

At the end, McPhee and his companions return to the riverbank and Chap Causey's crane—and then McPhee moves on, finishing both his journey and his story, which end with a canoe ride and a conversation with a young Jimmy Carter, then governor of Georgia.

McPhee is a master of framing; other frames he's employed in stories include a tennis match ("Centre Court," first published in *Playboy,* in which a championship game between Arthur Ashe and Clark Graebner provides the opportunity to profile not only both men but the sport of tennis itself) and a Monopoly game ("The Search for Marvin Gardens," first published in *The New Yorker* in 1972 in which McPhee tours Atlantic City). Each of these frames provides a narrative that leads the reader and leaves room for other information.

Wherever a writer chooses to start a story, there's usually a way to order the scenes—a larger connecting story with a clear beginning and end—so that it all comes together and makes sense to the reader.

The frames that McPhee uses, and the framing structure in most of the examples here, are rather narrow and specific—like fish surgery or a day in the life of a veterinarian. Eve Joseph's essay "Yellow Taxi" is loose and subtle, but the structural direction from beginning to end deals with her work and her experience at the hospice. Note that she begins the essay by indicating that she came to work at hospice in 1985. At the end of the essay she informs the reader that she left hospice work three years ago. Her hospice experiences and her reflections on death and dying may not be in chronological order, but they fit the scope and direction of the essay. Nothing she tells or shows us seems out of sync.

PARALLEL NARRATIVES

The frame for "Three Spheres" is narrower and more concise: Lauren Slater's initial experiences with her patient from the time she first learned of her to the time they met. (You could also call this the "public story.") But there's another frame—or potential frame—to "Three Spheres," Slater's own story as a borderline patient, the "personal story."

Slater introduces the personal story after the public or "therapist" story, but she could have easily framed it the other way—beginning with a memory from her childhood in the hospital and then flashing forward to the phone call from her supervisor. Or she could have started the story closer to the heat of the action by finding herself lost in memory as she headed toward the wrong bathroom during the break from her conference.

Slater chose to use the public story as the frame, but the personal story is as strong a narrative as the therapist's story narrative. She could have gone either way. So Slater has an essay with a parallel narrative—two primary stories, vying for the reader's attention simultaneously. This is good.

The more tension and suspense, the more likely it is the reader will keep reading. In a long-form essay, there can be three or four narratives going on at the same time. If a reader's interest wanes on one level or story, another is immediately available.

Parallel narratives are more easily developed in books because there's more space and time to flesh out plot, place, and characters. In *The Immortal Life of Henrietta Lacks*, Skloot develops many narratives in addition to Henrietta's, including the life and experiences of George Gey, the physician who discovers HeLa cells. In my book *The Best Seat in Baseball, But You Have to Stand*, I tell the story of a year in the life of a crew of National League umpires. But at the same time I help my readers see that year through the eyes of Art Williams, the first black umpire in the National League. I could have easily written the book from Williams's point of view; that would have been the overall narrative. And in retrospect, since it was so personal and since the story turned out to be about racism as well as baseball, it might have been the best bet.

Don't Make Promises You Can't Keep

We're in a diner witnessing a conversation between two psychopathic lovers who, while eating breakfast, decide to rob the place—the cash register and the customers as well. The robbers are ready to strike.

But suddenly we're swept back to the previous day and we meet a collection of eccentric and questionable characters, played by Bruce Willis, John Travolta, Samuel Jackson, Harvey Keitel, and Uma Thurman, all involved tangentially in a series of loosely related homicides, robberies, and swindles. Each of their stories stands alone, but their stories are ingeniously connected to one another in a web of violence and perversion.

Two hours of cinematic intensity later, two of the characters, Jackson and Travolta, decide to end a harrowing and exhausting all-nighter with a hearty breakfast at a diner—the diner which, when the viewer last saw it, was about to be robbed. I won't reveal the end of the movie, but suffice it to say we haven't heard anything from the psychopaths since the opening scene. Yet their story has lingered in our minds throughout the film. We know that the

---

EXERCISE 16

Try to identify and describe the frame of the excerpt from *The Immortal Life of Henrietta Lacks*. Then leaf through your favorite magazines and essay anthologies. Identify the frames. Take note of how often the writer breaks chronology. How does the author do it? Look for frames that are subtle and loose like "Yellow Taxi"—and others sharper and more targeted, like "Fixing Nemo." Do the essays you have been writing have a frame—and might it be more effective to make those frames narrower? It often is.

---

director, Quentin Tarantino, made a promise to us by introducing the two psychopaths at the start that he is bound to keep—and we expect he will, sooner or later. And he does in his iconic 1994 film *Pulp Fiction*.

Similarly, novelist Don DeLillo makes a promise to his readers in a 2003 *New Yorker* essay, "That Day in Rome." DeLillo and his wife are walking along the Via Condotto in Rome when they see, walking toward them, a "glamorous international movie star, wearing a shiny lavender blouse, suede pants and long boots and sporting a man on each arm." (Note the specificity of detail.)

Over the next couple of paragraphs, DeLillo describes the city, the atmosphere, and Rome's general cultural history. He points out also that the actress seems comfortable and happy. Eventually he tells us that it's been twenty-five years since this encounter. As he relives it for us in this essay, piecing together the details, he realizes he's "no longer certain, at this level of separation, who the movie star was."

From that point on in the essay DeLillo discusses movies he's enjoyed over the years and actresses who remind him of the mystery actress. He discusses disagreements with his wife over movies generally and actresses specifically—and tells us a bit about the challenges of married life. We learn about Anita Ekberg, James Bond, Sissy Spacek, Federico Fellini, and many other people of note he's acquainted with, but we don't learn who the actress was he spotted twenty-five years ago until near the end of the essay.

DeLillo teases his readers and keeps our interest—and keeps his promise in the end.

Clearly DeLillo wanted to write an essay about movies, marriage, and memory, but he's framed or "book-ended" his piece with the mysterious actress, teasing us that if we remain loyal to him through his ramblings, he'll provide her name—and finally he does: Ursula Andress.

Main Point of Focus

Many people confuse frame and focus. Remember that frame is structural. It's like the frame of a painting; it presents the venue or the rationale for the selection and order of your scenes.

Focus—the second way you can select and order scenes—represents theme or meaning or thesis, what it is the writer wants the reader to come away with at the end of the reading experience. In order for the scenes to fit together, they should reflect the same or similar themes.

In "Difficult Decisions," seven of the nine scenes have similar themes or meanings—all relating to the veterinarian's ability to end the lives of her patients or try to save them. Each time she faces this dilemma it is a "difficult decision." Most of the scenes reflect that focus.

In "Fixing Nemo," Rebecca Skloot states her focus about a third of the way into the essay—"the human-fish bond." Lauren Slater explains her focus in the paragraph beginning, "For I have learned how to soothe the hotspots."

Scenes that in no way relate to your focus, no matter how interesting or compelling, usually don't belong. For example, the veterinarian in "Difficult Decisions" was a prominent amateur tennis player—she changed into "whites" before leaving the office most days. But tennis didn't fit with goats or horses—so it didn't belong in "Difficult Decisions." This veterinarian also struggled for a half dozen years to be accepted into veterinary school. Until recently, women were thought to be physically unable to handle large animals, so veterinary schools enrolled mostly male students. I could have found a way to embed such information into the text, but chose to save it for another essay chapter focusing on the difficulties women veterinarians face in being accepted by their male colleagues.

FRAME REFLECTS FOCUS

In the best of worlds, the story structure or frame will have the same or a similar focus in most of the scenes. The more symmetry the better. Eve Joseph is discussing death and dying in a hospice context, and she is telling us that there is a beauty and a purpose in the process, for both the person who is dying and the person who is supporting his passing. The frame fits the focus. The frame and focus in the Skloot and Slater excerpts are also in sync. But the "day in the life" chronology in "Difficult Decisions" doesn't adhere to this pattern. Its scope is too broad; it doesn't reflect the difficult decisions the veterinarian confronts on a daily basis. It's okay; it works. But it could be sharper.

Can I make it better? Are there options I haven't taken advantage of? Let's think about this as we move forward.

STORIES (SCENES) ARE ELASTIC

Stories in this context—scenes—are receptacles; some stories can be stretched to contain a lot of information and many scenes, but some cannot. I've talked about scenes within scenes in relation to "Three Spheres" and "Fixing Nemo." In the latter, the frame is a surgical procedure—a rare and unlikely procedure. But it works in this essay because it communicates information and establishes the requisite sauce of suspense—will Nemo live? Think of a rubber band—the more you stretch it the tauter it becomes until it breaks. So too with a good story; it can be stretched so that the reader is tantalized with heightening suspense as the writer goes off on related tangents.

The goldfish procedure Skloot documents in "Fixing Nemo" is elastic— it contains information as well as other scenes and stories and people. And here the frame largely reflects the focus of the piece—this surgery wouldn't have taken place without the existing overarching theme: the human-fish bond. So it's a circle and a package.

Now let's go back to "Difficult Decisions." The "day in the life" chronology is acceptable. It works because the focus is clear from the beginning—and there's some inherent momentum in the narrative. The reader may suspect, however, that something could be happening.

Keeping in mind the elasticity of stories and the idea that frame may reflect focus for maximum impact and effectiveness, which of the scenes marked in yellow is elastic enough to hold all the other scenes, enhance suspense, and reflect focus? Let's take a look:

Certain scenes can be eliminated immediately. The disbudding scene (page 145) doesn't reflect focus. So that's out. And although the stories the veterinarian tells (Shadow, for instance) reflect focus, they're limited in scope and couldn't hold all the details and characters of the other stories.

To do that, we'd have to go back to the veterinarian and reinterview her, and even then we wouldn't know until we've invested a lot of time and trouble to see if any of her stories are large and elastic enough to contain the other stories.

Two stories or scenes are left—both recreations. The first, Ricki and Honey (page 141), might work from an elasticity point of view. But there's not a lot of suspense. We know from the start the veterinarian isn't going to put Honey down. But in contrast we don't know if the veterinarian is going to invest the time or money to treat the goat in the final scene of the essay—or make the difficult decision to euthanize her (page 148). That final scene contains the elasticity to accommodate all the other scenes in the essay, the potential of suspense to keep the reader riveted, and, obviously, the focus.

How would you do this? You'd play with time, starting the essay at the end of the day with the veterinarian examining the Nubian goat and pondering her difficult decision. But you wouldn't tell the reader what her decision will be; rather, you'd flash back to the beginning of the day, writing a foreshadowing transition that informs the reader that this is the kind of

EXERCISE 17

Rewrite "Difficult Decisions," not by changing the text but by moving or stretching out scenes/blocks of yellow. How will my suggestions work?

decision the veterinarian has been pondering all day—the difficult decision that haunts her profession. What will she do about the goat?

So the reader is hooked by the veterinarian's decision or indecision, but you don't tell the reader what the decision is until the rest of the day is complete. At the end of the essay, you keep your promise and dramatically reveal the veterinarian's decision. The story of the difficult decision is elastic enough to hold all the other stories you've included in the essay and enhance suspense—with only minor revision. In this case, I've moved information around but added very little. I've manipulated structure—not content.

First Lede/Real Lead: A Creative Nonfiction Experiment Precipitated by Ernest Hemingway and F. Scott Fitzgerald

"How much rewriting do you do?" an interviewer from the *Paris Review* asked Ernest Hemingway in 1956.

"It depends," he replied. "I rewrote the ending of *A Farewell to Arms* (1929) the last page of it, thirty-nine times before I was satisfied."

"Was there some technical problem there? What was it that had stumped you?"

"Getting the words right," Hemingway replied.

Hemingway, according to his biographers, was steadfast and persistent when it came to revision. As in the last chapter of *A Farewell to Arms*, he never gave up. Yet F. Scott Fitzgerald described significant parts of Hemingway's first book, one of his most well regarded, *The Sun Also Rises* (1926), as "careless and ineffectual."

This was when Hemingway thought he'd finished the novel. His editor, the legendary Maxwell Perkins, who was also Fitzgerald's and Thomas Wolfe's editor at Scribner's, was ready to publish the novel. But as the story goes, Hemingway was unwilling to proceed until he received feedback from Fitzgerald, his then friend in Paris.

Fitzgerald procrastinated—he didn't want to tell Hemingway what he thought of the book. But Hemingway persisted, and Fitzgerald finally wrote a letter in which he criticized the novel, page by page. Or at least the first part of the book. "It's fine from Chapter V," Fitzgerald wrote.

Hemingway was humiliated—and probably furious. But the more he examined the first few chapters of *The Sun Also Rises*, the more he realized he'd included unnecessary scenes and information that could either be eliminated or embedded further in the text. Eventually Hemingway cut the first four chapters from *The Sun Also Rises*, and the book we read today begins with the original chapter 5.

This story, along with *Creative Nonfiction*'s editors' long experience editing essays—eliminating unnecessary background information from the beginnings—led to an interesting and valuable experiment—first lede/real lead.

The text below is excerpted from *Creative Nonfiction*'s website (www.creativenonfiction.org). If you go to the website, you'll see the results of the first lede/real lead experiment. It begins here:

In textbook journalism, the lede covers the famous Five W's—who, what, when, where and why (and sometimes how). In creative nonfiction, the lede functions somewhat differently.

Because the primary purpose is not so much to communicate quickly the basic information of a story as it is to draw readers in, the beginning of a story may not capture the Five W's; often, some of the answers to those essential questions are purposely held back to enhance suspense and to allow the narrative to develop more organically. "The lede also has a more complex function for the writer; it tells the writer where to take the reader and when to introduce ideas, themes and characters. The lede, in other words, leads. It gets the writer going and fuels momentum.

While revising, however, the writer usually has to return to the beginning of the piece and decide whether the first lede is still necessary. Often it is not; the first lede was just a tool or triggering device that allowed the writer to get to the 'real lead.'

During the editing process for this issue, with the permission of the writers, we eliminated the original beginnings of three essays and started them a few paragraphs or pages later. Our goal was to make the beginnings more immediate, to eliminate some writerly throat-clearing, to help plunge readers into the heart of the story—the action, the theme, the substance—from the very beginning."

The pieces are . . . online as they were originally submitted, with graphics that demonstrate not only what was removed during editing, but also what was moved further into the pieces and, in some cases, what was added.

First lede/real lead demonstrates another vitally important consideration when you are crafting a scene: are your opening paragraphs as effective as you can make them? To use a baseball metaphor, are you winding up or throwing the ball? The former is interesting—the latter is essential.

CLARITY AND QUESTION MARKS

I annoy my students on a number of levels. I don't praise them enough; I'm always being critical, finding fault in their work. I make them commit to a writing project—choose the subject of their essays—almost immediately. I don't tolerate procrastination. And I make them go out into the world and do immersions.

In addition to reading books, they dig into Wikipedia, conduct a few telephone interviews, and write something. They have to be involved—which is the real-life aspect of creative nonfiction. But what they dislike more than anything else—what drives them to drink—are my constant question marks.

When I read their manuscripts and find something I don't completely understand, a reference or an idea that isn't totally clear, an image that doesn't make sense, I inscribe a series of question marks in the margins of their manuscripts. This is part of my ongoing campaign for clarity.

"Words," I say, "should embrace the reader and help tell the story—not confuse readers or divert them to a dictionary or back to the essay to see what they missed in context so that they can understand what the writer means."

"But you know what I am saying," my students object.

"I know what you're saying, more or less, but I've known you through the semester and I know what you're writing about. We've discussed your story frequently."

Sometimes at this point my students will explain to me what they mean by a phrase or a sentence or an image. "Will you be around to explain to your readers every time they're stymied?" I ask.

"My wife (boyfriend, mother, roommate) read this and knew exactly what I was saying," they often counter.

"Well, maybe you should send your wife (boyfriend, mother, roommate) to the editor of the magazine when you submit it for publication, just so they'll be around for explanations and clarifications."

Most of the writing-oriented chapters in this book deal with structure—not line editing. Shape and structure are the major challenges. As you play with and revise structure and shape scenes, you're also revising and sharpening your scenes and sentences. Much line editing is accomplished in that manner. But sooner or later, you'll be happy enough with the shape of your essay and you'll be ready to focus on your word-by-word prose. I'm not talking about grammar and punctuation; I'm referring to word efficiency, word choice (diction), and clarity. This is no easy job.

EXERCISE 18

Clarity includes efficiency. Go over a scene you've recently written. Are you showing your readers what you want them to know? Are you also telling your readers what you're showing? Do you need to tell and show? Probably not. Edit your prose with concision and precision in mind. Don't be afraid of cutting. It's often surprising how much more effective a piece of writing can be when it's trimmed. Circle word multiples. Do you need to repeat words three or four times in a paragraph? Probably not. Isolate your phrases and metaphors from their context. Do they still make sense? Don't just read and reread your sentences and paragraphs—x-ray them.

John McPhee once told me it takes him about nine months to research and write an average long-form *New Yorker* piece. He dedicates most of his writing time to shape and structure and doesn't worry about how he puts his words together until later in the game. But it's as polished and perfect as he can make it by the time he sends it off to his editor at *The New Yorker*. And invariably at some point in the editing process, he'll take a train from Princeton to New York and huddle side by side with his editor, and they'll go over every word, sentence, image, or phrase on each page, polishing, defining, and seeking clarity. This process takes anywhere from one to two full eight-hour days, says McPhee. That's a lot of question marks.

THE DRAWER PHASE

Question: After I feel certain about structure and clarity and I've x-rayed and revised, am I ready to submit?

Answer: Yes. You're ready to submit your manuscript to your desk drawer. Put the essay or chapter away for a couple of weeks; don't look at it. We all tend to love what we've written right after we've finished it. But the sense of perfection can wear off when we establish some distance. You want editors to see your best work—not something with potential. Most editors will give serious consideration to your work only once, and if it's less than terrific, a rejection follows.

Question: But I need to be published, don't I? How else will I prove myself and make a living? I need published writing samples.

Answer: But you want to be published well. You don't want mediocre samples. You want work that will impress your readers—editors and friends alike—and not haunt or embarrass you ten years down the road. So take your time and take your best shot. You'll be published sooner or later, and when that magical day arrives, you'll be proud to showcase your work to the world.

REMEMBER THAT WRITING IS REVISION

In the introduction to Part II, I make the case for revision. In fact, I find it difficult to distinguish between writing and revision for they happen simultaneously. Almost every sentence, every paragraph, every page we write we will revise and rewrite a number of times before we actually say it is a rough or first draft. The techniques, exercises, and ideas about writing presented in Part II cannot be subdivided. Writing is a singular, synchronized creative process. And it is ongoing and unyielding. Your work is never good enough; it can always be made better. Winston Churchill said it all: "Never, never, never give up."

Now That I Know Everything I Ever Wanted to Know About Creative Nonfiction, What Happens Next?

MFA IN THE USA

Master of Fine Arts (MFA) degrees in fiction and poetry have been around since 1936, when the Iowa Writers' Workshop—the country's first MFA program in creative writing—was founded. About twenty years ago I helped start the first MFA program in creative nonfiction at the University of Pittsburgh, and the idea has caught on at colleges and universities everywhere since then. There are no reliable statistics available as far as I know, but I estimate there are more than seventy-five colleges and universities in the United States and abroad where you can earn a master's level creative nonfiction degree. And there are another half dozen institutions offering a PhD in creative nonfiction or in creative writing with a creative nonfiction concentration, including the University of Missouri, University of Nebraska–Lincoln, and Ohio University, among others.

Low residency creative nonfiction MFA programs are also becoming increasingly popular. Instead of attending regular weekly classes, students work mostly online or through telephone conversations with a nonfiction writing mentor. Students and faculty get together two or three times a year, from seven to ten days for classes and workshops. "Low res" tuition is about the same as on campus tuition, but the low residency requirement allows students to work or live at home, making the educational experience more cost-effective, although not necessarily so "real and intense."

Are MFA programs good for the creative nonfiction writer? Who should attend such a program—and when? Here are some questions to ask before you decide to invest what could be tens of thousands of dollars, along with a two- to three-year commitment.

1. How much have you suffered—or experienced?

This is a serious question, especially if you're just completing an undergraduate degree. The idea of writing a memoir and recounting the tribulations of your first twenty-one years is tempting. But most young people haven't experienced enough to have something significant to say about life, especially to readers who are older than they are. The standing joke among faculty in creative nonfiction programs is how many "dead grandmother" stories they've received in any given semester. Losing a grandparent is often the worst thing that's happened to a twenty-one-year-old student with a newly minted bachelor's degree.

I'm not contending here that young people can't write with power and beauty or that they haven't suffered. But it's often better to join the Peace Corps, take a job driving a taxi, or interact with a different culture before studying writing on a master's degree level. If nothing else, you'll have more material, more reference points, more ideas and experiences to draw on. And it doesn't mean you're giving up the dream of being a writer; rather, you're living the creative nonfiction life, which means that you're experiencing new worlds—and writing about them in your spare time and on a regular schedule. With a good stockpile of new material, you'll maximize your MFA investment when you finally get there.

Even if something awful or fascinating (or both!) did happen to you as a child and you and your family suffered a great deal, you may not have accrued enough distance and insight to be able to reflect on the experience passionately and intelligently enough to share with readers. Periodically I work with private clients who have interesting stories to tell and don't want to participate in a writing program. Recently I helped someone write about the death of her grandmother. But this writer is sixty-five years old.

2. *What do you know?*

This question relates to your subject. If you've had a rich life, with rare and fascinating personal experiences to share, then you might write memoir—or two or three memoirs. But remember that the mission of creative nonfiction is to communicate information—to teach readers about various subjects, from motorcycles to menopause to mountain climbing to mathematics. The more you know, the more interesting you are to a publisher, especially if you're a professional or an academic.

Recently I co-coordinated a series of lectures and workshops, Rewriting Your Thinking and Rethinking Your Writing, intended for an audience of mostly faculty and postdoctoral students at Arizona State University. The first session—The Age of the Expert—featured a literary agent who discussed the importance and popularity of nonfiction narrative. To support his argument, he'd made a survey of nonfiction (mostly narrative) book proposals sold during 2010, mostly by academics. The survey was anecdotal; the agent had analyzed announcements in the online *Publisher's Lunch*, which is hardly inclusive, but the results were surprisingly indicative of enthusiastic interest.

There were 108 titles, divided among the subject areas of history, politics, current affairs, science, business, health, and religion; these were sold to fifty-nine different publishers, among them Knopf, Norton, Penguin, and Crown. Ten of those titles received six-figure advances; one, more than $500,000. Obviously, many other lucrative deals weren't announced online and not included in the survey, but if academics and scholars could learn to transform their research into compelling and accessible stories using creative nonfiction techniques, there would be a motivated trade press market eager to publish their work. The agent left no doubt that "the age of the expert" is upon us, especially if the expert can master narrative.

These sessions were mostly for academics, but the lesson is for all aspiring writers. There's so much we need or want to know in this world, but we don't have much time to learn it. Many people want to learn in a pleasurable way, and the creative nonfiction writer with knowledge, commitment, and an understanding of story can fulfill those needs. So what do you know, what can you share with the world of readers?

To return to question 1, the graduating college senior who wants to stay in a university setting could go on to study biology, physics, business, or any other subject. The idea is to acquire an in-depth body of knowledge and then use it as writing material.

3. What do you want to accomplish by earning an MFA in creative nonfiction?

If you want to teach writing in a university, then an MFA degree would be helpful. Since most writing programs offer an MFA degree, most prefer that their faculty members have an MFA. But this is not a universal requirement.

For one thing, most prestigious writers in creative nonfiction today don't have MFA degrees and don't want to take the time to get them. And second, a degree won't guarantee a teaching job; you'll still need publications—at least one well-reviewed book, maybe more. A book, or two or three published books, is usually more valuable as a credential than an MFA degree. The ideal, of course, is to publish your MFA writing manuscript as your first book, but that rarely happens. There are, of course, exceptions. Many of my students have done very well with their MFA manuscripts. One, excerpted in this book, is Rebecca Skloot. Another is the author of *The Knock at the Door: A Journey Through the Darkness of the Armenian Genocide* (2007). Margaret Anhert has earned many awards for her efforts.

Many people enroll in creative nonfiction programs because they have a book they want to write but don't care about getting an MFA degree or teaching. Many creative nonfiction students are midcareer professionals with no intention of giving up their day jobs; they're simply seeking more avenues to explore writing.

MFA programs have helped motivated writers who have a specific book in mind they want to write. In such a program you might get three or four different faculty mentors to work with you on a one-to-one basis. The program provides a community you can share your early drafts with that will support you along the way. Being a writer means accepting a certain amount of isolation—and so having a community, even if the members of that community are not in the same city, can be valuable.

There are alternatives to MFA programs. You could hire a mentor, for example, to assist you for as long as you like, at a cost much less than the $30,000–$40,000 that an MFA program might cost. Many students I've talked with, especially midcareer professionals, have entered MFA programs because they've been unaware of other options. The Creative Nonfiction Foundation offers mentoring help, for example. Go to the website for more information on this program, www.creativenonfiction.org.

All MFA creative nonfiction programs are not the same. Some are easier to be admitted to than others. There's not much quality control. In most programs, in addition to finishing your course work, you are expected to turn in a 100- to 200-page "publishable" manuscript—similar to the requirement for a master's thesis. Obviously "publishable" is a subjective term—we all have different values and standards. And producing a "publishable" manuscript doesn't guarantee that you'll be published.

My strong advice is:

- Do some serious research into writing programs before you send in your registration fee. Don't feel flattered at being accepted into a program, even if you were chosen in an allegedly competitive situation. Program administrators tend to exaggerate.
- Apply to programs with high standards and well-known faculty. Find out where the program graduates go after graduation and whether they succeed—where their work has been published or will be published—before making a commitment.
- Find out who your professors will be during the two to three years you'll be in the program. Familiarize yourself with their work. Do you like how they write? Do they have something to teach you? Make certain they have teaching experience. A good writer may not be a good teacher—or may not want to devote the time nec-

essary to mentor you. Some universities use poets and fiction writers with limited nonfiction experience to teach in creative nonfiction programs in an attempt to be efficient at the student's expense. Instead, look for programs with faculty who publish and teach creative nonfiction as their specialty—not a sideline.

- Be discerning. If you don't get into the program you feel is best suited for you, then spend a year polishing your writing sample and try again. The sample is what's going to get you accepted or rejected, so the best way to begin your writing career is by writing and submitting the best work you can produce to the best programs—and waiting patiently to get where you want to go. Remember, you're still writing, compiling material, moving in the right direction. Timing is crucial. If you enter an MFA program before you're ready, you'll spend your first semester or your first year trying to find a writing project.

PUBLISH OR PERISH

Yes, that's the old adage, especially for academics; if you don't publish books and critical essays, you probably won't get tenure. And to a certain extent, the same is true for writers. If you don't publish, your work seems unofficial. And being unpublished is depressing. Laboring alone and writing material no one seems to be paying attention to is frustrating. When people learn that you are a writer, they will want to know what you've published lately or where they've read your work.

In every art or profession, it takes a while to get good at what you're doing, and sometimes it takes longer for the world (or the publishing industry) to recognize your worth. It takes time to be recognized. Margaret Mitchell's Pulitzer Prize–winning 1936 novel *Gone with the Wind* was rejected nearly forty times by prominent publishers before it found a home at Macmillan. J.K. Rowling was nearly destitute while she was writing *Harry Potter and the Philosopher's Stone*, the first of seven Potter books that have brought her fame and fortune. Joseph Heller devoted a dozen years to *Catch 22*, which was published in 1961 by Simon & Schuster.

Over the years I've learned to protect myself; I rarely tell people what I'm working on—or even what my profession is, unless I'm literally cornered. I'd rather listen to other people talking (that's where I get some of my best material), and most people would rather talk than listen, anyway.

Listening is an anchoring element of the creative nonfiction life. Discussing your work with others can be self-destructive; talking it out can siphon the energy, the spontaneity of insight and discovery that is essential when you're writing creative nonfiction. I'm not recommending a "writer as a hermit" approach, only that you be circumspect and allow your unpublished work room to breathe, and when published, to speak for itself.

Don't Worry, Be Happy—and Smart

I know this seems easy for me to say since I've published many books, but I believe we need to care more about the quality of our work than its dissemination. Your work will probably be published if it *deserves* to be published, and when it is, as I have said before, you want it to reflect the best you can do. Which is not to say you shouldn't try to publish after that drawer phase is over and you feel you're ready—only that you shouldn't become overly anxious. If your story is good, your intent is serious, your research is solid, and you remain dedicated to producing the highest quality of work possible, your day will most likely come.

At the same time, you can hasten the process and help yourself by understanding the writing and publishing business. Read about the industry. *Publishers Weekly* is available in most libraries. The *New York Times Book Review* is available online; find out what's being published these days and how it's reviewed. The daily *Times* also reviews books and covers the publishing industry. Not that you should devote your day to newspapers. I use Google alerts, so I know what's going on in the publishing world, and I receive daily Google alerts on the latest news related to whatever I'm writing about. Although there aren't as many bookstores as there once were, it's helpful to visit your nearest independent or Barnes & Noble and browse the shelves. See what's being published and where the books similar to yours are shelved. Be aware of your competition because at some point you'll have to pitch your own book.

There's a lot to say about selling, marketing, and publishing creative nonfiction—enough to fill another book—but here are a few points to ponder:

- Forget the major magazines. *Harper's*, the *New Yorker*, the *Atlantic*, and others like them rarely if ever publish unsolicited manuscripts. Try literary magazines like *Creative Nonfiction, Georgia Review, Colorado Review*, or *Prairie Schooner*. There are hundreds of them in the United States. They are always seeking good writing no matter what the subject, and they do not shy away from daring or experimental work, even in a longer form, as many as 5,000 words, for example. The pay is poor for publication in literary journals—sometimes you only get complimentary copies. But book editors and agents seeking emerging talents pay attention to these journals. Every issue published by *Creative Nonfiction* brings inquiries from agents and editors about the writers we publish.
- Get a literary agent when you have a product you're proud of—after the drawer phase. Be as discerning when choosing an agent—even more discerning—as you were when you chose an MFA program. Interview the agent, talk to his or her clients and see what they publish. Don't allow the flattery of an agent's taking you on to go to your head. Also, remember that agents are almost always seeking entire book manuscripts or proposals for book manuscripts. Rarely will an agent submit essays on your behalf. The best way to find an agent is through a friend or colleague who can endorse and recommend one. You can also go to the website of the Association of Author's Representatives (http://aaronline.org) and learn more about the process of finding and working with an agent—and reviewing a long list of agents seeking authors.
- Learn everything you can about writing book proposals, especially for "public" creative nonfiction. Writing a good book proposal can

be more challenging than writing the book itself. They are often long (50 pages is not unusual), with the writer describing in great detail the project he or she is proposing. Book proposals usually include sample chapters. Rebecca Skloot's proposal was nearly 20,000 words, about one-fourth the length of her finished book. I suggest you seek out a mentor to help you with your proposal. The Creative Nonfiction mentoring program can help, or you may wish to attend a writers' conference featuring presentations by editors or agents. There are a number of how-to-write-a-book-proposal books on the market. Any one of them will be helpful. It is not necessarily the form that agents and editors are concerned about; it is, obviously, the content. Don't underestimate the value of putting time and attention into the proposal. Many creative nonfiction books are sold on the basis of a proposal—not a finished book.

- Consider small presses. The big boys are prestigious—Simon & Schuster, HarperCollins, Random House—but the recession and the digital age have altered their landscape in negative ways, and they're still reeling from the aftershocks. Recently university presses and smaller independent presses have filled the serious literature gap the big publishers have left. Presses like the University of Nebraska, Coffee House, Princeton University Press, and Sarabande are a few you might think about querying. Although small presses don't have large marketing budgets, big publishers don't do much marketing anymore, either. The large publishers usually devote their time and energy to established or brand name writers, people like John Grisham and Danielle Steele.

- Learn about marketing and promoting yourself. Rebecca Skloot conducted her own marketing campaign and book promotion tour at her own expense, which led to a cover story in *Publishers Weekly*. And then reviewers—and subsequently readers—began paying attention. As wonderful and powerful as her book is, she knows that it took her marketing ingenuity and persistence to help it along.

A Final Word:
Read This Book Again

Now that you've read this book—whether from the beginning or the middle, or bit by bit, please read it again. I want you to remember what we creative nonfiction writers are all about: our mission, our life, our literature, and our passion.

And remember to write and revise and rewrite. That is my message. Write, revise, and rewrite—write, revise, and rewrite until you're certain you can't go any farther, that you've achieved your best work. And then start something new.

And remember the words and message of Winston Churchill. Don't give up and don't give in if you don't get published right away or if, when you are published, the critics lambast or ignore you. Just keep writing. Publication and prestige will happen when it happens, but high-quality writing, prose to be proud of, is your primary mission.

I can't promise you fame and fortune—I can't even promise satisfaction, since writers are never satisfied or happy for very long, if ever. But if you read this book again and consider what I've said in these pages, it will provide you with the information and inspiration you need to succeed in the world of creative nonfiction.

After all, let's remember who's talking to you, and guiding you, and exhorting you, in fact.

The Godfather.

APPENDIX: THEN AND NOW:
GREAT (AND NOT SO GREAT) MOMENTS
IN CREATIVE NONFICTION, 1993–2010

This unofficial history and time line of creative nonfiction was put together by Hattie Fletcher to celebrate the (2010) transition of the literary journal *Creative Nonfiction* to the quarterly magazine it is today. Fletcher is managing editor of *Creative Nonfiction* and coordinator of the move from journal to magazine. Perhaps you can add to the timeline for 2012—and beyond!

The term "creative nonfiction" may be relatively recent, but what it describes is hardly new. People have been telling true stories in interesting ways since some hunter came back to the cave and tried to describe the light on the grass as he crept up on a bird, and how it reminded him of afternoons when his father taught him how to hunt. And there's a long list of writers since then whose work blends style and substance and uses scene, dialogue, and other literary tools in the service of true stories. Augustine, Montaigne, Thoreau, Woolf, Hemingway, Orwell . . . they probably wouldn't have called themselves creative nonfiction writers, but hey—they didn't know any better.

But now we know, and in the years since issue 1 of *CNF* rolled off the press, creative nonfiction has come into its own, both as a literary form and as a highly popular (and lucrative) sector of the publishing industry. Have there been some rough patches? Yes, but that's to be expected—perhaps twenty years from now we will look back on the Age of Frey as a sort of rebellious adolescent period.

As for what's coming next, who knows? Not us, that's for sure. All we can tell you is where we've been.

Just to be perfectly clear: this is speculation! We weren't there and can't confirm this story; nevertheless, we believe it to be a plausible account of events that might have transpired. (We assume that you'll assume that, but people have gotten in trouble for that kind of thing, on occasion.)

1993 First issue of *Creative Nonfiction*, a literary journal devoted exclusively to long-form narrative nonfiction, is published.

- "Is It Fiction? Is It Nonfiction? And Why Doesn't Anyone Care?" *New York Times* critic Michiko Kakutani laments, "We are daily assaulted by books, movies and television docudramas that hopscotch back and forth between the realms of history and fiction, reality and virtual reality, with impunity."

- Susanna Kaysen, *Girl, Interrupted:* memoir of the author's years of hospitalization for mental illness.

1994 The Association of Writers and Writing Programs (AWP) counts 534 degree-conferring creative writing programs; sixty-four offer a Master of Fine Arts.

- John Berendt, *Midnight in the Garden of Good and Evil:* Edmund White calls this true-crime story "the best nonfiction novel since 'In Cold Blood' and a lot more entertaining"; it remains on the *New York Times* best-seller list for four years; tour buses descend on Savannah.

- More memoirs of troubled girlhood: Lucy Grealy, 31, explores "the deep bottomless grief . . . called ugliness," in *Autobiography of a Face;* Elizabeth Wurtzel, 26, arrives on the scene with *Prozac Nation: Young and Depressed in America.*

- Sherwin Nuland's *How We Die: Reflections on Life's Final Chapter,* a study informed by the author's family experiences, wins the National Book Award for nonfiction.

- Justin Hall, a Swarthmore College sophomore, begins an online diary chronicling events in his life; is later dubbed "the founding father of personal blogging" by the *New York Times Magazine.*

1995 *This American Life,* now a nationally syndicated program hosted by Ira Glass featuring mainly first-person narratives by the likes of David Sedaris and Sarah Vowell, first airs on Chicago Public Radio.

- Sixty-six-year-old TV repairman and Holocaust survivor Herman Rosenblat wins a *New York Post* Valentine's Day contest for a true story about a young girl who threw apples to him over a concentration camp fence; later he met and married her.

- David Sedaris, *Naked:* Sedaris's collections of stories about his family and other topics go on to sell more than 7 million copies (and counting) worldwide.

- Mary Karr, *The Liars' Club:* comes to be seen as the beginning of a "memoir craze"; also published this year, to less fanfare: a memoir by *Harvard Law Review* editor Barack Obama.

1996   The craze continues: publication of *Angela's Ashes,* Frank McCourt's best-selling memoir of Irish childhood, which goes on to win a Pulitzer Prize and the National Book Critics Circle Award.

- "The Age of the Literary Memoir Is Now." Critic James Atlas announces, in the *New York Times Magazine,* "Fiction isn't delivering the news. Memoir is. At its best, in the hands of a writer able to command the tools of the novelist . . . the memoir can achieve unmatchable depth and resonance."

- The first Mid-Atlantic Creative Nonfiction Summer Writers' Conference, the first such event dedicated to the genre, is held at Goucher College.

- Oprah Winfrey starts a book club.

- Binjamin Wilkomirski, *Fragments: Memories of a Wartime Childhood:* this Holocaust-survival memoir, first published in German, is awarded the National Jewish Book Award.

- Herman Rosenblat appears on Oprah Winfrey's show to recount what Oprah calls "the single greatest love story . . . we've ever told on air."

1997   Brent Staples observes, in the *New York Times,* "the memoir is seizing ground once held by the novel. The presumption that only a novelist's gift can transform life into literature has clearly been put to rest."

- Reviewing in *Vanity Fair* "the new, confessional school of writing known as 'creative nonfiction,'" critic James Wolcott complains, "Never have so many shared so much of so little." In the same article, Wolcott dubs *Creative Nonfiction* editor Lee Gutkind "the godfather behind creative nonfiction."

- Kathryn Harrison, *The Kiss:* the author is widely criticized for her decision to write a nonfiction account of her incestuous relationship with her father, a plot she first explored in a 1992 novel, *Thicker Than Water.*

- Stranger than fiction: Misha Defonseca's *Misha: A Memoire of the Holocaust Years* recounts a young Jewish girl's journey across Europe on foot in search of her deported parents; a pack of wolves protects her.

- Maya Angelou, *The Heart of a Woman:* Oprah Book Club's first nonfiction selection.

- "Disaster nonfiction" comes into vogue: Jon Krakauer's *Into Thin Air: A Personal Account of the Mount Everest Disaster* and Sebastian Junger's *The Perfect Storm: A True Story of Men Against the Sea* combine reporting and research with speculation to recount dramatic tragedies.

- Mark Kurlansky's *Cod: A Biography of the Fish That Changed the World* ushers in an era of what *New Yorker* critic Adam Gopnik later calls "little-thing/big-thing" books, narratives about subjects from seasonings

(2003: *Salt: A World History*; 1999: Nathaniel's *Nutmeg: Or the True and Incredible Adventures of the Spice Trader Who Changed the Course of History*) to the rainbow (2001: *Mauve: How One Man Invented a Color That Changed the World*; 2002: *Color: A Natural History of the Palette*).

- *Brevity*, an online journal of concise nonfiction edited by Dinty W. Moore, posts its first issue.

1998 The year's top-selling nonfiction book: Mitch Albom's *Tuesdays with Morrie*, an inspirational account of the author's weekly visits to a former professor dying of Lou Gehrig's disease.

- Edward Ball's *Slaves in the Family*, the author's exploration of his family's slaveholding past and its repercussions, wins the National Book Award for nonfiction.

- Scandal! A Swiss journalist questions the veracity of Wilkomirski's *Fragments*; a detailed investigation funded by the author's literary agency proves the "memoir" was mostly fiction.

- "Too good to be true": Stephen Glass, associate editor at the *New Republic*, is fired after editors discover that at least twenty-seven of forty-one stories he wrote for the magazine contained fabrications.

1999 Personal blogging spreads widely with the introduction of LiveJournal, Pitas.com, and blogger.com.

- Edmund Morris, *Dutch: A Memoir of Ronald Reagan:* the acclaimed biographer himself appears as a fictionalized character in the story. Defending his controversial technique on PBS's NewsHour, Morris explains, "I am the projector of a documentary movie about Ronald Reagan, which is absolutely authentic and thoroughly documented."

- John McPhee's *Annals of the Former World*, a four-part epic of North American geography centered on the 40th parallel, wins the Pulitzer Prize in general nonfiction

2000 First season of *Survivor:* America's obsession with reality television begins.

- Staggering ambivalence? Dave Eggers's best-selling memoir *A Heartbreaking Work of Staggering Genius* begins with extensive caveats, apologies, and disclaimers; later editions contain an appendix, "Mistakes We Knew We Were Making."

- Nasdijj, *The Blood Runs Like a River Through My Dreams:* the first of three memoirs by a Navajo writer who claims that he "became a writer to piss on all the many white teachers and white editors out there (everywhere) who said it could not be done. Not by the stupid mongrel likes of me."

2001   Barbara Ehrenreich, *Nickel and Dimed:* the Harper's writer goes under-cover as a house cleaner, waitress, and Walmart employee to see how the working poor make ends meet.

-   Ken Kesey, acclaimed novelist whose psychedelic parties featured promi-nently in Tom Wolfe's *The Electric Kool-Aid Acid Test* and Hunter S. Thompson's *Hell's Angels,* dies at age 66.

-   Hollywood falls in love with nonfiction: *A Beautiful Mind,* adapted from Sylvia Nasar's biography of Nobel laureate John Nash, wins four Acad-emy Awards, including best picture. Also this year: big-screen adapta-tions of Mark Bowden's *Black Hawk Down* and Elizabeth Wurtzel's *Prozac Nation.*

2002   Stranger than fiction: Augusten Burroughs's *Running with Scissors,* the author's memoir of an adolescence spent living with his mother's psy-chiatrist's unconventional family, starts a two-year stay on the *New York Times* best-seller list.

-   Otherwise (just between us), a curiously slow year for nonfiction.

2003   Carlos Eire's *Waiting for Snow in Havana: Confessions of a Cuban Boy* wins the National Book Award for Nonfiction. Erik Larson's historical real-life thriller *The Devil in the White City* is a runner-up.

-   Memoir on steroids: James Frey swaggers onto the literary scene. In a *New York Observer* interview, he promises, "I'm going to try to write the best book of my generation and I'm going to try to be the best writer. And maybe I'll fall flat on my fucking face." His memoir, *A Million Little Pieces,* is generally well received; blurber Pat Conroy calls the book "the *War and Peace* of addiction." (Janet Maslin of the *New York Times*—she's a sharp one—points out that the book was originally shopped around as a novel: "Little problem: This story is supposed to be all true.")

-   George Plimpton, founder of the *Paris Review* and writer who would try anything once for the sake of a story, dies at 76.

-   Pictures worth thousands of words: Marjane Satrapi's *Persepolis,* a graphic memoir of an Iranian girlhood, is translated into English.

-   Scandal: Jayson Blair, a 27-year-old *New York Times* national reporter, resigns in disgrace after revelations that many of his stories were plagia-rized or fabricated.

-   First-day sales of Hillary Rodham Clinton's memoir, *Living History,* top 200,000 copies, helping the book's publisher, Simon & Schuster, recoup the record $8 million advance it paid Clinton.

2004 Bill Clinton's *My Life* (advance: $15 million) sells nearly 935,000 copies
      in the first week, setting a new nonfiction sales record.

-   *Creative Nonfiction* celebrates its tenth (ish) anniversary with *In Fact:
    The Best of Creative Nonfiction* (Norton).

-   Documentary fever: Michael Moore's *Fahrenheit 9/11* wins the Palme
    d'Or at the Cannes Film Festival, only the second documentary to be so
    honored. The film goes on to become the highest-grossing documentary
    of all time. Also in theaters this year: Morgan Spurlock's *Super Size Me,*
    for which the filmmaker ate only McDonald's food for a month, gaining
    24.5 pounds in the process.

2005 Oprah's Book Club selects *A Million Little Pieces;* James Frey appears on
      an episode entitled "The Man Who Kept Oprah Awake at Night." The
      Oprah edition of the paperback sells more than 2 million copies.

-   *The Year of Magical Thinking,* Joan Didion's exploration of grief and the
    year following her husband's unexpected death, wins the National Book
    Award for nonfiction.

-   Scandal? The family of Dr. Rodolph H. Turcotte files suit against Au-
    gusten Burroughs and his publisher, St. Martin's, for invasion of privacy
    and defamation of character based on Burroughs's depiction of the fam-
    ily in *Running with Scissors.* The case settles for an undisclosed amount;
    Burroughs describes the settlement as "a victory for all memoirists" but
    agrees to changes in the author's note in future printings.

-   Hunter S. Thompson, father of Gonzo journalism, commits suicide at
    the age of 67.

-   The *Atlantic Monthly* announces that it will stop including a short story
    in each month's issue and begins publishing a yearly fiction issue. The
    editors explain that lack of space in the magazine is a factor, "at a time
    when in-depth narrative reporting . . . has become more important than
    ever."

-   Satirist Stephen Colbert introduces the word "truthiness" in the first
    episode of his new show, *The Colbert Report.*

-   Scandal! Reclusive, transgendered, formerly homeless and drug addicted
    male prostitute—and autobiographical novelist—J. T. LeRoy, whose
    work appeared in *Zoetrope, McSweeney's, Vogue,* and the *New York Times*
    (among other publications), is discovered by *New York* magazine to be
    a fictional front for writer (and former sex-call operator) Laura Albert.
    The *San Francisco Chronicle* calls the ruse "the greatest literary hoax in a
    generation."

2006   Scandal! The Smoking Gun website posts "A Million Little Lies: Exposing James Frey's Fiction Addiction," detailing inaccuracies in the bestseller. Frey responds on his website: " . . . let the haters hate, let the doubters doubt, I stand by my book, and my life, and I won't dignify this bullshit with any sort of further response." A few days later, Frey appears on *Larry King Live* to discuss the veracity of his book; Oprah calls in to support him. Two weeks later, on her own show, Oprah berates Frey and his editor, Nan Talese, and apologizes to her audience. "I gave the impression that the truth does not matter," she says. "I made a mistake."

- Scandal! *LA Weekly* reveals that Navajo memoirist Nasdijj is actually Timothy Patrick Barrus, a white guy from Lansing, Michigan, otherwise best known as a writer of gay and sadomasochistic erotica.

- *US News & World Report* notes that "the convergence of all three scandals [Leroy, Frey, and Nasdijj] at once [has] the feel of a Triple Crown of hoaxery, with the grand losers being accuracy, truth, and literature itself."

- *Creative Nonfiction* responds to the James Frey controversy with a special issue, "A Million Little Choices: The ABCs of CNF," later expanded and republished by W. W. Norton as *Keep It Real: Everything You Need to Know About Researching and Writing Creative Nonfiction.*

- Merriam-Webster's dictionary names "truthiness" its Word of the Year (the runner-up, trailing 5 to 1: "google").

- *Smith* online magazine begins soliciting six-word memoirs, eventually publishing a best-selling collection "from writers famous and obscure."

- *Creative Nonfiction* launches PodLit, a literary podcast focusing on nonfiction and literary trends.

- Elizabeth Gilbert's *Eat, Pray, Love:* Millions of readers buy, read, envy. (And take up yoga.)

2007   Norman Mailer—novelist, New Journalist, cofounder of the *Village Voice,* Pulitzer Prize winner—dies at 84.

- Scandal! Sort of. Maybe. Alex Heard fact-checks four David Sedaris books and concludes in the *New Republic* that the best-selling humorist often goes too far for his work to count as nonfiction, "even if you allow for an extra-wiggly definition of 'exaggerate.'" Readers are apparently too busy laughing to feel outraged.

- According to Michael Cader of Publishers Lunch, which tracks publishing trends, publishers this year acquire 295 memoirs, and only 227 debut novels. Further, reports *USA Today,* 12.5 percent of nonfiction book deals in 2007 were for memoirs, compared with 10 percent in 2006 and 9 percent in 2005.

- W. W. Norton publishes volume 1 of a new annual collection, *The Best Creative Nonfiction*, edited by Lee Gutkind.

2008   Margaret B. Jones, *Love and Consequences: A Memoir of Hope and Survival:* a half white, half Native American foster child and Bloods gang member makes good. In a February *New York Times* review, Michiko Kakutani calls the story "remarkable" and says Jones writes with "a novelist's eye for the psychological detail and an anthropologist's eye for social rituals and routines"; *Entertainment Weekly* gives the book an A-rating, warns that readers "may wonder if Jones embellished the dialogue."

- Scandal! Misha Defonseca admits her Holocaust memoir "is not actual reality, but was my reality." In actual reality the author, Monique de Wael, is the orphaned daughter of two Catholic members of the Belgian resistance.

- Scandal! In March, Margaret B. Jones turns out to be Margaret Seltzer, a white girl raised (and sent to private school in North Hollywood) by her biological parents. Her publisher, Riverhead Books, recalls all copies and offers refunds to readers.

- *Smith's Not Quite What I Was Planning: Six-Word Memoirs by Writers Famous and Obscure:* a *New York Times* best-seller.

- Scandal! Weeks before publication, Herman Rosenblat's memoir, *Angel at the Fence: The True Story of a Love That Survived,* is canceled after Rosenblat admits to having fabricated significant details. The author insists, "I wanted to bring happiness to people."

2009   Fed up with the poor quality of fraudulent survivor memoirs, *Heeb* magazine announces a (self-described) "self-aggrandizing and somewhat offensive publicity stunt": a Fake Holocaust Memoir Competition.

- Frank McCourt dies at age 78.

- AWP counts 822 degree-conferring creative writing programs, 153 offering the MFA.

- Former vice presidential candidate Sarah Palin turns in her 413-page memoir, *Going Rogue* (reported advance: $5 million), four months after the book deal is announced.

- *CNF* invites submissions of 130-character true stories to a daily Twitter contest.

2010   *Creative Nonfiction:* now a magazine.

BIBLIOGRAPHY

Anhert, Margaret. *The Knock at the Door: A Journey Through the Darkness of the Armenian Genocide.* New York: Beaufort, 2007.

Berendt, John. *Midnight in the Garden of Good and Evil.* New York: Random House, 1994.

Bissinger, Harry Gerard, *Friday Night Lights.* New York: Da Capo, 1990.

Bouton, Jim. *Ball Four.* New York: Macmillan, 1970.

Bowling for Columbine. Directed by Michael Moore. Dog Eat Dog Films, 2002.

Burroughs, Augustine. *Running with Scissors.* New York: Picador, 2002.

Capote, Truman. *In Cold Blood.* New York: Random House, 1965.

Churchill, Winston. Speech to Students. Harrow School, October 1941.

Clancy, Tom. *The Hunt for Red October.* Annapolis, MD: Naval Institute Press, 1984.

D'Agata, John. *The Next American Essay.* St. Paul, MN: Graywolf, 2002.

Defoe, Daniel. *Robinson Crusoe.* London: W. Taylor, 1719.

DeLillo, Don. "That Day in Rome." *New Yorker,* October 20, 2003.

Didion, Joan. "Why I Write." *New York Times Magazine,* December 5, 1976.

Dillard, Annie. *Pilgrim at Tinker Creek.* New York: Harper's, 1975.

———. *The Writing Life.* New York: Harper & Row, 1989.

Easy Rider. Directed by Dennis Hopper. Columbia Pictures, 1969.

Eggers, Dave. *Zeitoun.* San Francisco: McSweeney's, 2009.

Fahrenheit 9/11. Directed by Michael Moore. Miramax Films, 2004.

Filkins, Dexter. *The Forever War.* New York: Knopf, 2008.

Finkel, Michael. *True Story: Murder, Mayhem, Mea Culpa.* New York: Harper-Collins, 2005.

Frank, Anne. *The Diary of Anne Frank.* New York: Random House, 1956.

Franzen, Jonathan. *The Corrections.* New York: Picador, 2001.

Frey, James. *A Million Little Pieces.* New York: Random House, 2003.

Gardiner, Muriel. *Code Name "Mary": Memoirs of an American Woman in the Austrian Underground*. New Haven: Yale University Press, 1983.

Garreau, Joel. *Radical Evolution: The Promise and Peril of Enhancing Our Minds and Bodies and What It Means to Be Human*. New York: Doubleday, 2005.

Gilbert, Elizabeth. *Eat Pray Love*. New York: Penguin, 2006.

Glass, Stephen. *The Fabulist*. New York: Simon & Schuster, 2003.

Gutkind, Lee. *Almost Human: Making Robots Think*. New York: Norton, 2007.

———. *The Best Seat in Baseball, But You Have to Stand*. Carbondale: Southern Illinois University Press, 1975.

———. *Bike Fever*. New York: Avon, 1973.

———. "Difficult Decisions." *Prairie Schooner*, Winter 1996.

———. *In Fact: The Best of Creative Nonfiction*. New York: Norton, 2004.

———. *Keep It Real: Everything You Need to Know About Researching and Writing Creative Nonfiction*. New York: Norton, 2008.

———. *Many Sleepless Nights*. Pittsburgh: University of Pittsburgh Press, 1988.

———. *One Children's Place: Inside a Children's Hospital*. New York: Plume, 1990.

———. *The People of Penn's Woods West*. Pittsburgh: University of Pittsburgh Press, 1984.

Gutkind, Lee., and S. Gutkind. *Truckin' with Sam*. New York: Excelsior Editions/State University of New York, 2010.

Harrison, Kathryn. *The Kiss*. New York: Avon, 1994.

Heard, Alex. "This American Lie: A Midget Guitar Teacher, a Macy's Elf, and the Truth About David Sedaris." *New Republic,* March 19, 2007. http://tinyurl.com/86apdqa.

Heller, Joseph. *Catch 22*. New York: Simon & Schuster, 1961.

Hellman, Lillian. *Pentimento*. New York: Little, Brown, 1973.

Hemingway, Ernest. *Death in the Afternoon*. New York: Scribner's, 1932.

———. *A Farewell to Arms*. New York: Scribner's, 1929.

———. E. *In Our Time*. New York: Boni & Liveright, 1925.

———. *A Moveable Feast*. New York: Scribner's, 1964.

———. *The Nick Adams Stories*. New York: Scribner's, 1972.

———. *The Sun Also Rises*. New York: Scribner's, 1926.

Hemley, Robin. *Confessions of a Navel Gazer*. Athens: Ohio University Press, 2011.

Hillenbrands, Laura. *Unbroken: A World War II Story of Survival, Resilience, and Redemption*. New York: Random House, 2010.

Harmon, William. *A Handbook to Literature*. 12th ed. Saddle River, NJ: Prentice Hall, 2011.

JFK. Directed by Oliver Stone. Warner Bros., 1991.

Joseph, Eve. "Yellow Taxi." In Lee Gutkind, ed., *At the End of Life: True Stories About How We Die*. Pittsburgh: Creative Nonfiction, 2012.

Julia. Directed by F. Zinneman. 20th Century Fox, 1977.

Junger, Sebastian. *The Perfect Storm*. New York: Norton, 1997.

Kahn, Roger. *The Boys of Summer*. New York: Harper & Row, 1972.

Karr, Mary. *The Liars Club*. New York: Penguin, 1995.

Kerouac, Jack. *On the Road*. New York: Viking, 1957.

Kidder, Tracy. *House*. Boston: Houghton Mifflin, 1985.

The King's Speech. Directed by T. Hooper. UK Film Council, See-Saw Films, and Bedlam Productions, 2011.

Kurlansky, Mark. *Cod*. New York: Penguin, 1997.

Lawrence of Arabia. Directed by David Lean. Horizon Pictures, 1962.

Leavitt, David. *While England Sleeps*. New York: Houghton Mifflin, 1993.

Liebling, Abbott Joseph. *The Sweet Science*. New York: North Point, 1951.

Lopate, Phillip. *The Art of the Personal Essay*. New York: Doubleday, 1994.

Malcolm, Janet. "In the Freud Archives." *New York Review of Books*, 1983.

March of the Penguins. Directed by Luc Jacquet. 2005.

Marszalek, Keith I. "David Sedaris' Latest Book, *Realish*." *New Orleans Times-Picayune*, June 4, 2008. http://tinyurl.com/7jbdxpn.

McAdams, Dan. *The Redemptive Self*. New York: Oxford University Press, 2005.

McCourt, Frank. *Angela's Ashes*. New York: Scribner's, 1996.

McCullough, David. *The Great Bridge: The Epic Story of the Building of the Brooklyn Bridge*. New York: Simon & Schuster.

McPhee, John. "Centre Court." *Playboy*, June 1971.

———. *The Curve of Binding Energy: A Journey into the Awesome and Alarming World of Theodore B. Taylor*. New York: Farrar, Straus & Giroux, 1994.

———. *The Founding Fish*. New York: Farrar, Straus & Giroux, 2002.

———. *Oranges*. New York: Farrar, Straus & Giroux, 1966.

———. *The Survival of the Bark Canoe*. New York: Farrar, Straus & Giroux, 1975.

———. "Travels in Georgia." *New Yorker*, April 28, 1973.

———. *Uncommon Carriers*. New York: Farrar, Straus & Giroux, 2006.

Michael Jordan Nike Commercial, 2008. http://www.youtube.com/watch?v=fCpElwU_hiI.

Miller, Arthur. *Death of a Salesman*. New York: Penguin, 1949.

Mitchell, Margaret. *Gone with the Wind*. New York: Macmillan, 1936.

Morris, Edmund. *Dutch: A Memoir of Ronald Regan*. New York: Random House, 1999.

Mortenson, Greg. *Three Cups of Tea: One Man's Mission to Promote Peace*. New York: Penguin, 2006.

Nabokov, Vladimir. *Speak Memory: An Autobiography Revisited.* New York: Putnam's, 1966.

Nixon. Directed by Oliver Stone. Cinergi Pictures, 1995.

Orlean, Susan. *The Orchid Thief.* New York: Random House, 1998.

Orwell, George. *Down and Out in Paris and London.* London: Victor Gollancz, 1933.

Patton. Directed by Frank Schaffner. 20th Century Fox, 1970.

Pollan, Michael. *The Botany of Desire.* New York: Random House, 2001.

———. *The Omnivore's Dilemma.* New York: Penguin, 2001.

Pulp Fiction. Directed by Quentin Tarantino. Miramax Films, 1994.

Purpura, Lia. *On Looking.* Louisville: Sarabande, 2006.

Rankine, Claudia. *Don't Let Me Be Lonely: An American Lyric.* St. Paul, MN: Graywolf, 2004.

Robinson, John Elder. *Look Me in the Eye: My Life with Asperger's.* New York: Random House, 2007.

Robinson, Margaret. *The Long Journey Home.* New York: Spiegel & Grau, 2011.

Roger and Me. Directed by Michael Moore. Warner Bros., 1989.

Rosenblat, Herman. *Angel at the Fence.* New York: Berkley Books, 2009.

Roth, Phillip. *Goodbye Columbus.* New York: Vintage International, 1959.

Rousseau, Jean Jaques. *Confessions.* Paris: Cazin, 1769.

Rowling, Joanne Kathleen. *Harry Potter.* London: Bloomsbury, 1997–2007.

Sack, Kevin. "Shared Prayers, Mixed Blessings." *New York Times,* June 4, 2000.

Sedaris, David. *Naked.* New York: Little, Brown, 1997.

Sheehan, Susan. *Is There No Place on Earth for Me?* New York: Vintage, 1982.

Sicko. Directed by Michael Moore. Dog Eat Dog Films, 2007.

Skloot, Rebecca. *The Immortal Life of Henrietta Lacks.* New York: Crown, 2010.

Slater, LLauren. *Love Works Like This: Moving from One Kind of Life to Another.* New York: Random House, 2002.

———. *Lying: A Metaphorical Memoir.* New York: Penguin, 2000.

———. *Opening Skinner's Box.* New York: Norton, 2004.

———. *Prozac Diary.* New York: Penguin, 2000.

———. *Welcome to My World.* New York: Doubleday, 1996.

Slaughter, Frank. *The New Science of Surgery.* New York: J. Massner, 1946.

The Social Network. Directed by David Fincher. Columbia Pictures, 2010.

Spender, Stephen. *World Within World.* New York: Brace Harcourt, 1951.

Talese, Gay. *Fame and Obscurity.* New York: Doubleday, 1970.

———. "Frank Sinatra Has a Cold." *Esquire,* 1966.

———. *Honor Thy Father.* New York: World, 1971.

Tall, Deborah, and John D'Agata. "*Seneca Review* Promotes Lyric Essay." *Seneca Review,* Fall 1997.

Thompson, Hunter. *Hell's Angels.* New York: Random House, 1967.

Thoreau, Henry David. *Walden.* Boston: Ticknor & Fields, 1854.

Twain, Mark. *The Adventures of Huckleberry Finn.* Chatto & Windus, 1884.

Walls, Jeanette. *The Glass Castle.* New York: Scribner's, 2005.

Weisberger, Lauren. *The Devil Wears Prada.* New York: Doubleday, 2003.

Wolcott, James. "Me, Myself, and I." *Vanity Fair,* October 1997.

Wolfe, Tom. *The New Journalism.* New York: Harper & Row, 1973.

———. *The Right Stuff.* New York: Farrar, Straus & Giroux, 1979.

———. *This Boy's Life.* New York: Grove, 1989.

Woodward, Bob, and Carl Bernstein. *All the President's Men.* New York: Simon & Schuster, 1974.

Wouk, Herman. *Marjorie Morningstar.* New York: Little, Brown, 1955.

PERMISSIONS

From "Frank Sinatra Has a Cold" by Gay Talese, reprinted by permission of the author; from *Truckin' with Sam A Father and Son, the Mick and the Dyl, Rockin' and Rollin' on the Road* by Lee Gutkind and Sam Gutkind, reprinted by permission of SUNY Press; from "Issues in Science & Technology" by Meera Lee Sethi and Adam Briggle, reprinted by permission of the American Academy of Sciences; "Difficult Decisions" by Lee Gutkind, reprinted by permission of the author; "Three Spheres" by Lauren Slater, reprinted by permission of the Creative Nonfiction Foundation; "Yellow Taxi" by Eve Joseph, reprinted by permission of the author; from *The Immortal Life of Henrietta Lacks* by Rebecca Skloot, used by permission of Crown Publishers, a division of Random House, Inc.; "Fixing Nemo" by Rebecca Skloot used by permission of the author; "Then and Now: Great (and Not So Great) Moments in Creative Nonfiction, 1993–2010," used by permission of the Creative Nonfiction Foundation.

INDEX